GOGO
LONDON

GOGO LONDON: Autumn/ Winter 2015-16
ISBN: 978-2-919474-15-8
6th edition

———•———

© Gogo City Guides 2011-15

———•———

Gogo City Guides Ltd., Pinnacle House, 1st Floor, 31 Cross Lances Road, Hounslow, TW3 2AD, UK.
www.gogocityguides.com

This book is produced sustainably using plantation timber, and printed in the destination market on demand reducing wastage and excess transport.

Cover photo by Anna Watts. www.anna-watts.com

LONDON

Autumn / Winter 2015-16

Biannual Edition

Welcome to London

6 ► **THIS SEASON IN LONDON**

12 ► **CENTRE**
30 ► **WEST**
40 ► **NORTH**
50 ► **EAST**
66 ► **SOUTH**

76 ► **HOTELS**
78 ► **DIRECTORY A-Z**
82 ► **TRANSPORT**
86 ► **INDEX** • ALPHABETICAL
92 ►   • BY TAGS

THIS SEASON
in
LONDON

AUTUMN / WINTER
2015–16

NEWS & TRENDS

FOOD *The Relaunched Ivy*

Built in 1917, the legendary West End restaurant *The Ivy* (pg 17) reopened in June after undergoing a five-month-long redesign by Martin Brudnizki Design Studio. The celeb haunt retains its Art Deco feel and signature harlequin stained glass windows but has more of an airy feel, with a glitzy 20-seat bar as its centerpiece. The 5-star service and style remains. **the-ivy.co.uk**

NEWS *Alexander McQueen to grace £20 note?*

For its new £20 note, to go into circulation by 2020, the Bank of England will honour a historic visual artist (including architects, photographers, filmmakers, designers…) – and for the first time it's asking the public to decide which one. William Blake and JMW Turner are, of course, possibilities, but Bank governor Mark Carney is urging people to think beyond the most obvious. Alexander McQueen's name is on the list of 592 personalities nominated by UK citizens, alongside Alfred Hitchcock, Marie Tussaud, Stanley Kubrick and Charlie Chaplin… with the winner to be selected next spring.

FASHION *New Era for Matthew Williamson*

London fashion luminary *Matthew Williamson* closed his Mayfair flagship in July, moving his label online where he'll present six collections per year, immediately available to shop. But a new showroom is set to open this season, next to the studio in Queen's Park, and will be open for appointments, fittings and online order collection. **www.matthewwilliamson.com**

FOOD *Modern Pantry*

Anna Hansen inaugurates a second *Modern Pantry* in the City's Finsbury Square (Alphabeta Building, 14-18 Finsbury Sq, EC2) this September. With a Scandinavian-inspired design, the all-day dining venue with tapas bar opens seven years after the celebrated Clerkenwell original (pg 18). **themodernpantry.co.uk**

TRANSPORT *Night Tube inaugurated*

In the early hours of 12 September, London's night time Tube service starts operations. In tune with London's 24-hour lifestyle, the service will run round-the-clock on Fridays and Saturdays, on five lines: the Jubilee, Victoria, and most of the Central, Northern and Piccadilly lines. Across the Night Tube lines, you will be able to travel between Central London and the outskirts of the city, complementing the existing night bus services and London taxi and private hire vehicles. **www.tfl.gov.uk/NightTube**

FASHION *Mr. Hare Launches Ready-to-Wear*

The elegant-urban-cool men's shoe label **Mr. Hare** launched a menswear collection for SS16. Croydon-born Marc Hare, the company's founder and designer, owned a surf shop in London before launching Mr. Hare in 2008; it was quickly picked up by Dover Street Market. He now has two shops – in Mayfair (pg 24) and Notting Hill – all his own. The video that introduced the new menswear line imagined "what The People's Democratic Republic of the Future might look like," Hare told i-D magazine. The collection was influenced by African tribal wear, with loose trousers that recall ceremonial dress – and make you want to dance! mrhare.com

THEATRE *Hussein Chalayan Presents Gravity Fatigue at Sadler's Wells*

Performance art venue Sadler's Wells will host fashion designer Hussein Chalayan's first-ever dance work, **Gravity Fatigue**, in October. The Central Saint Martin grad and MBE has always combined performance, art and fashion; here he acts as artistic director, leading choreographer Damien Jalet. Expect a minimalist, experimental production, much like his clothes. Chalayan's history at the theatre dates back to his FW00 collection, which included his infamous convertible table/dress; he has also designed costumes for Sadler's Wells productions in the past. The 13 dancers in **Gravity Fatigue** will, of course, be clad in his designs. sadlerswells.com

FOOD *Broadgate Circle in the City*

New dining hub Broadgate Circle, just a stone's throw from Liverpool Street Station, opened this spring with a worldly range of eating options. Our favourites: A new outpost for the star Brixton pizzeria **Franco Manca** (pg 70), and for **Yauatcha** – which already boasts a Michelin-starred outpost in Soho (pg 19) – serving fresh contemporary Chinese cuisine; for dessert, take home his inventive chocolates, mini cakes and macarons (matcha pistachio, vanilla orchid, yuzu, sesame…). www.broadgate.co.uk/BroadgateCircle

FASHION *House of Holland Launches Men's Line*

Over at Selfridge's car park this June, the London-based designer Henry Holland presented his first-ever House of Holland menswear line (the womenswear line launched back in 2008). On sale immediately following the London Collections: Men presentation, the "young playful menswear brand" (as Holland told *Vogue*) is called Season 0001. British photographer **Martin Parr** was commissioned for the line's campaign; in his typical, satirical fashion, he shot in Holland's hometown, Ramsbottom, juxtaposing trendy models with everyday locations like a laundromat and butcher. houseofholland.co.uk

SHOPPING *Dover Street Market moves to West End*

Ten years after **Dover Street Market** opened in Mayfair and subsequently transformed the area, the influential concept shop has surprised the fashion world, announcing plans to quit Dover Street and move to Haymarket in March 2016. The change of venue – to the original Burberry building from 1911, vacated by the brand eight years ago – is sure to alter the landscape south of Piccadilly Circus. Owned by Comme des Garçons, DSM has a knack for setting up shop in unexpected neighbourhoods, most recently in New York City's Curry Hill. doverstreetmarket.com

FASHION *London Fashion Week Moves to Soho*

At stately Somerset House since 2009, LFW is moving to **Brewer Street Car Park** in Soho starting this September. The edgy location is a better fit for London's cutting-edge fashion scene, and it also aims to bring the biannual event closer to West End shopping strips – Bond, Mount, Dover, Regent and Oxford, to name a few. Dating to 1929, the Art Deco building still functions as a car park while doubling as a creative space for art exhibits and audio-visual installations curated by **The Vinyl Factory**. Another change: this season LFW will feature a programme of free talks open to the public. londonfashionweek.co.uk

SHOPPING
Cambridge Satchel Company Opens First Men's Store

This June the Cambridge Satchel Company – the UK-made purveyor of classic and colourful leather satchels – opened a men's shop (pg 22) in the same Seven Dials location as its first-ever bricks-and-mortar store. The story behind the brand is entrepreneurial legend: Julie Deane and her mum founded it in 2008 to pay to send her daughters to private school; today the brand is worn by the likes of Taylor Swift and Alexa Chung, recently launched a collab with Dame Vivienne Westwood and turns over more than £10 million annually. The brand's six-storey Covent Garden flagship is steps from the new outlet, which also offers made-to-order trunks and free embossing.
cambridgesatchel.com

ART Hayward Gallery Closes for Renovations

On the back of Carsten Höller's spectacular interactive exhibition *Decisions*, the Southbank Centre's contemporary artspace has closed for two years of renovations as the entire Festival Wing – comprising the Queen Elizabeth Hall, Purcell Room and Hayward Gallery – undergoes significant repair and maintenance. The replacement of the iconic roof lights and the installation of a new integrated blind system together with changes to the plant and the repair of the external sculpture terraces will broaden the range of artwork which can be shown there. The local skateboard community can rejoice as the Queen Elizabeth Hall undercroft remains open for the duration!
www.southbankcentre.co.uk

FASHION Marques'Almeida Scoops Influential LVMH Prize

This March, London-based **Marques'Almeida** label scooped up the prestigious LVMH Prize for Young Fashion Designers. Selected by heavyweights like Phoebe Philo, Karl Lagerfeld and Nicolas Ghesquière, it comes with €300,000 plus a year of mentoring from LVMH. Portuguese designers Marta Marques and Paulo Almeida met while students at Central Saint Martins and launched their label in 2011 after graduation. Known for their creative ways with jeans, Marques'Almeida plans to use the new funding to expand their team of five and their vision of "raw, undone luxury." The cash prize, established in 2014, is the biggest for up-and-coming designers.
marquesalmeida.com

SHOPPING
Shifting scene on Mayfair's Mount Street

Scottish fashion designer **Christopher Kane**, who graduated Central Saint Martins in 2006 and has a studio in Dalston, opened his first-ever standalone this spring at 6–7 Mount Street (pg 22), alongside London Fashion Week designers **Roksanda** (pg 25), **Roland Mouret** (pg 25) and **Nicholas Kirkwood** (pg 24). And innovative contemporary jewellery designer **Delfina Delettrez** (pg 23) opened her first stand-alone store outside Italy at 109 back in March. Joining them this autumn will be other Brit label **J&M Davidson**, known for its leather bags and accessories (as well as a line of ready to wear), at number 104.

NEWS Paris Imports

One of Paris' hippest hotels, boudoir celeb haunt the **Hôtel Costes** is set to occupy a Victorian apartment building at One Sloane Gardens, transforming into a gleamy 40-room luxury hotel in 2016. Designed by Liberty architect Edwin Thomas Hall, it's located in boutique-filled Sloane Square, down the road from Knightsbridge. Expect a new epicentre of the fashion week scene. And revered Paris table Taillevent, which opened post-**WWII** will open a brasserie in London's Cavendish Square in the West End this September. Named **Les 110 de Taillevent**, it will offer 110 types of vin by the glass and pair each dish with four choices of wine. And finally, the multi-floor concept shop **Merci**, an anchor in Paris' trendy north Marais neighbourhood, is set to open a branch in King's Cross area – although details beyond that are hush-hush.
➤➤➤

WHAT'S ON

ART *Ai Weiwei, Royal Academy of Arts*
Ai became widely known in Britain after his sunflower seeds installation in Tate Modern's Turbine Hall in 2010 but this is the first major institutional survey of his work ever held in the UK. Curated in collaboration with the artist from his studio in Beijing, the exhibition presents some of his most important works from the time he returned to China from the US in 1993 up to the present day. Among new works created specifically for the show are a number of large-scale installations, as well as works showcasing everything from marble and steel to tea and glass. With typical boldness, the chosen works draw on his own experience to comment on creative freedom, censorship and human rights, as well as examining contemporary Chinese art and society. Sat 19 Sep–Sun 13 Dec · www.royalacademy.org.uk

PHOTO *Audrey Hepburn, National Portrait Gallery*

From her early years as a chorus girl in London's West End through to her philanthropic work in later life, **Portraits of an Icon** celebrates one of the world's most photographed and recognisable stars. A selection of more than 70 images define Hepburn's iconography, including classic and rarely seen prints from leading twentieth-century photographers such as Richard Avedon, Cecil Beaton, Terry O'Neill, Norman Parkinson and Irving Penn. An array of vintage magazine covers, film stills, and other archival material complete her story. Until Sun 18 Oct · www.npg.org.uk

ART *The Alice Look, V&A Museum of Childhood*
Get a whole new view of Lewis Carroll's heroine in this display marking the 150th anniversary of Alice's Adventures in Wonderland. Follow Alice's evolution from follower-of-fashion to trend-setter through a selection of garments, photographs, rare editions and a brand new commission by Roksanda pattern-cutter Josie Smith. The display shows how Alice has been adopted and adapted around the world, and how she has inspired many of the most celebrated designers, stylists and photographers including Vivienne Westwood, Annie Liebovitz, Gwen Stefani, Avril Lavigne and Aerosmith.
Until 1 Nov · www.vam.ac.uk/moc

ART *Frieze 2015*
The 13th edition of the contemporary art fair presents over 160 of the world's leading contemporary galleries, from almost 30 countries. The Sculpture Park returns to the English Gardens in the Regent's Park featuring new and historical works from both Frieze London and Frieze Masters galleries. **Frieze Talks**, curated by the editors of frieze magazine, will continue to present an exciting programme of lectures and conversations. The **Frieze Projects** programme of new works commissioned specifically for the fair will be curated by Nicola Lees for the third year. And dedicated to performance and participatory work, **Live** develops in breadth and innovation from its critically acclaimed debut in 2014.
Wed 14–Sat 17 Oct · friezelondon.com

ART *Artist & Empire, Tate Britain*
The first major presentation of the art associated with the British Empire from the 16th century to the present day explores how artists from Britain and around the world have responded to its dramas, tragedies and experiences. Featuring a vast array of objects from collections across Britain, including maps, flags, paintings, photographs, sculptures and artefacts, the exhibition examines how the histories of the British Empire have shaped art past and present. Contemporary works within the exhibition suggest that the ramifications of the Empire are far from over. Wed 25 Nov – Sun 10 Apr · www.tate.org.uk

ART *Fourth Plinth: Hans Haacke*
The Fourth Plinth Programme invites world-class artists to make new works to complete an empty plinth in Trafalgar Square. **Gift Horse**, the 2015 Commission by Hans Haacke, is a wry comment on the equestrian statue of William IV originally planned for the plinth, depicting a skeletal, riderless horse. The horse is derived from an etching by George Stubbs, the famous English painter whose works are represented in the National Gallery at Trafalgar Square. Tied to the horse's front leg is an electronic ribbon displaying live the ticker of the London Stock Exchange, completing the link between power, money and history. www.london.gov.uk

ART *Hyundai Commission 2015: Abraham Cruzvillegas*

Mexican artist Abraham Cruzvillegas will undertake the inaugural Hyundai Commission, a new series of annual commissions by renowned international artists for the Tate Modern's monumental Turbine Hall. Cruzvillegas was among the key figures of a new wave of emerging conceptual artists in Mexico in the 1990s and 2000s and is best known for creating sculptural works from local found objects and materials. For the past few years, Cruzvillegas has created a body of work under the title *autoconstrucción* or 'self-construction', a term which usually refers to the way Mexicans of his parents' generation arriving in the capital from rural areas in the 1960s, built their own houses in stages, improvising with whatever materials they could source.
Tue 13 Oct – Sun 20 Mar · www.tate.org.uk

ART *The Line*

Walk The Line between the O2 and the Queen Elizabeth Olympic Park to see sculptures from artists including Martin Creed, Damien Hirst, Thomas J Price, Antony Gormley and Eduardo Paolozzi. London's new sculpture trail leads walkers along three miles of waterways including London's Royal Docks and along the River Lea. Born from a crowdfunding campaign, the project proposal raised over £140,000 in less than eight weeks to bring existing works out of warehouses and into the public eye. The ten works installed this year will be on loan to **The Line** for two years, with new pieces introduced each year.
the-line.org

PHOTO *Christina Broom, Museum of London*

Considered as the UK's first female press photographer, Broom boldly took her camera to the streets and captured thousands of images of people and events in London, from parades of First World War soldiers and Suffragette processions to royal occasions and sporting events. Self-taught, Broom turned photography into a business venture to support her family, and her observations of London life at the start of the 20th century brought her substantial commercial success until her death in 1939. Showcasing many images never seen before on public display, this is the first ever exhibition dedicated solely to Broom, featuring prints and original glass plate negatives, as well as a selection of her popular picture postcards of London.
Until Sun 1 Nov · www.museumoflondon.org.uk

FASHION *Shoes: Pleasure & Pain, V&A*

Extremes of footwear from around the globe – from a sandal decorated in pure gold leaf from ancient Egypt to the most elaborate designs by contemporary makers – are on display, exploring the cultural significance and transformative capacity of shoes. Examples from famous shoe wearers and collectors are shown alongside a dazzling range of historic shoes, many of which have not been displayed before. The latest developments in footwear technology are also explored with the ever higher heels and dramatic shapes.
Until Sun 31 Jan · www.vam.ac.uk

London Fashion Week · Women's SS16 collections · 18–22 Sep · www.londonfashionweek.co.uk

Skate at Somerset House · Nov–Jan · www.somersethouse.org.uk

Hyde Park Winter Wonderland · 19 Nov–Jan 3 2016 · www.hydeparkwinterwonderland.com

New Year's Eve fireworks · Dec 31, South Bank

London Fashion Week · Mens AW16 collections · 8–11 Jan · www.londonfashionweek.co.uk

---

➤ *Follow us on Twitter & Instagram @_gogolondon*
or Facebook (GogoLondon) for more ideas on where to go and what to see.

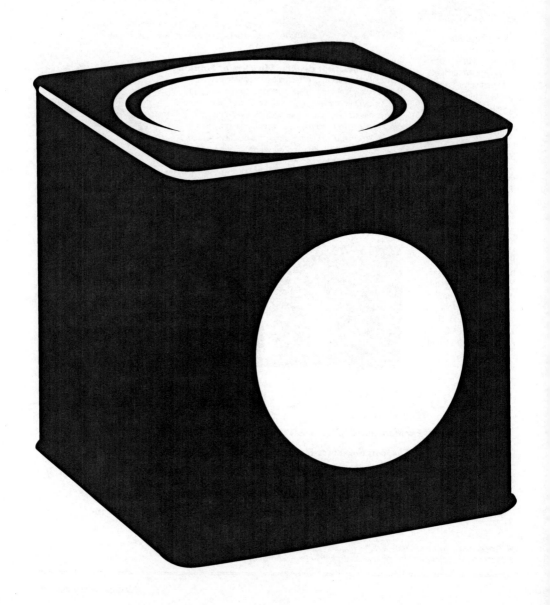

CENTRE

The Oxford & Regent St area is a SHOPPING nexus, flaunting major flagships including a vast Topshop. Piccadilly's THEATRES & classic arcades attract tourists, while the newly buzzing shopping hub of Carnaby St runs parallel into nearby SOHO. Famous GALLERIES are to be found around Trafalgar Square, while the delights of theatreland & the tourist-friendly COVENT GARDEN are a short stroll south of Shaftesbury Ave. West of Oxford Circus, MONIED Bond St & Mayfair host leading UK galleries, LUXE department stores like Selfridges & Comme des Garçon's avantgarde temple Dover Street Market. Respite is to be had north in Marylebone Village, a continental cluster of restaurants & shopping that pivots around the charming High St, or in LEAFY MECCA Bloomsbury, home to the British Museum & literary London. Continue east to the grown-up delights of Clerkenwell, CHICHI Exmouth Market or the Brutalist arts' complex the Barbican Centre.

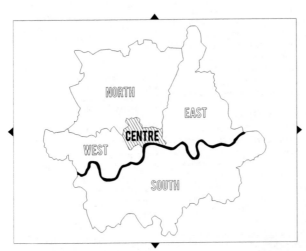

GETTING AROUND

Shoppers should get out at **Bond St** and head to Selfridges before nipping down quaint **Marylebone Lane** towards the **High St** for lunch. Loop back down to **Oxford Circus** for the major chains, then either head south towards **Piccadilly** via Dover St or take **Carnaby Street** into the maze of Soho, pausing for coffee at **Greek St.** Get out at **Holborn** for museums and sights, where it's a short stroll past **Covent Garden's Seven Dials** on into **Trafalgar Square**, or north towards the **British Museum** and idyllic **Russell Square**.

NEW *Babaji, Bao, Bar Termini, Blacklock, Cambridge Satchel Company Mens, Chiltern Firehouse, Christopher Kane, City Social, Delfina Delettrez, Duck & Rice, Hubbard & Bell, The Ivy, Kitty Fisher's, Portland, Smoking Goat, Spring, Victoria Beckham...*

ART CULTURE DESIGN

Barbican
ART / DANCE / FILM / LATE / LIVE MUSIC / WOW

No longer viewed as a Brutalist monstrosity, the '60s arts complex has become a much-loved icon. Consistently great exhibitions, dance and concerts plus a delightful indoor greenhouse.
The City: Silk St, EC2 ·
9am (10am Sun)– 11pm ·
www.barbican.org.uk

British Museum
LATES / MUSEUM

Vast and eternal as Norman Foster's domed Great Court piazza, with a collection spanning prehistoric and modern culture. Don't miss the Chinese ceramics, Egyptian mummies and star exhibits like the Rosetta stone and Parthenon marbles.
Bloomsbury: Great Russell St, WC1 ·
10am–5.30pm (8.30pm Fri) ·
www.britishmuseum.org

Curzon Soho DON'T MISS
FILM

The independent cinema chain may have branded bar snacks now, but the Soho branch continues to charm with its appealing underground bar (witness to the soliloquy of many a drunken actor) and consistently thoughtful programming. Sunday double bills.
Soho: 99 Shaftesbury Ave, W1 (+ branches) · www.curzoncinemas.com

David Zwirner DON'T MISS
ART

The pioneering New York gallery opened in London in 2012. Enjoy three gorgeous floors of exhibition space inside a quintessential London townhouse in the city's historic fine arts district.

Mayfair: 24 Grafton St, W1 ·
10am–6pm. Closed Sun, Mon ·
www.davidzwirner.com

Hauser & Wirth
ART

With owner Iwan Wirth frequently topping the art world's power lists, the London supergallery continues to flex the curatorial muscle, showing artists from Martin Creed and Paul McCarthy through to the estate of Louise Bourgeois.
Mayfair: 23 Savile Row, W1 ·
10am–6pm. Closed Sun, Mon ·
www.hauserwirth.com

ICA
ART / FILM / LATE / LIVE MUSIC

The cult arts institution with the not-for-profit ethos beats the experimental drum. Muse in the bookshop, cinema and galleries, then get down with the cultural elite at the bar or arty club nights.
St James's: The Mall, SW1 ·
11am–11pm. Closed Mon · www.ica.org.uk

Lazarides
ART

London's pre-eminent street art gallery. Two floors curated by Steve Lazarides, the man who was a catapult for Banksy's career.
Fitzrovia: 11 Rathbone Place, W1 ·
11am–7pm. Closed Sun, Mon ·
www.lazinc.com

Museum of London
MUSEUM

After a £20 million revamp, five new interactive galleries trace London's history from 1666 to the present. The fashion display is enticing (galleon hats by Philip Treacy) and continues in the shop with Westwood and Tatty Devine.
The City: 150 London Wall, EC2 ·
10am–6pm · www.museumoflondon.org.uk

National Gallery
ART / MUSEUM

Boasting over 2,300 of Western Europe's finest artworks covering the Middle Ages to the 20th century, the National Gallery is one of the most visited art museums in the world – and for good reason. Don't miss masterpieces by artists including Da Vinci, Botticelli, Rembrandt, Turner, Renoir or Van Gogh.
Trafalgar Square: Trafalgar Square, WC2 ·
10am–6pm (9pm Fri) ·
www.nationalgallery.org.uk

National Portrait Gallery
ART / MUSEUM / PHOTO

Royals, scientists, artists... footballers: observe the changing times in this temple to significant Brits. Don't miss the haunting Chandos portrait of Shakespeare.
Trafalgar Square: 2 Saint Martin's Place, WC2 · 10am–6pm (9pm Thu, Fri) ·
www.npg.org.uk

The Photographers' Gallery
DON'T MISS / ART / PHOTO

London's premier public photography gallery reopened in mid 2012 after an ambitious renovation. It's a slick showcase dedicated to high-profile artists and emerging talent. It also hosts talks and the annual Deutsche Börse Photography Prize.
Soho: 16-18 Ramillies Street, W1 ·
10am–6pm (8pm Thu); Sun 11.30am–6pm ·
thephotographersgallery.org.uk

Royal Academy of Arts
MUSEUM

Offering loan exhibitions on a par with the building's Palladian splendour, the RA has dropped its stuffy image and even enticed provocatrice Tracey Emin onto the governing board.
Piccadilly: Burlington House, Piccadilly, W1 ·
10am-6pm (10pm Fri) ·
www.royalacademy.org.uk

Sadie Coles HQ DON'T MISS
ART

A London institution since the mid '90s, Sadie (wife of Juergen Teller) shows Richard Prince, Matthew Barney and a host of high-end Brits, including a generous crop of the (now not so) Young British Artists, many of whom she ushered onto the international scene.
Mayfair: 69 South Audley St, W1 & 62 Kingly St, W1 ·
11am–6pm. Closed Sun, Mon ·
www.sadiecoles.com

Sir John Soane's Museum
DON'T MISS / MUSEUM

Maintained just as it was on the eponymous architect's death, this series of intricate interconnected rooms is a treasure trove stuffed with models, sculptures and cultural curiosities like the Seti sarcophagus in the basement. A place to lose hours.
Holborn: 13 Lincoln's Inn Fields, WC2 ·
10am–5pm. Closed Sun, Mon ·
www.soane.org

Somerset House DON'T MISS
ART

A Neoclassical dream set around a breathtaking courtyard off the Strand. Peruse the Courtauld Gallery's old masters and Impressionists then get your skates on in winter for a whizz around London's favourite ice rink.
Charing Cross: **The Strand, WC2** · 10am–6pm · www.somersethouse.org.uk

Stephen Friedman
ART

One of the leaders on the contemporary art scene presents his artists, including the emblematic Brit talent David Shrigley, behind a huge shop window.
Mayfair: **11 & 25–28 Old Burlington St, W1** · 10am–6pm; Sat 11am–5pm. Closed Sun, Mon · www.stephenfriedman.com

Stuart Shave / Modern Art
ART

A leading light on the conceptual art scene, this gallery continues to take risks, supporting some of the edgier artists on the international scene.
Clerkenwell: **4-8 Helmet Row, EC1** · 11am–6pm. Closed Sun, Mon · www.modernart.net

The Wallace Collection
MUSEUM

A sumptuous but approachable collection of Louis XIV furniture and 18th-century masters including Frans Hals's *The Laughing Cavalier*.
Marylebone: **Hertford House, Manchester Square, W1** · 10am–5pm · www.wallacecollection.org

White Cube Mason's Yard
DON'T MISS / ART

This contemporary gallery promotes international talents including Steve McQueen, Kelley Walker, Glenn Ligon and Abraham Cruzvillegas.
St James's: **25-26 Mason's Yard, SW1** · 10am–6pm. Closed Sun, Mon · whitecube.com

EAT & COFFEE

The Ape & Bird ££
BAR / BRITISH / PUB

The first foray into the contemporary (gastro) pub from the brains behind Polpo is a 3-floor extravaganza boasting 4 bars, a restaurant, a funked-up décor and great British grub.
Covent Garden: **142 Shaftesbury Ave, WC2** · 020 7836 3119 · Noon–11.30pm; Sun noon–10.30pm · apeandbird.com

Ask for Janice £
BAR / BREAKFAST / BRITISH / COCKTAILS

A modish distressed décor for this all-day café that takes pride in everything it serves, from the modern Brit small plates menu, to the long list of gin cocktails and craft beers in the hidden basement bar.
Farringdon: **50–52 Long Lane, EC1** · 020 7600 2255 · 7.30am–12.30am. Closed Sun · askforjanice.co.uk

The Attendant £
BREAKFAST / BRUNCH / COFFEE

Formerly a Victorian toilet, built circa 1890 and mothballed in the '60s, today a unique espresso & food bar designed around the original porcelain urinals.
Fitzrovia: **27a Foley Street, W1** · No reservations · 8am–6pm; Sat 10am–5pm. Closed Sun · www.the-attendant.com

Babaji ££ NEW / DON'T MISS
BRUNCH / TURKISH

Restaurateur Alan Yau has been converting Londoners to the joys of exotic cuisine for years. After great Japanese at Wagamama, Thai at Busaba Eathai and Cantonese at Hakkasan, this venture brings the best of Istanbul to the heart of Soho with a fingerlicking menu of Turkish pides, grills and salads.
Soho: **53 Shaftesbury Ave, W1D** · 020 3327 3888 · Noon–11pm (11.30 Sat, Sun); Noon–10pm Sun · www.babaji.com.tr

Bao ££ NEW / DON'T MISS
SMALL PLATES / TAIWANESE

The flavours are sensational at this slick Taiwanese street food affair.
Soho: **53 Lexington St, W1** · No reservations · Noon–3pm; 5.30–10pm. Closed Sun · www.baolondon.com

Bar Italia £
BUDGET / COFFEE / ITALIAN / LATE / MYTHIC / TERRACE

The Soho institution has been serving up a slice of authentic Italy to Mods, coffee afficionados and star fans like Francis Ford Coppola since 1949. The coffee, prepared with an ancient Gaggia machine, is best sipped at a pavement table made for watching the girls and boys go by.
Soho: **22 Frith Street, W1** · No reservations · Open 24/7 · www.baritaliasoho.co.uk

Barnyard ££
BRITISH / COCKTAILS

The second restaurant from Michelin-starred chef Ollie Dabbous and mixologist Oskar Kinberg is a relaxed, no-reservations affair serving Brit comfort food – like bubble and squeak with black pudding, apple chutney and fried egg – within a distressed farm setting in Fitzrovia.
Fitzrovia: **18 Charlotte St, W1** · No reservations · Noon–11pm (11.30pm Fri); Sat, 10am–11.30pm; Sun 10am–9pm · www.barnyard-london.com

Barrafina Adelaide St £££
NEW / DON'T MISS / SPANISH / TAPAS

A second address for London's favourite Spanish restaurant. Like the Frith Street address, you may have to queue for the privilege of enjoying London's finest tapas.
Charing Cross: **10 Adelaide St, WC2** (+ branches) · No reservations · Noon–3pm, 5–11pm; Sun 1–3.30pm, 5.30–10pm · barrafina.co.uk

Berners Tavern £££ DON'T MISS
BAR / BREAKFAST / MODERN EURO

The all-day restaurant ('a new kind of gathering place') belonging to luxe hotel The London Edition. Jaws drop upon entering the gorgeous space, overloaded with mouldings and art. The modern Brit menu was devised by the hyperactive and Michelin-starred Jason Atherton.
Fitzrovia: **10 Berners Street, W1** · 020 7908 7979 · 7am–midnight · www.bernerstavern.com

Bird of Smithfield £££
BAR / BREAKFAST / BRITISH / COCKTAILS / TERRACE

A club with no members. Over 5 floors of an old Georgian townhouse, chef Alan Bird (ex The Ivy) brings together great modern Brit cuisine across two different dining areas, a basement cocktail bar The Birdcage and a fantastic rooftop terrace.

Clerkenwell: 26 Smithfield St, EC1 ·
020 7559 5100 · 7.30am (10am Sat)–
midnight. Closed Sun ·
birdofsmithfield.com

Bob Bob Ricard £££
BRUNCH / BURGERS / WOW

Wildy flamboyant décor and a surreal
all-day menu that serves up an Orient
Express-style kitsch in the sober heart of
Mayfair. Lie back and order via high-tech
table-top buttons in the booths then
watch as the turquoise-clad staff ferry
you more champagne.
Mayfair: 1 Upper James St, W1 ·
020 3145 1000 · 12.30–3pm, 6pm–
midnight, daily · www.bobbobricard.com

Blacklock £ NEW
CHOPS

It's great chops or great chops at this
trendy basement chop house with its
clever slash ironic 80s electro soundtrack.
Soho: 24 Great Windmill St, W1 ·
No reservations · Mon–Wed noon–3pm,
5–11.30pm; Thu–Sat noon–11.30pm.
Closed Sun · theblacklock.com

Bodega Negra ££
BAR / MEXICAN

Don't be put off by the sex shop
exterior, because the experience begins
at the door. Inside, Day of the Dead
paraphernalia and Mexican wrestling
masks contribute to the décor, but that
shouldn't distract from the tasty menu
and long list of tequilas and mezcals at
this hyped spot.
Soho: 9 Old Compton St, W1 ·
020 7758 4100 · 6pm–1am (midnight Sun) ·
labodeganegra.com

Bone Daddies £
JAPANESE

Walk in, grab a stool and start slurping
at this rowdy NYC-inspired 'rock 'n'
roll' ramen bar. Customise your richly
flavoured pork broth with everything
from bean sprouts to cock scratchings,
from noodles to spicy ground chicken.
Soho: 31 Peter St, W1 · No reservations ·
Noon–11pm (10pm Mon; midnight Thu, Fri;
9.30pm Sun) · bonedaddiesramen.com

Burger & Lobster Mayfair ££
BURGERS

A welcome antidote to the burden
of choice, this buzzing yet relaxed
Mayfair spot has only three things
on the menu: burgers, lobster or lobster
roll, with cocktails themed to match.
Now with branches in Soho (36 Dean
Street), Farrringdon and The City.

Mayfair: 29 Clarges St, W1 (+ branches) ·
020 7409 1699 · Noon–10.30pm (5.30pm
Sun) · www.burgerandlobster.com

Busaba Eathai £
BUDGET / THAI

Communal tables in a soothing wood-
filled Oriental space and Thai cooking
that punches way above its weight
make this Alan Yau enterprise a perfect
lunch spot.
Soho: 106-110 Wardour St, W1
(+ branches) · No reservations ·
Noon–11pm (11.30pm Fri, Sat); Sun
noon–10.30pm · www.busaba.com

Caravan Exmouth ££
BREAKFAST / BRUNCH / CAKES / PACIFIC RIM

Exporting the chef and the Antipodean
flavours of Marylebone's Providores
& Tapa Room, this cool-looking and
slick outfit attracts the Clerkenwell
crowds. Don't miss the fry-up
and impeccable cakes.
Clerkenwell: 11–13 Exmouth Market,
EC1 (+ branches) · 020 7833 8115 ·
8am–10.30pm; Sat, Sun 10am–10.30pm
(4pm Sun) ·
www.caravanonexmouth.co.uk

Ceviche ££
BAR / PERUVIAN

This fun and laid-back pisco bar and
Peruvian kitchen serves London's best
ceviche. You might not find better
in Lima. Seriously.
Soho: 17 Frith St, W1 · 020 7292 2040 ·
Noon–11.30pm (10.15pm Sun) ·
cevicheuk.com

Cha Cha Moon £
BUDGET / CHINESE / COCKTAILS / TAKE AWAY

Inspired by Hong Kong noodle bars,
Alan Yau's mini-chain sticks to the
winning fast-food Asian-style formula
he developed for the Wagamama chain,
in a supremely stylish central location.
Great lychee cocktails.
Soho: 15-21 Ganton St, W1 · 020 7297
9800 · 11.30am–11pm (Fri, Sat, 11.30pm);
Sun noon–10.30pm ·
www.chachamoon.com

Chiltern Firehouse £££ NEW
DON'T MISS / AMERICAN / BRUNCH

Nuno Mendes is in the open kitchen
at American hotel impresario André
Balazs's (Chateau Marmont, The
Mercer) hyper-stylish first London
address. Expect stellar food and A-list
dining companions.

Marylebone: 1 Chiltern St, W1 ·
020 7073 7676 ·
8am (11am Sat, Sun)–10.30pm ·
www.chilternfirehouse.com

City Social £££ NEW
BAR / BRITISH / COCKTAILS / VIEW

An elegant and glamorous Art Deco
inspired affair from chef Jason Atherton
and decorated by Russell Sage. Step
out of the lifts to admire the London
skyline before plunging into the modern
Brit menu, featuring dishes like pigs
trotter and ham hock with crispy black
pudding, apple and Madeira.
The City: Tower 42, 25 Old Broad St, EC2 ·
020 7877 7703 · Noon–2.30pm; 6–10.30pm.
Closed Sun · www.citysociallondon.com

Cocomaya
AFTERNOON TEA / CAKES / CHOCOLATE / TAKE AWAY

This beautiful artisan bakery
and chocolatier serves freshly baked
morning goods, delicious cakes,
sandwiches, quiches and salads using
only the finest ingredients.
Marylebone: 12 Connaught St, W2 ·
No reservations · 8am–7pm (6pm Sun) ·
cocomaya.co.uk

Copita £££
SPANISH / TAPAS

Like the Spanish joints it takes after,
Barrica-owner Tim Luther's latest is
strictly standing room only on weekends.
If you're more keen on sampling the
food than the sherry and Spanish wines,
a lunch of razor clams and *ajo blanco*
(white soup) may be a better bet.
Soho: 26 d'Arblay St, W1 ·
020 7287 7797 · Noon–4pm, 5.30–10.30pm;
Sat 1pm–10.30pm. Closed Sun ·
copita.co.uk

Dabbous £££ DON'T MISS
BAR / MODERN EURO

The first and eponymous table from
hot young chef Ollie Dabbous. Now
reservations are actually attainable,
so you too can try the light, inventive
delights – like avocado, basil and
almonds in a chilled fig leaf broth, or
barbecued octopus with violet mustard
and Jerusalem artichoke. Downstairs is
buzzy Oskar's Bar.
Fitzrovia: 39 Whitfield St, W1T ·
020 7323 1544 · Noon–11.30pm.
Closed Sun, Mon · www.dabbous.co.uk

The Delaunay £££
MODERN EURO

The Wolseley's sister restaurant reprises the continental grand café thing, with added Viennese flair (think Weiner Schnitzel and perfect Sachertorte). Media types can't get enough of the ice cream Coupe Lucian (Freud, naturally).

Covent Garden: 55 Aldwych, WC2 · 020 7499 8558 · 7am (8am Sat)–midnight; Sun 9am–11pm · www.thedelaunay.com

Dept of Coffee & Social Affairs £
COFFEE / TAKE AWAY

A contemporary iteration of an Italian espresso bar, serving two single origin espresso options plus two filter options. There's also a short food menu.

Piccadilly: 15 Sherwood St, Regent St Quadrant, W1 · No reservations · 7am–5.30pm; Sat 10am–7pm. Closed Sun · departmentofcoffee.com

Ducksoup ££ DON'T MISS
MODERN EURO / SSHHH

Discreetly signposted, and boasting the minimal New York vibe currently all the rage on the Soho dining scene, Ducksoup is the impressive brainchild of several former Mark Hix protégés. The best bit? You can even bring your own vinyl to play on the in-house record player.

Soho: 41 Dean St, W1 · 020 7287 4599 · Noon–10.30pm; Sun 1–6pm · www.ducksoupsoho.co.uk

Duck & Rice ££ NEW
BEER / BRUNCH / CHINESE / DIM SUM / PUB

A new-gen Brit pub with a proper Chinese kitchen serving modernised Hong Kong and Cantonese classics, plus a dim sum menu which really hits the spot for weekend brunch. Beers from traditional brewers marry well with the spicy flavours, including the Pilsner Urquell, from the Czech Republic.

Soho: 90 Berwick St, W1 · 020 3327 7888 · Noon–11.30pm (midnight Fri, Sat); Sun noon–10.30pm · www.theduckandrice.com

Fernandez & Wells £
BUDGET / BREAKFAST / BRUNCH / CAKES / COFFEE / TAKE AWAY

This ever-expanding London café chain's soul is in Soho. The original Lexington St branch offers a killer array of sandwiches (at night it's a wine and charcuterie bar) and the smaller Beak St outpost rolls out superlative coffee, *afogatos* and custard tarts in one of Soho's best window seats.

Soho: 73 Beak St, W1 · No reservations · 7.30am (9am Sat, Sun)–6pm.
Food/wine: 43 Lexington St, W1 · No reservations · 11am (noon Sun)–10pm (11pm Thu, Fri). Sat, noon–11pm · www.fernandezandwells.com

Flesh & Buns ££
JAPANESE

Spacious, noisy and hidden in a basement, this upbeat Japanese joint is unexpected in quaint Seven Dials. Here the signature dish is DIY hirata steamed buns with a choice of filling; there's also a long list of sushi and small dishes.

Covent Garden: 41 Earlham St, WC2 · 020 7632 9500 · Noon–3pm, 5–10.30pm (11.30pm Wed–Fri); Sat, Sun noon–11.30pm (9.30pm Sun) · www.fleshandbuns.com

Gymkhana £££ DON'T MISS
INDIAN

Excellent contemporary Indian cuisine using seasonal British ingredients, with a strong focus on the tandoori oven. The menu offers *chatpatta* sharing dishes inside a moody dining room referencing British Raj India.

Mayfair: 42 Albemarle St, W1 · Noon–2.30pm; 5.30–10.30pm. Closed Sun · 020 3011 5900 · www.gymkhanalondon.com

Hakkasan Mayfair £££
CHINESE / COCKTAILS / DIM SUM

Sexy and sophisticated contemporary Cantonese cuisine flaunts luxury ingredients including foie gras, abalone, crab, lobster and wagyu to please an A-list clientele.

Mayfair: 17 Bruton St, W1 · 020 7907 1888 · Noon–5.30pm, 6pm–12.30am · www.hakkasan.com

Hix £££ DON'T MISS
BRITISH / COCKTAILS

As a former Caprice Holdings director, Mark Hix certainly attracts a starry (art world) crowd. At his second London outpost, you can enjoy seasonal British classics before getting merry on historical cocktails in the very hip basement bar.

Soho: 66-70 Brewer St, EC1 · 020 7292 3518 · Noon (11am Sat)–11.30pm (10.30pm Sun) · www.hixsoho.co.uk

Holborn Dining Room £££
BAR / BREAKFAST / BRITISH

Attached to the Rosewood Hotel, this grand bar and brasserie pushes a 'café society' approach to all-day drinking and dining. The copious and very British menu covers everything, including breakfast, gourmet sandwiches or high tea.

Holborn: 252 High Holborn, WC1 · 020 3747 8633 · 7am (8am Sat)–11.30pm; Sun 8am–10.30pm · www.holborndiningroom.com

Hubbard & Bell ££ NEW
AMERICAN / BAR / BREAKFAST / BRUNCH / COCKTAILS / COFFEE / SUNDAY ROAST

This trendy all-day Brooklyn style restaurant from the Soho House group – located on the ground floor of hot new hotel Hoxton Holborn – specialises in grilled meats, seafood and small plates. Or just drop in for coffee and doughnuts at the café. DJs take over the bar on the weekends.

Holborn: 199-206 High Holborn, WC1 · 0207 661 3030 · 7am–midnight (11pm Sun) · www.hubbardandbell.com

The Ivy £££ NEW
BAR / MODERN EURO

The longstanding theatreland celebrity haunt celebrates its centenary with a total refurbishment by Martin Brudnizki Design Studio. A stunning central bar replaces the old cramped one, and you'll even find Damien Hirsts on the walls. Happily the impeccable service and style remain.

Covent Garden: 1–5 West St, WC2 · 020 7240 2565 · Noon–11.30pm (midnight, Thu-Sat); Sun noon–10.30pm · www.theivy.co.uk

J Sheekey Oyster Bar £££
OYSTERS / TAKE AWAY

Borrowing the décor and the class of the star-studded fish restaurant next door, but offering a more informal setting and more affordable prices, this is a theatreland gem.

Leicester Square: 28–35 St Martin's Court, WC2 · 020 7240 2565 · Noon–midnight (11pm Sun) · www.j-sheekey.co.uk

Kitty Fisher s £££ NEW
BRITISH / COCKTAILS

Don't be deceived by the clubbish, old-fashioned dining room, this buzzing restaurant serves excellent modern British fare that's been passed over the wood grill, maybe Cornish crab, barbecued cucumber, dill and seaweed.

Mayfair: 10 Shepherd Market, W1 · 020 3302 1661 · Noon–2.30pm, 6.30–9.30pm. Closed Sat lunch & Sun · kittyfishers.com

Koya Bar £
BREAKFAST / BRUNCH / JAPANESE

A pared-down modern Japanese counter specialised in udon. Extra points for the exotic breakfast and brunch menus.

Soho: 50 Frith St, W1 · No reservations · 8.30am (9.30am Sat)–11pm (10.30 Mon–Wed); Sun 9.30am–10pm · www.koyabar.co.uk

Life ££
BAR / JAPANESE / LIVE MUSIC / SUSHI

Authentic Japanese fare in a relaxed ground-floor restaurant – go the unagi/avocado maki sushi, the beef carpaccio or the deep-fried karaage dishes. The chilled basement bar has DJs on the weekend from 11pm.

Barbican: 2-4 Old St, EC1 · 020 7250 3737 · Noon–3pm, 6–11pm. Closed Sun · www.life-oldst.com

Look Mum No Hands! £
BAR / BUDGET / CAKES / COFFEE

The fixed-gear brigade's favourite hangout is this café-bar with secure cycle parking and a one-man workshop. The café serves Square Mile coffee and simple platters, with cakes to fuel the ride home.

Clerkenwell: 49 Old St, EC1 (+ branches) · 020 7253 1025 · 7.30am (8.30am Sat, 9am Sun)–10pm · www.lookmumnohands.com

Maison Bertaux £ DON'T MISS
CAKES / MYTHIC

Dating back to 1871, London's oldest pâtisserie mixes Continental charm with an eclectic bohemian décor. The cakes aren't cheap, but more than worth it: starving St Martins' students famously saved up for weeks to get their hands on one of the exquisite French delicacies.

Soho: 28 Greek St, W1 · No reservations · Daily 8.30am–11pm; Sun 9.30am–8pm · www.maisonbertaux.com

Mishkin's £
DELI

Russell Norman and Richard Beatty's (of Polpo & Spuntino) enticing take on New York Jewish delis. Cue salf beef with pickles and bagels and lox. Mmm!

Covent Garden: 25 Catherine St, WC2 · 020 7240 2078 · Noon–11.30pm (10.30pm Sun) · mishkins.co.uk

Monmouth Coffee £ DON'T MISS
COFFEE / TAKE AWAY

London's pioneering coffee fanatics started roasting and retailing from the basement of this store back in 1978. They're still making superlative coffee, served with organic Jersey whole milk and organic cane sugar from Costa Rica.

Covent Garden: 27 Monmouth St, WC2 · 8am–6.30pm. Closed Sun · www.monmouthcoffee.co.uk

Monocle Café £
BREAKFAST / CAKES / COFFEE

Just around the corner from the Monocle HQ and Shop, this café serves simple dishes and drinks from dawn till dusk (an event/meeting space is available for hire to the magazine's subscribers too). Stop by for a coffee and a creamy roll cake from the Japanese pastry chefs.

Marylebone: 18 Chiltern St, W1 · No reservations · 7am–7pm; Sat 9am–6pm; Sun 10am–6pm · cafe.monocle.com

The Modern Pantry ££
BRUNCH / PACIFIC RIM / TAKE AWAY

Attractive café and dining rooms serving fusion across two floors of a Georgian townhouse. Book for weekend brunch.

Clerkenwell: 47–48 St John's Square, EC1 · 020 7553 9210 · 8am–11am, noon–10.30pm; Sat 9am–4pm, 6pm–10.30pm; Sun, 10am–4pm, 6.30pm–10pm · www.themodernpantry.co.uk

Morito ££
SHERRY / SPANISH / TAPAS

The little sibling of Sam and Samantha Clark's Moro next door, this simple space with open kitchen is all about the food: Middle Eastern and Spanish flavour combinations coaxed into tapas with serious flair.

Clerkenwell: 32 Exmouth Market, EC1 · 020 7278 7007 · Noon–11pm (4pm Sun) · morito.co.uk

Moro ££
SPANISH

Much lauded Moorish cuisine in a buzzing spot on Exmouth Market means you'll have to book 48 hours ahead. A favourite of London thesps.

Clerkenwell: 34-36 Exmouth Market, EC1 · 020 7833 8336 · Noon–10.30pm; Sun 12.30–2.45pm · www.moro.co.uk

Nopi ££££
MEDITERRANEAN / VEGETARIAN

The dazzling first true restaurant from Yotam Ottolenghi, who has a string of eponymous delis around town, has the critics raving, and prices to match.

Soho: 21-22 Warwick St, W1 · 020 7494 9584 · 8am–3pm, 5.30–10.15pm; Sat, Sun 10am–10.30pm (4pm Sun) · www.nopi-restaurant.com

Nordic Bakery £££
BUDGET / CAKES / COFFEE / SCANDINAVIAN

Clad in sleek navy and pine décor, and perching on a delightful square, this is a tranquil space to stop off for a slice of Scandinavia, like delicious cinnamon buns and rye rolls topped with salmon.

Soho: 14 Golden Square, W1 (+ branches) · No reservations · 7.30am (8.30am Sat)–8pm; Sun 9am–7pm · www.nordicbakery.com

The Palomar ££ DON'T MISS
ISRAELI

This loud, buzzing address serves the food of modern-day Jerusalem, so fusion dishes mixing up Jewish, Arabic and Mediterranean traditions, maybe a pork belly tajine with ras el hanout, dried apricots & Israeli couscous. Sit up at the zinc counter and watch the chefs singing, dancing and cooking!

Soho: 34 Rupert St, W1 · 020 7439 8777 · Noon–2.30pm, 5.30pm–12.30am; Sun noon–5pm · thepalomar.co.uk

Pollen Street Social £££
TAPAS / VEGETARIAN

Star chef Jason Atherton knows how to put the fun into fine dining. Have drinks and tapas in the social room, splash out on the gourmet tasting menu or simply pop in for dessert.

Mayfair: 8 Pollen St, W1 · 020 7290 7600 · Noon–3.30pm, 5.30pm–close; Sat, noon–11pm. Closed Sun · www.pollenstreetsocial.com

Polpetto £££
ITALIAN

The highly anticipated relaunch of the popular Soho restaurant sees chef Florence Knight wowing them from an open kitchen in a more upscale space. The cocktails are excellent too. Reservations are only taken at lunch.

Soho: 11 Berwick St, W1 · 020 7439 8627 · Noon–11pm (4pm Sun) · www.polpetto.co.uk

♪ TO LISTEN TO
BELLE & SEBASTIAN
GIRLS IN PEACETIME WANT TO DANCE (MATADOR)

Polpo Soho ££
ITALIAN / SMALL PLATES

This is where it all started for this now cult mini-empire of Venetian *bàcari*: humble restaurants serving simple food and good wines. Here, this translates as a lively Italian tapas and wine bar with a chic, no-design interior. Reservations are only taken at lunch.
Soho: 41 Beak St, W1 (+ branches) · 020 7734 4479 · Noon–11pm (10pm Sun) · www.polpo.co.uk

Portland ££ NEW / DON'T MISS
MODERN EURO

Owned and run by Daniel Morgenthau (ex 10 Greek St) and Will Lander (Quality Chop House), Portland's got good pedigree. The unfussy all-day restaurant serves the very best produce, cooked simply but with imagination. And of course the wine list is special too, with great vintages available by the glass.
Fitzrovia: 113 Great Portland St, W1 · 020 7436 3261 · Noon–2.30pm, 6–11pm. Closed Sun · portlandrestaurant.co.uk

Princi £
BREAD / BREAKFAST / ITALIAN / PIZZA

This principal stop for 'sohemians' offers an authentic Italian experience for breakfast, lunch and dinner. Designed by minimalist master Claudio Silvestrin, the sleek sandstone and marble interior emphasises the sumptuous array of baked-on-site pâtisserie, focaccia and pizza. It's difficult to find a seat at peak times, but well worth the wait.
Soho: 135 Wardour St, W1 · No reservations · 8am–midnight; Sun 8.30am–10pm · www.princi.com

The Providores & Tapa Room £££
BRUNCH / PACIFIC RIM / WINE BAR

Fine dining upstairs and an all-day wine bar/café downstairs featuring award-winning Pacific Rim fusion from chef Peter Gordon. A killer miso and maple syrup porridge makes this the best brunch in town.
Marylebone: 109 Marylebone High St, W1 · 020 7935 6175 · 9am–10.30pm (10pm Sun) · theprovidores.co.uk

Quo Vadis £££ DON'T MISS
BAR / BREAD / BREAKFAST / BRITISH / TERRACE

This classy Soho institution now serves breakfast in the bar, prepared with their own delicious bread; it's a reliable and charming option for breakfast, lunch or dinner, or just a drink in the bar (noon-midnight. Closed Sun).

Soho: 26-29 Dean St, W1 · 020 7437 9585 · 8am (noon Sat)–3pm, 5.30–11pm; Sun 1–3.30pm · www.quovadissoho.co.uk

Regency Café £
BREAKFAST / BRITISH / BUDGET / MYTHIC

An authentic greasy spoon whose striking Art Deco exterior has featured in a host of adverts and films.
Pimlico: 17–19 Regency St, SW1 · No reservations · 7am–2.30pm, 4–7.15pm; Sat 7am–noon. Closed Sun.

Riding House Café ££
DON'T MISS / BRITISH

A triumph of salvage chic, this all-day brasserie features ex-theatre seats and a private dining room forged from an old riding stable. Breakfast spans peanut-butter smoothies and muesli, while lunch and dinner have a gastropub vibe.
Fitzrovia: 43–51 Great Titchfield St, W1 · 020 7927 0840 · 7.30am–10pm. Sat, Sun 9am–9.30pm · www.ridinghousecafe.co.uk

Roti Chai £
INDIAN / TAKE AWAY

Simple and delicious Indian street food. We prefer the more relaxed upstairs space, the Street Kitchen, to the downstairs Dining Room, with its pricier and more elaborate menu.
Marylebone: 3 Portman Mews South, W1 · 020 7408 0101 · Noon–10.30pm; Sun 12.30–9pm · www.rotichai.com

Sake No Hana £££
JAPANESE / SUSHI

This fancy Japanese boasts an exquisite bamboo-lined interior by architect Kengo Kuma. Highlights of the authentic but modern menu are charcoal grill, Toban and Kamameshi dishes, and the sushi and sashimi are prepared to order.
Mayfair: 23 Saint James's St, SW1 · 020 7925 8988 · Noon–3pm (4pm Sat), 6–11pm (11.30pm Fri, Sat). Closed Sun · sakenohana.com

Sketch ££££ DON'T MISS
AFTERNOON TEA / MODERN EURO / WOW

Animated by a consistently beautiful Euro clientele, the stylish hotspot is the brainchild of superchef Pierre Gagnaire and Momo's Mourad Mazouz. The afternoon tea in the parlour is legendary, the futurist toilet pods above the decadent gallery restaurant even more so.

Mayfair: 9 Conduit St, W1 · 020 7659 4500 · Afternoon tea 12.30–6pm. Dinner & bar 6.30pm–2am · www.sketch.uk.com

Smoking Goat ££ NEW
BAR / BBQ / LIVE MUSIC / THAI

A tiny Thai bbq and drinking den on Soho's famous Denmark Street. The short menu brings together excellent produce sourced from Cornish farms with wood smoke, chilli, fermented and palm sugar flavours, and aromatic herbs ground on site. The street's musical heritage lives on with a spot-on vinyl collection and the resident sax player, Hans.
Soho: 7 Denmark St, WC2 · No reservations · Bar menu from 3pm, full menu 7pm–midnight. Closed Sun.

Social Eating House £££
BAR / MODERN EURO

Another great address from Jason Atherton the team behind Mayfair's fab Pollen Street Social. The ground-floor restaurant offers mid-priced bistro fare, in the basement a chef's table plus a small bar, and upstairs sample the cocktails at The Blind Pig.
Soho: 58-59 Poland St, W1 · 020 7993 3251 · Noon–2.30pm, 6–10.30pm. Closed Sun · www.socialeatinghouse.com

Spuntino ££
AMERICAN / GRUNGY

A speakeasy-style eatery famed for its tattooed staff, grungy Lower East Side vibe and college rock soundtrack. Food may be Italian-American, but it's more mini-burgers and pizzette than shake and fries. No booking so turn up before 7pm or face queues.
Soho: 61 Rupert St, W1 · No reservations · Noon–midnight (1am Thu–Sat, 11pm Sun) · www.spuntino.co.uk

Spring £££ NEW
MODERN EURO

Acclaimed Australian-born chef Skye Gyngell's first solo venture brings her ingredient led cooking to a beautiful 19th-century dining space set in the New Wing of the iconic Somerset House. Here, food is celebrated for its conviviality and the joy of sharing seasonal produce.
St James's: Somerset House, Lancaster Place, WC2 · 020 3011 0115 · Noon–2.30pm, 6–10.30pm. Sun, noon– 3pm · www.springrestaurant.co.uk

St John £££ DON'T MISS
BRITISH / MYTHIC

Fergus Henderson spearheaded the modern British cooking scene from this sparse Smithfields base. His seasonal and simple ingredients and nose-to-tail ethos continue to make it a carnivore's paradise. (The St John Bread & Wine branch in Spitalfields is equally good.)
Clerkenwell: 26 St John St, EC1 · 020 7251 0848 · Noon (6pm Sat)–11pm; Sun 1–3pm · www.stjohnrestaurant.co.uk

Sushi Tetsu £££ DON'T MISS
JAPANESE / SUSHI

This elegant and minimal hole-in-the-wall serves London's best sushi to just 7 lucky punters.
Clerkenwell: 12 Jerusalem Passage, EC1 · 020 3217 0090 · 11.45am–2pm, 5–9.30pm; Sat 5–9.30pm. Closed Sun & Mon · sushitetsu.co.uk

The Wolseley £££
AFTERNOON TEA / BREAKFAST / WOW

Continental grand café in an exquisite vaulted Art Deco room from the pair behind The Ivy and Sheekey. Spot the capital's power players over breakfast served by impeccably-clad staff.
Piccadilly: 160 Piccadilly, W1 · 020 7499 6996 · 7am (8am Sat, Sun) – midnight (11pm Sun) · www.thewolseley.com

Workshop ££
BREAKFAST / BRUNCH / COFFEE / VEGETARIAN

Workshop's relaxed Clerkenwell HQ is of course a destination for great coffee – they're dedicated to sourcing, roasting and serving the very best – but not only. It's a great all-day café with a food and drinks menu that demonstrates the same passion for quality and flavour.
Clerkenwell: 27 Clerkenwell Rd, EC1 · 020 7253 5754 · 7.30am (8am Sat, Sun)–10pm (6pm Sat–Mon) · www.workshopcoffee.com

Yauatcha ££
AFTERNOON TEA / CAKES / DIM SUM

Much talked-about all-day teahouse and basement restaurant serving exquisite dim sum. From the décor to the pâtisseries, everything here is seriously stylish, but don't let that fool you – it's held a Michelin star since 2005.
Soho: 15 Broadwick St, W1 (+ branches) · 020 7494 8888 · Noon–11.30pm (10.30pm Sun) · www.yauatcha.com

PARTY

Annabel's
MEMBERS CLUB / MYTHIC

If you can get into this ridiculously posh member's club and veritable London institution, you are likely to rub shoulders with a pot-pourri of Brit aristocrats, Hollywood celebs, Eurotrash, members of the Royal family, plus royalty from the rock and art worlds.
Mayfair: 44 Berkley Square, W1 · 8pm–3am. Closed Sun · www.annabels.co.uk

Bar Termini NEW / DON'T MISS
BAR / COCKTAILS / COFFEE

A terribly elegant new Italian style coffee and aperitivo bar from cocktail maestro Tony Coniglario (69 Colebrooke Row) and coffee virtuoso Marco Arrigo. Make sure to hit up the house Negronis.
Soho: 7 Old Compton St, W1D · 7.30am–11.30pm (midnight Fri); Sat, 9am-midnight; Sun, 10.30am-10.30pm · www.bar-termini.com

BYOC
BAR / BYO / COCKTAILS / SSHHH

Juice bar by day, basement speakeasy by night. Lacking a liquor licence, BYOC ('bring your own cocktail') asks guests to come with their own bottles – as many as they want, from standards to rare libations that'll put the bartender to the test. He rolls right up to the table with a trolley full of mixers; for £20, get two hours with him and unlimited custom-made drinks.
Covent Garden: 28 Bedfordbury, WC2 · 6pm–midnight. Closed Sun, Mon · www.byoc.co.uk/london

Cirque Le Soir
CLUB

Sip your cocktail in a glam burlesque atmosphere alongside live circus performances, ranging from snake charmers and dwarves to contortionists and stilt walkers.
Soho: 15-21 Ganton St, W1 · 10.30pm–3.30am. Closed Tue, Sun · cirquelesoir.com

Coach & Horses
BAR / MYTHIC

This Soho landmark is famed for its louche literary associations, and offers a welcome reprieve from some of its more populist neighbours. There are weekly piano sing-alongs named in memory of the legendary former landlord.
Soho: 29 Greek St, W1 · 11am–11.30pm (midnight Fri, Sat); Sun noon–10.30pm · www.coachandhorsessoho.co.uk

Compagnie des Vins Surnaturels
BAR / COCKTAILS

The French crew behind the Experimental Cocktail Club empire has brought some sophistication to hippy Neal's Yard. Their two-floor *bar à vin* has an immaculate interior and a 'supernatural' menu offering small dishes, desserts, bubbly and hundreds of wines from small producers around the world.
Covent Garden: 8-10 Neal's Yard, WC2 · Noon (10am Sat)–midnight · www.cvssevendials.com

Disco
CLUB

Get down at this pricey but fun Soho club with an outrageous 70s theme. Speed entry by signing onto the guest list online.
Soho: 13 Kingly Court, W1 · Thu–Sat 10pm–3am · disco-london.com

Experimental Cocktail Club
DON'T MISS / COCKTAILS / SSHHH

The Paris speakeasy has won a firm place in Londoners' hearts since opening in late 2010. Make sure you e-mail in advance to ensure an easy passage at the door, and you'll be rewarded with two floors of fin-de-siècle chic, and decadent, reasonably-priced cocktails.
Soho: 13A Gerrard St, W1 · 6pm–3am (midnight Sun) · www.chinatownecc.com

Fabric DON'T MISS
CLUB / GRUNGY / MYTHIC

The capital's best club made its name championing underground talents such as Ricardo Villalobos and Ellen Allien. It gets invariably messy but it's still the place to dance all night to the world's foremost DJs.
Farringdon: 77a Charterhouse St, EC1 · Fri–Sun 11pm–6am (8am Sat) · www.fabriclondon.com

French House
BAR / BUDGET / COCKTAILS / MYTHIC

The legendary watering place of poets, artists and modern-day aesthetes serves up a potent mix of cheap *kir royales* and surreal conversation.
Soho: 49 Dean St, W1 · Noon–11pm (10.30pm Sun) · frenchhousesoho.com

Heaven
CLUB / LIVE MUSIC

Home to the G-A-Y nightclub, this atmospheric dungeon-like space under Charing Cross station also hosts gigs by a progressive roster of left-field and established indie acts.
Charing Cross: 9 The Arches, Villiers St, WC2 · 11pm–late. Closed Sun, Tue, Wed · www.heavennightclublondon.com

The Lucky Pig
BAR / COCKTAILS / WOW

A stylish addition to Fitzrovia's many old-man boozers, this Art Nouveau meets old-style New York cocktail bar oozes plushness. Grab a cubbyhole, stow your valuables in a lockable vintage trunk and knock back the champagne.
Fitzrovia: 5 Clipstone St, W1 · 5pm (6pm Sat)–late. Closed Sun, Mon · theluckypig.co.uk

Mahiki
CLUB / COCKTAILS

Mayfair's long-running tiki bar serves potent tropical rum-based cocktails and a short 'island grill' menu in a glam but fun setting. Celebrity hangout. (Expect to pay to get in after 9.30pm.)
Mayfair: 1 Dover St, W1 · 6pm–3am. Closed Sun · www.mahiki.com

Mark's Bar DON'T MISS
BAR / COCKTAILS

Go to Mark Hix's Soho speakeasy for sophisticated evening drinking. It has justly been labelled London's coolest place to drink and its cocktail list is rousing.
Soho: 66-70 Brewer St, W1 · 11.30am–1am · www.marksbar.co.uk

Momo
BAR / COCKTAILS / MOROCCAN

A Marrakesh souk in the middle of Mayfair set up by restaurateur Mourad Mazouz. After princely Moroccan cuisine in the upstairs restaurant/café and boho outdoor terrace, head downstairs to the tiny Kemia cocktail bar (Tue–Sat 7pm–3am) for edgy DJs and live world music.
Mayfair: 25 Heddon St, W1 · Noon (11am Sat)–1am (noon Sun) · www.momoresto.com

Mr Fogg's
BAR / COCKTAILS

'Home to the eccentric British adventurer,' this fabulous Victorian-themed bar is named after the dashing Mr Phileas Fogg, the hero of Jules Verne's *Around the World in Eighty Days*, who, we must believe, liked a cocktail.
Mayfair: 15 Bruton Lane, W1 · 5.01pm (4.01pm Thu, Fri; 3.01pm Sat)–1.01am. Closed Sun · mr-foggs.com

New Evaristo Club
DON'T MISS / CLUB / GRUNGY / SSSHH

The ultimate antidote to the bland and touristy pubs in Soho, this small speakeasy with a chaotic '60s style may not be signposted, but it is always rammed with a hip and beautiful crowd. It's like stumbling across a houseparty that's as unexpected as it is brilliant.
Soho: 57 Greek St, W1 · 020 7437 9536 · 5.30pm–1am.

The Scotch
CLUB

The legendary meeting place for London's rock elite in the 1960s has reopened after a 20-year slumber. It's still a late-night music venue for carefully selected friends and those 'in the know' (so dress up!).
St James's: 13 Masons Yard, SW1 · 10.30pm–late Thu–Sat · www.the-scotch.co.uk

The Social
BAR / CLUB

Smallish and perfectly formed bar from the people behind Heavenly Recordings (Doves, St Etienne.) As you'd expect, the music policy is spot-on, the clientele eclectic and up for it.
Fitzrovia: 5 Little Portland St, W1 · 9.30pm (6pm Sat)–1am (midnight Mon, Tue). Closed Sun · www.thesocial.com

Zetter Townhouse DON'T MISS
BAR / COCKTAILS

Resembling a magical antique shop stuffed with curios, this hotel cocktail lounge is a pretty romantic place to spend an evening. Cocktails are by 69 Colebrooke Row star Tony Conigliaro, and snacks by The Zetter's Bruno Loubet. What's not to like?
Clerkenwell: 49-50 St John's Square, EC1 · 7am–midnight (1am Thu–Sat) · www.thezettertownhouse.com

SHOPPING

Agent Provocateur
LINGERIE

The legendary boudoir cum boutique has long ruled the roost for stylish suspenders, accessories and undergarments, and continues to lord it over sleazy Soho neighbours.
Soho: 6 Broadwick St, W1 (+ branches) · 11am–7pm (8pm Thu); Sun noon–5pm · www.agentprovocateur.com

Alexander McQueen
FASHION / MENS

Under Sarah Burton, the cult label continues to deliver the exquisite tailoring and elaborate, yet sensitive, celebrations of the female form the late fashion genius and national treasure was known for.
Mayfair: 4-5 Old Bond St, W1 · 10am (noon Sun)–6pm (7pm Thu) · www.alexandermcqueen.com

Alexander McQueen Menswear DON'T MISS
MENS

McQueen's move to London's home of tailoring Savile Row typifies the brand's dedication to fine cuts. This is its largest menswear space in the world, and it is curated by Sadie Coles, who adds artwork that underscores the stylistic value of emblematic McQueen motifs.
Mayfair: 9 Savile Row, W1 · 10am–6pm. Closed Sun · www.alexandermcqueen.com

Alfies Antiques Market
ANTIQUES / DESIGN / INTERIORS / VINTAGE

A treasure trove of 20th-century fashion and design plus a charming rooftop café. Don't miss pristine Dior, YSL et al at Sparkle Moore's stylist-tipped The Girl Can't Help It outlet.
Marylebone: 13-25 Church St, NW8 · 10am–6pm. Closed Sun, Mon · www.alfiesantiques.com

Antoni & Alison
COFFEE / FASHION

This pioneering fashion duo, a fixture on the London fashion week calendar, is renowned for their trompe-l'oeil digital prints.
Clerkenwell: 43 Rosebery Ave, EC1 · Thu 12.30am–5.30pm; Fri 11.30am–7.30pm; Sat noon–5pm · www.antoniandalison.co.uk

Apple Store

Expect permanent swarms of tech hippies queuing patiently for a go on the latest iGizmo at Apple's swanky London HQ.

Mayfair: 235 Regent St, W1 · 10am–9pm; Sun noon–6pm · www.apple.com/uk

Aquascutum
FASHION / MENS

The flagship of the luxury Brit heritage brand, founded in 1851, is home to the full men's and women's collections as well as a junior line, all flaunting the understated and elegant tailoring the label's famous for.

Soho: 24 Great Marlborough St, W1 (+ branches) · 10am–8pm (7pm Mon–Wed); Sun noon–6pm · www.aquascutum.co.uk

Bang Bang
EXCHANGE / VINTAGE

Grab a pristine second-hand designer bargain (Comme des Garçons, BIBA) or sell your own clothes and get a voucher to spend here, or in the equally good Goodge St branch.

Soho: 9 Berwick St, W1 (+ branches) · 11am–6.30pm. Closed Sun · bangbangclothingexchange.co.uk

Barbour Heritage
FASHION / MENS

The place to go for a bit of British legacy. The garments, including their famous hand-manufactured wax jacket, are inspired by the best of the 19th- century Barbour fashion archives.

Oxford Circus: 29 Fouberts Place, W1 (+ branches) · 10am–7pm (8pm Thu); Sun noon–6pm · www.barbour.com

Ben Sherman
MENS / MYTHIC

In Carnaby Street since 1968, this brand is forever associated with the UK Mod scene. In their flagship, 'the shirt bar' is testament to their signature item, but you'll find a complete British wardrobe for the sharply dressed man of today.

Carnaby Street: 50 Carnaby St, W1 (+ branches) · 10am–8pm (9pm Thu–Sat); Sun noon–6pm · www.bensherman.com

Blackout II
FASHION / MENS / VINTAGE

This Aladdin's cave of vintage threads has been open for over two decades. Upstairs you'll find pristine accessories (think 1950s sunglasses and cocktail rings), while downstairs you can pore over thousands of shoes and clothing from the '20s to the '80s.

Covent Garden: 51 Endell St, WC2 · 11am–7pm; Sat 11.30am–6.30pm. Closed Sun · www.blackout2.com

Bookmarc
BOOKS

Possibly London's coolest bookstore, in the basement of Marc by Marc Jacobs. It offers chichi stationery, classic written works and the best coffee-table literature. You can even pick up original David Bowie flyer art, or a signed edition of Allen Ginsberg's *Reality Sandwiches*.

Mayfair: 24-25 Mount St, W1 · 11am–7pm; Sun noon–6pm · www.marcjacobs.com

Brompton Junction
BIKES

The first retail venture for the cult British folding bike, designed and built in a factory in London. Browse and buy Brompton bikes in a rainbow of colours, get advice from mechanics and stock up on accessories and spare parts, then refuel downstairs in the Canteen.

Covent Garden: 76 Long Acre, WC2 · 9am–7pm; Sat 10am–6pm; Sun noon–5pm · www.bromptonjunction.com

Browns & Browns Focus
FASHION / MENS / MULTIBRAND / MYTHIC

Joan Burstein continues to blaze a trail as the elder stateswoman of London fashion across the ready-to-wear main store and the more avant-garde Browns Focus next door.

Mayfair: 24-27 South Molton St, W1 · 10.30am–7pm (7.30pm Thu). Closed Sun · www.brownsfashion.com

Burberry
FASHION / MENS

The Regent Street flagship gleams behind the British label's iconic tartan pattern and flaunts the label's oh-so-famous, and must-have, classic: the trench. Founded in 1856, the label and its designs scream luxe Britishness.

Mayfair: 121 Regent St, W1 · 10am–10pm; Sun noon–6pm · burberry.com

Cambridge Satchel Company Mens NEW
BAGS / MENS

The on-trend retro Brit bag company has opened its first dedicated mens store, in Seven Dials, selling the iconic satchel, but also backpacks, trunks and even the 'batchel,' the clever satchel/ briefcase hybrid. The new shop also includes a bespoke embossing service.

Covent Garden: 15 Shorts Gardens, Seven Dials, WC2 · 10am–7pm; Sun noon–6pm · www.cambridgesatchel.com

Céline DON'T MISS
FASHION

The first London mecca for Phoebe Philophiles. An ode to art and artisanat, and fashion of course, it displays the label's bags, shoes and ready-to-wear in a unique and beautiful space designed by Philo herself.

Mayfair: 103 Mount St, W1 · 10am–6.30pm. Closed Sun · www.celine.com

Charlotte Olympia
BAGS / SHOES

Nostalgic for a bygone era of old Hollywood glamour, the London label signs playful and feminine shoe collections.

Mayfair: 56 Maddox St, W1 · 10am–6pm (7pm Thu). Closed Sun · charlotteolympia.com

Christopher Kane NEW / DON'T MISS
FASHION / MENS

A first flagship for the Brit fashion talent, now backed by the Kering group. The heritage building has been transformed by John Pawson into a hyper minimal backdrop for Kane's distinctive, textural collections.

Mayfair: 6-7 Mount St, W1 · 10am–6.30pm. Closed Sun · www.christopherkane.com

Claire de Rouen Books
BOOKS / PHOTO

The only specialist photography and fashion bookshop in London stocks photobooks, fashion monographs, micropublishing, rare, signed and limited-edition books, international magazines, lookbooks and artist publications.

Soho: 1st Floor, 125 Charing Cross Rd, WC2 · 11am–7pm. Closed Sun · clairederouenbooks.com

Coco de Mer
FASHION / LINGERIE

Feminist activist Sam Roddick started this cheeky 'erotic lifestyle' company as a tool to transform peoples lives through sex. Its products are a favourite with liberated Londoners.

Covent Garden: 23 Monmouth St, WC2 · 11am–7pm (8pm Thu); Sun noon–6pm · www.coco-de-mer.com

Cos
FASHION / MENS

The flagship of H&M's sophisticated sister brand has a slick and enticing layout, which means you won't be fighting to get to the rails. Expect classic separates and spot-on interpretations of catwalk trends.
Soho: 222 Regent St, W1 · 10am–9pm (8pm Sat); Sun noon–6pm · www.cosstores.com

Darkroom
CONCEPT STORE / FASHION / INTERIORS / JEWELLERY / MENS

Fashion and interior crossovers in this impeccably curated temple to design. Think rope necklaces that would look equally at home hung on the wall, and saddle-inspired leather satchels for men and women.
Fitzrovia: 52 Lamb's Conduit St, WC1 · 11am–7pm (6pm Sat); Sun noon–5pm · www.darkroomlondon.com

Daunt Books
BOOKS

The deservedly popular indie bookshop is a dream for bibliophiles and has a particularly celebrated travel section.
Marylebone: 83 Marylebone High St, W1 (+ branches) · 9am–7.30pm; Sun 11am–6pm · www.dauntbooks.co.uk

Delfina Delettrez NEW
JEWELLERY

A first stand-alone store outside Italy for the innovative contemporary jewellery designer's conceptual pieces, all handmade in her atelier in Rome.
Mayfair: 109 Mount St, W1 · 10am–6pm. Closed Sun · www.delfinadelettrez.it

Dover Street Market DON'T MISS
CONCEPT STORE / FASHION / MENS

The concept store curated by Comme Des Garçons stocks an edgy range of complementary designs – think Raf Simons and Lanvin – alongside its own collections, vintage copies of *Interview* and gardening wares by Labour and Wait.
Mayfair: 17–18 Dover St, W1 · 11am–7pm; Sun noon–5pm · www.doverstreetmarket.com

Dunhill
BAGS / MENS

Home to the iconic UK brand that supplies high-end men's leather goods. On top of a bespoke tailoring service you can also get a shave, a spa treatment and even throw back a bourbon, James Bond style.
Mayfair: 2 Davies St, W1 · 10am–7pm. Closed Sun · www.dunhill.com

Folk
FASHION / MENS / SHOES

Understated clothing with an emphasis on high-quality fabric and playful details have made Folk a go-to brand for capsule wardrobe essentials. The newer footwear lines for men and women are worth a look too.
Bloomsbury: 49 & 53 Lamb's Conduit St, WC1 · 11am–7pm (6pm Sat); Sun noon–5pm · www.folkclothing.com

Fortnum & Mason
AFTERNOON TEA / CAKES / DELI / TAKE AWAY

Gilded, chandeliered and absurdly luxuriant, the fine food hall is official supplier to the Royal family. Peruse the world-class hampers before withdrawing for high tea in the genteel oasis of the St. James's Restaurant.
Piccadilly: 181 Piccadilly, W1 · 10am–8pm; Sun 11.30am–6pm · www.fortnumandmason.com

Foyles
BOOKS

The renowned bookseller and literary landmark has moved down Charing Cross Road a bit to a massive new flagship. Designed to be 'a bookshop for the 21st century,' the light-filled Deco space was completely gutted and rebuilt and is the largest bookstore to be built in the UK this century!
Soho: 107 Charing Cross Rd, WC2 · 9.30am–9pm; Sun 11.30am–6pm · www.foyles.co.uk

Globe-Trotter
BAGS / MENS / MYTHIC

A new flagship for this heritage leather goods brand. Founded in 1897 by Englishman David Nelken, it has since played a supporting role in British history, accompanying Scott on his Antarctic mission, Winston Churchill on his state business and the Queen on her honeymoon.
Mayfair: 35 Albemarle St, W1 (+ branches) · 10am–6pm. Closed Sun · www.globetrotter1897.com

Hunter
FASHION / MENS / SHOES

Now with Alasdhair Willis (Mr Stella McCartney) at the helm, the heritage Wellington rubber boot specialist has opened its first flagship. Over three floors, it presents more than just the iconic Wellies, but complete footwear, accessories and outerwear collections, including the new Field line of specialised performance wear.
Soho: 83-85 Regent Street, W1 · 10am–8pm; Sun, noon–6pm · www.hunterboots.com

Jaeger
FASHION / MENS

This traditionally Brit brand gets an overhaul, bringing its classic and elegant tailored cuts up to date.
Oxford Circus: 200-206 Regent St, W1 · 10am–8pm; Sun noon–6pm · www.jaeger.co.uk

Koenig Books
BOOKS

A handy central London branch of the Serpentine Gallery's impeccable art, architecture and photography bookshop. Think Gerhard Richter show catalogues and Steidl tomes on the likes of William Eggleston.
Soho: 80 Charing Cross Rd, WC2 · 11am–8pm (9pm Thu). Closed Sun · www.koenigbooks.co.uk

Kokon To Zai DON'T MISS
FASHION / MENS / MULTIBRAND

Get noticed sporting cutting-edge fashion from radical design duo Marjan Pejoski and Sasha Bezovski.
Soho: 57 Greek St, W1 · 11am–7.30pm; Sun noon–6pm · www.kokontozai.co.uk

Lazy Oaf
FASHION / MENS

Home to the cult London clothing label and its pop, print focused illustration collections.
Soho: 2 Ganton St, W1 · 10.30am–7pm (8pm Thu); Sun noon–6pm · www.lazyoaf.com

Liberty
DEPARTMENT STORE / FASHION / MYTHIC

From the '20s mock-Tudor façade to the intricate window displays, Liberty has become as much a part of the London fabric as its celebrated print designs. Expect all the right luxe labels and homewares alongside the famed haberdashery.
Soho: Regent St, W1 · 10am–8pm; Sun noon–6pm · www.liberty.co.uk

Linda Farrow Gallery
EYEWEAR

The London luxury eyewear label has opened a first London flagship that fuses the minimal with the baroque. Check the full gamut of their designer collabs including Erdem, Dries van Noten, The Row or Matthew Williamson. *Mayfair*: 91 Mount St, W1 · 10.30am–7pm; Sun noon–6pm · lindafarrow.com

Loewe
BAGS / FASHION / MENS

Now with Brit fashion talent JW Anderson at the helm, this venerable Spanish fashion and accessories label has undergone an exciting overhaul. *Mayfair*: 125 Mount St, W1 · 10am–6.30pm (7pm Thu). Closed Sun · www.loewe.com

Machine-A
FASHION / MENS / MULTIBRAND

This indie shop/ gallery space showcases avant-garde young fashion designers such as Noki or Louise Gray, as well as curating an array of cool events, window installations and exhibitions. *Soho*: 13 Brewer St, W1 · 11am–7pm (8pm Thu–Sat); Sun noon–6pm · www.machine-a.com

Magma
BOOKS

The original address for this first-rate bookstore dedicated to contemporary visual arts, fashion, photography, graphics, design etc. *Covent Garden*: 8 Earlham St, WC2 (+ branches) · 11am–7pm; Sun noon–6pm · www.magmabooks.com

Margaret Howell
FASHION / MENS

From the fine Harris tweeds to the pared-down designs, there's something reassuringly old-fashioned about Margaret Howell. Alongside simple (but not cheap) pieces you'll keep for years, her shops now stock reissued British homewares from Ercol et al. *Marylebone*: 34 Wigmore St, W1 · 10am–6pm (7pm Thu); Sun noon–5pm · www.margarethowell.co.uk

Monocle Shop
DESIGN / FASHION / INTERIORS / MENS

Covering only 9m² but packing a punch, the London outlet of the design bible stocks a ready-made gift selection of back issues, stationery, knitwear and bags. *Marylebone*: 2A George St, W1 · 11am–7pm; Sun noon–5pm · monocle.com

Mouki Mou
CONCEPT STORE / FASHION / MENS

An exclusive selection of fashion, accessories, beauty and lifestyle pieces described by owner Maria Lemos as 'objects with unique brilliance and character'. The 2-floor space's minimal design is by William Russell of Pentagram. *Marylebone*: 29 Chiltern St, W1 · 11am–7pm; Sat 10am–6pm; Sun noon–5pm · www.moukimou.com

Mr Hare DON'T MISS
MENS / SHOES

A fave among London's contemporary elite, Mr Hare is one to watch. This first flagship demonstrates how the 'shoeist' adds a little stylistic fervour and romance to men's classics like the brogue and loafer. *Mayfair*: 8 Stafford St, W1 (+ branches) · 10.30am–7pm. Closed Sun · www.mrhare.com

Mulberry
BAGS / FASHION

This flagship is decked out with an authentic Cotswold drystone wall and British oak, representing the Britishness of this company that was founded in 1971 and has since become an international luxury brand. A Mulberry handbag remains a must for fashionistas. *Mayfair*: 50 New Bond St, W1 · 10am–7pm; Sun noon–6pm · www.mulberry.com

Neal's Yard Dairy
CHEESE

London's artisanal cheese kings helped kickstart the British wholefood movement, and these days there's an unending stream of gourmets lining up for a fix of Wensleydale or Cornish Yarg. (Another branch at Borough Market.) *Covent Garden*: 17 Shorts Gardens, WC2 (+ branches) · 10am–7pm. Closed Sun · www.nealsyarddairy.co.uk

Neal's Yard Remedies
BEAUTY / ORGANIC

This is where it all started 30 years ago for the pioneering UK organic skincare company. As well as the range of skin and body care, with its signature blue bottles, there's a huge range of dried herbs available for your own concoctions. *Covent Garden*: 15 Neal's Yard, WC2. (+ branches) · 10am–7.30pm (8pmThu); Sun 11am–7.30pm · www.nealsyardremedies.com

Nicholas Kirkwood
SHOES / WOW

Every fashion editor's favourite, Nicholas Kirkwood's creations mystically combine a sculptural aesthetic with comfort of wear. See if you can spy the Brit designer at work in his studio upstairs. *Mayfair*: 5 Mount St, W1 · 11am–7pm; Sun 1–5pm · www.nicholaskirkwood.com

Nicole Farhi
FASHION

London-based French fashion designer Nicole Farhi has been fusing French style with British eccentricity since the 80s. This flagship showcases the breezy tailoring of her characteristically cool, graceful and playful designs. *Mayfair*: 25 Conduit St, W1 · 10am–6pm (7pm Thu, Sat); Sun noon–6pm · www.nicolefarhi.com

Oliver Spencer DON'T MISS
MENS

Bridging streetwear and traditional tailoring, Oliver Spencer's elegant clothes are the discerning gent's garb of choice. Influences range from hunting and the military to Japan, all melded seamlessly into his English aesthetic. *Bloomsbury*: 62 Lambs Conduit St, WC1 (+ branches) · 11am–7pm; Sun noon–5pm · oliverspencer.co.uk

Opening Ceremony
DON'T MISS / FASHION / MENS

OC's first European outpost sells its generation-defining selection of world brands including cult US creators Patrik Ervell or Proenza Schouler. British designer Faye Toogood was commissioned to interpret the space and did so with Tinker, a furniture-based art installation. There's also a Claire de Rouen bookshop-in-shop. *Covent Garden*: 35 King St, WC2 · 11am–8pm; Sun noon–6pm · www.openingceremony.us

Other Criteria
ART / BOOKS / JEWELLERY / KNICK KNACKS

Damien Hirst's publishing company now stocks artist-designed T-shirts, jewellery and prints alongside its award-winning art book selection by Brit icons like Banksy and Tracey Emin. *Marylebone*: 14 Hinde St, W1 (+ branches) · 10am–6pm; 11am–7.30pm Sun · othercriteria.com

Other Shop DON'T MISS
CONCEPT STORE / FASHION / MENS / MULTIBRAND

Kirk Beattie and Matthew Murphy, the talented duo behind the now closed B Store, launched this replacement retail concept to support new avant-garde fashion names and labels. Those on show include British talent Awai, Peter Jensen and Marwood.
Oxford Circus: 21 Kingly St, W1 · 10.30am–6.30pm; Sun noon–5pm · www.other-shop.com

Paxton & Whitfield
DON'T MISS / CHEESE / MYTHIC

Exceptional cheesemongers for over 200 years, they stock a plethora of excellent cheeses from around the UK and Europe, matured on site in underground cellars.
St James's: 93 Jermyn St, SW1 · 9.30am–6pm; Sun 11am–5pm · www.paxtonandwhitfield.co.uk

Penhaligon's
BEAUTY / PERFUME

Court barber and perfumer to Queen Victoria, William Penhaligon founded this company in the 1860s. Still made in England, the original scents are refashioned for the modern nose.
Covent Garden: 41 Wellington St, WC2 · 10am (noon Sun)–6pm (7pm Thu–Sat) · www.penhaligons.com

Percival
MENS

Here the emphasis is on quality British workmanship, timeless styling and clever detailing such as playful linings, buttons and unexpected colours for an eccentric British gentlemen vibe.
Soho: 43 Berwick St, W1 · 11am–7pm; Sun noon–5pm · www.percivalclo.com

Philip Treacy
HATS

London's other star milliner produces from his Belgravia shop extravagant creations that don't always resemble hats.
Belgravia: 69 Elizabeth St, SW1 · 10am–6pm; Sat 11am–5pm. Closed Sun · www.philiptreacy.co.uk

Phonica Records
VINYL

Impeccable selection of dance, house and electronica, bubble chairs and excellent service make this the coolest record shop in Soho.

Soho: 51 Poland St, W1 · 11.30am–7.30pm (8pm Thu, Fri); Sun noon–6pm · www.phonicarecords.com

Poste Mistress
SHOES

The beautiful and considerably more chic elder sister to High Street brand Office stocks avant-garde footwear from Vivienne Westwood and Dries Van Noten alongside edgier newcomers like Chloe Sevigny for Opening Ceremony.
Covent Garden: 61-63 Monmouth St, WC2 · 10am–7pm (8pm Thu); Sun 11.30am–6pm · www.office.co.uk

Pringle of Scotland
FASHION / MENS

One of the oldest luxury knitwear manufacturers in the world. 'Luxury with an edge' defines the mainline women's and men's collections, which you can peruse here, in the Mayfair flagship.
Mayfair: 94 Mount St, W1 · 10am–6.30pm (7pm Thu). Closed Sun · www.pringlescotland.com

Rigby & Peller
LINGERIE

Royal service is a given at the Queen's official *corsetière*. Arrive early or make an appointment to be measured, and expect a 6-week delay for the unbeatable bespoke service. Brands include Aubade and Fantasie.
Mayfair: 22A Conduit St, W1 · 9.30am–6pm (7pm Thu). Closed Sun · www.rigbyandpeller.co.uk

Roksanda
FASHION

An extension of the collections, the store's interior references the London-based designer's use of geometry, symmetry and bold colour.
Mayfair: 9 Mount Street, W1 · 10am–6.30pm. Closed Sun · roksanda.com

Roland Mouret
FASHION

The London-based French designer's first and only stand-alone store displays his complete range of figure-hugging collections, designed with the red carpet in mind.
Mayfair: 8 Carlos Place, W1 · 10am–6.30pm (7pm Thu). Closed Sun · www.rolandmouret.com

Rupert Sanderson
SHOES

This Brit designer takes a 'less-is-more' attitude to his collections of shoes for women, all designed in London and hand-made in Italy.
Mayfair: 19 Bruton Place, W1 · 10am (11.30am Sat)–6.30pm. Closed Sun · www.rupertsanderson.com

Selfridges
DEPARTMENT STORE

This giant, centennial, Oxford Street landmark now competes with Harvey Nichols in the high fashion stakes, but if fashion's not your thing, head straight to the devastating food hall.
Oxford Street: 400 Oxford St, W1 · 9.30am–9pm; Sun 11.30am–6.15pm · www.selfridges.com

SHOWstudio Shop
ART / KNICK KNACKS / WOW

Nick Knight's groundbreaking interactive fashion website now offers unique collectors' items from shoots and catwalk shows alongside original photographic prints and one-off creations by fashion luminaries.
Belgravia: 19 Motcomb St, SW1 · 11am–6pm. Closed Sat, Sun · showstudio.com/shop

Sister Ray
CDS / VINYL

For all you audiophiles out there, this is the largest, longest-running indie record store in London's West End. It sells new releases, a huge range of classic albums plus a selection of rare and second-hand vinyl.
Soho: 34–35 Berwick St, W1 (+ branches) · 10am–8pm; Sun noon–6pm · www.sisterray.co.uk

Smythson
BAGS / STATIONERY

One of London's oldest surviving brands, the heritage luxury stationery maker is today increasingly fashion oriented, with its smart and colourful range of handbags, purses, travel wallets and leather diaries.
Mayfair: 40 New Bond St, W1S (+ branches) · 9.30am (10am Sat)–7pm (8pm Thu); Sun noon-6pm · www.smythson.com

Solange Azagury-Partridge
JEWELLERY

This spectacular, two-floored boutique showcases the classy costume jewellery that has made the iconoclastic London-born designer the toast of everyone from Tilda Swinton to the Design Museum.

Mayfair: 5 Carlos Place, W1 · 10am–6pm. Closed Sun · solange.co.uk

Stella McCartney
FASHION / KIDS / LINGERIE / SHOES

Make a pilgrimage to the apartment-style Mayfair flagship of London's exemplary catwalk designer.

Mayfair: 30 Bruton St, W1 (+ branches) · 10am–7pm. Closed Sun · www.stellamccartney.com

Stephen Jones Millinery
FASHION / HATS

This London milliner burst onto the London fashion scene during its explosion of street style in the late 70s and has since worked with everyone from John Galliano to Rei Kawakubo.

Covent Garden: 36 Great Queen St, WC2 · 11am–6pm (7pm Thu). Closed Sat–Mon · www.stephenjonesmillinery.com

Tatty Devine DON'T MISS
JEWELLERY

Plastic Fantastic sums up the appeal of London's most inventive accessory makers. Their much-imitated bright acrylic necklaces and badges are artworks in themselves and fast becoming cult classics.

Covent Garden: 44 Monmouth St, WC2 (+ branches) · 11am–7pm; Sun noon–5pm · www.tattydevine.com

Topshop
FASHION

Approach the hub of the Topshop empire with military precision: head there in the morning, hit the edgy Boutique and capsule collections, have a quick browse of the basement shoes before getting your nails done at nail art phenomenon Wah Nails, and then get out with your sanity!

Oxford Circus: 214 Oxford St, W1 (+ branches) · 9am–9pm (10pm Wed–Fri); Sun 11.30am–6pm · www.topshop.com

Tracey Neuls
SHOES

The Cordwainers' graduate designs timeless yet ultra-fashionable leather heels and flats that display a love of detail. The shop is a delight: shoes hang elegantly from the ceiling or are piled pêle-mêle on the mantelpiece.

Marylebone: 29 Marylebone Lane, W1 · 11am–6.30pm; Sat, Sun noon–5pm · www.traceyneuls.com

Urban Outfitters
FASHION / MENS / MULTIBRAND / INTERIORS

Quieter than the Oxford Circus branch but featuring the same selection of edgy but affordable clothing and accessories alongside boutique collections from the likes of Acne, Vanesso Bruno and Peter Jensen.

Covent Garden: 42-56 Earlham St, WC2 (+ branches) · 10am–7pm (8pm Thu, Fri); Sun noon–6pm · www.urbanoutfitters.co.uk

Victoria Beckham NEW
FASHION

The celebrity designer's first flagship, just up the road from the iconic Dover Street Market, is modern and minimal, dominated by a dramatic stairway in polished concrete.

Mayfair: 36 Dover St, W1 · 11am–7pm; Sun, noon–5pm · www.victoriabeckham.com

The Vintage Showroom
DON'T MISS / MENS / VINTAGE

Forget tatty retro, this impeccable Covent Garden boutique stocks prime vintage menswear, with an archive covering early to mid 20th century workwear, military garb and English tailoring.

Covent Garden: 14 Earlham St, WC2 · 11.30am–7.30pm; Sun noon–6pm · www.thevintageshowroom.com

Wah Nails Topshop
NAILS

Wah began as a fanzine dedicated to hip-hop culture and is now an international nail art phenomenon. Their nail bar on the ground floor of Topshop is a firm favourite with London fashionistas looking for the most out-there custom designs.

West End: Lower ground floor, Topshop, 214 Oxford St, W1 · Noon–11pm (10.30pm Sun) · wah-nails.com

Windle & Moodie
HAIR

With its tagline 'from catwalk to the kerb', Windle & Moodie is much loved for its speed-styling service – namely fashion-savvy cuts from hairdressers who also work backstage at shows.

Covent Garden: 41-45 Shorts Gardens, WC2 · 10am–6.15pm (7.15pm Wed–Fri); Sat 9.30am–5.30pm. Closed Sun · www.windleandmoodie.com

Burlington Arcade
FASHION / MYTHIC / SHOES / WOW

Luxury runway meets historic gem in this gorgeous arcade from 1819. Enjoy luxury leather from Monocle faves Thomas Lyte, vintage Rolexes and Jimmy Choo's first standalone menswear shop. And watch out for the top-hatted beadles who keep the peace.

Piccadilly: Burlington Arcade, W1 · 9am–7.30pm. Sun 11am–6pm · www.burlington-arcade.co.uk

Carnaby Street
MYTHIC

Having a second wind after its '60s Pop Art and Mod heyday, the regenerated shopping district now features classy chains on the main strip and interesting independents hidden in the three-tiered Kingly Court complex.

Charing Cross Road Bookshops
ART / BOOKS / BUDGET / DESIGN

A cluster of secondhand bookshops that stretch south down Charing Cross Rd, between Shaftesbury Ave and Leicester Square, this is one stretch of London that (mercifully) hasn't changed in decades. Expect everything from rare poetry first editions to hip typography tomes.

St. James's Park
PARKS & GARDENS

Skirted by Buckingham Palace and the Houses of Parliament, this is London's prettiest and most genteel green stretch. Stop for lunch at Oliver Peyton's idyllic café/brasserie Inn the Park.

St. Paul's Cathedral
MONUMENT / VIEW / WOW

'If you seek a monument, look around you' is inscribed on architect Sir Christopher Wren's tomb in the crypt. Sights include an alterpiece by Bill Viola, a memorial to Lawrence of Arabia and vertiginous views of the capital from the Golden Gallery.

The City: St Paul's Churchyard, EC4 · 8.30am–4pm · Sun services only · www.stpauls.co.uk

HANGOUTS
Natasha Davis

✕ ✕ ✕

*Natasha is a buyer and bookseller at **Daunt Books**, at the handsome, original branch in Marylebone, famous for its Edwardian interior comprising long oak galleries, skylights and William Morris prints, and specialized in travel titles. A decade on, Natasha still finds Daunt a wonderful place to work, and is busy preparing the third Daunt Festival, coming up in March 2016. A born and bred Londoner, she lives on Russell Square in Bloomsbury.*
www.dauntbooks.co.uk

Towpath
There's nothing nicer than eating their fried eggs on buttery toast on a sunny morning whilst watching the joggers, cyclists, dogs and swans go past on the canal.
towpathcafe.com

Morito
Their eclectic playlist as well as their delicious tapas always makes for a fun evening. The chickpea salad is a must!
morito.co.uk

Tokyobike
A fantastic bike shop where I have my bike serviced but also always manage to buy something from their carefully curated selection of Japanese design products.
tokyobike.co.uk

Peter Harrington
My favourite place to browse exquisite first editions. A book-lover's heaven!
peterharrington.co.uk

Courtauld Gallery
I studied at King's College next door to the Courtauld many moons ago and would often find myself here rather than in the library in between lectures. It's a heavenly space, and Manet's Bar at the Folies-Bergere never ceases to beguile.
www.courtauld.ac.uk

Hampstead Heath
A swim in the ladies ponds in the summer or a stomp up Parliament Hill in the winter are ultimate life-affirming ways to spend a Sunday morning .
www.hampsteadheath.net

NOTES

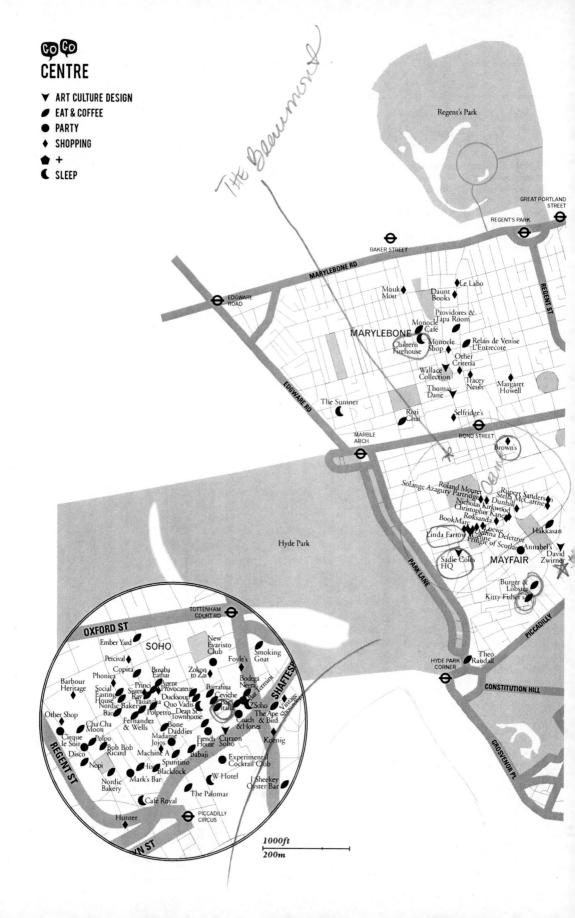

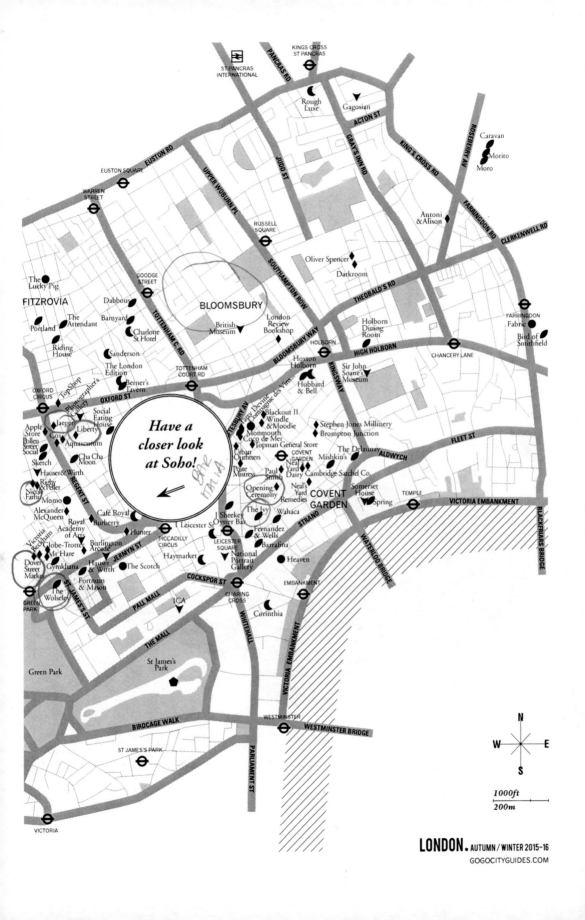

KINGS CROSS
ST PANCRAS

ST PANCRAS
INTERNATIONAL

PANCRAS RD

ACTON ST

KING'S CROSS RD

ROSEBERY AV

Rough
Luxe

Gagosian

Caravan
Morito
Moro

EUSTON RD

EUSTON SQUARE

UPPER WOBURN PL

JUDD ST

FARRINGDON RD

CLERKENWELL RD

WARREN
STREET

RUSSELL
SQUARE

Antoni
&Alison

THEOBALD'S RD

SOUTHAMPTON ROW

GRAY'S INN RD

Oliver Spencer
Darkroom

The
Lucky Pig

GOODGE
STREET

FITZROVIA

Dabbous

BLOOMSBURY

London
Review
Bookshop

Holborn
Dining
Room

FARRINGDON

Fabric

Portland

The
Attendant

Barnyard

TOTTENHAM C. RD

Charlotte
St Hotel

British
Museum

BLOOMSBURY WAY

HOLBORN

HIGH HOLBORN

Bird of
Smithfield

Riding
House

Sanderson

HOLBORN

Hoxton
Holborn

KINGSWAY

CHANCERY LANE

The London
Edition

Berner's
Tavern

TOTTENHAM
COURT RD

Sir John
Soane's
Museum

OXFORD
CIRCUS

TopShop

Photographer's
Gallery

OXFORD ST

Hubbard
& Bell

FLEET ST

Apple
Store
Pollen
Street
Social

Jaeger
Cos

Liberty

Social
Eating
House

AERAY DEVINE

Compagnie des Vins

Blackout II.
Windle
&Moodie

Stephen Jones Millinery

Brompton Junction

ALDWYCH

Aquascutum

Cha Cha
Moon

Monmouth
Coco de Mer

Topman General Store

The Delaunay

Sketch

REGENT ST

SHAFTESBURY AV

Urban
Outfitters

COVENT
GARDEN

Mishkin's

Hauser&Wirth

Poste
Mistress

Paul
Smith

Dairy
Yard

Cambridge Satchel Co.

Somerset
House

Have a
closer look
at Soho!

BAR
ITALIA

Nicola
Farhi

Rigby
&Peller

Opening
Ceremony

Neal's
Yard
Remedies

COVENT
GARDEN

Spring

TEMPLE

VICTORIA EMBANKMENT

Momo

Alexander
McQueen

The Ivy

Wahaca

STRAND

Café Royal

Burberry

Hunter

J Sheekey
Oyster Bar

Royal
Academy
of Arts

PICCADILLY
CIRCUS

Leicester St

LEICESTER
SQUARE

Fernandez
& Wells

Barrafina

WATERLOO BRIDGE

BLACKFRIARS BRIDGE

Victoria
Beckham

Globe-Trotter
Mr Hare

Burlington
Arcade

JERMYN ST

Haymarket

National
Portrait
Gallery

Heaven

Dover
Street
Market

Gymkhana

Hauser
& Wirth

The Scotch

The
Wolseley

ST JAMES'S ST

Fortnum
& Mason

COCKSPUR ST

CHARING
CROSS

EMBANKMENT

GREEN
PARK

PALL MALL

ICA

WHITEHALL

Corinthia

VICTORIA EMBANKMENT

Green Park

THE MALL

St James's
Park

St James's
Park

BIRDCAGE WALK

WESTMINSTER

WESTMINSTER BRIDGE

ST JAMES'S PARK

PARLIAMENT ST

N
W E
S

1000ft
200m

VICTORIA

LONDON. AUTUMN / WINTER 2015-16
GOGOCITYGUIDES.COM

GOGO
WEST

CHELSEA × KNIGHTSBRIDGE × NOTTING HILL × PADDINGTON
PORTOBELLO ROAD × SOUTH KENSINGTON × WESTBOURNE GROVE

Ah, West London – land of SLOANES, TRUSTAFARIANS
& BOHO CHIC, where life is divided between upmarket
boutiques, elegant mansions & stellar EXHIBITIONS.
Notting Hill Gate, Ladbroke Grove & Westbourne Park enclose
dainty SQUARES & neighbourhood RESTAURANTS,
while Portobello Market & Westbourne Grove/Ledbury Rd entice
the SHOPPERS. Beyond Hyde Park, plush Knightsbridge, home
to Harrods & 'Harvey Nicks', & the Gallic/jet-set South Ken
& Chelsea, embody GENTRIFICATION. Once known
as 'Albertopolis', the area counts endless MUSEUMS including
the V&A, funded by the Prince off the back of the 1851
Great Exhibition. As gilded as the man's memorial, the famous
King's Rd – centre of the HIPPIE COUNTERCULTURE –
has lost its cred but gained Saatchi's IMPRESSIVE HQ since 2008.

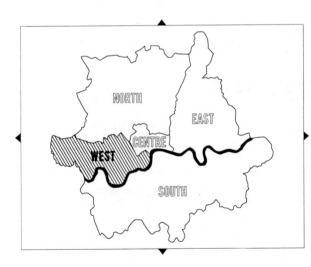

GETTING AROUND

From **Notting Hill** tube stroll along
shop-lined **Pembridge Rd** before taking
Portobello Rd and walking north
towards the Westway and Westbourne
Park, looking up for the Trellick Tower.
South Ken is the main artery for the
museums around **Thurloe Place**, while
Sloane Square leads to the **King's
Rd** shops. If you can't face navigating
the chichi streets on foot (Hyde Park
will take you from Notting Hill to South
Ken in around 20 min) hop on the No.9
Routemaster at Royal Albert Hall, exiting
at **Brompton Rd**, home to the luxe
department stores of **Knightsbridge**.

ART CULTURE DESIGN

Natural History Museum
DON'T MISS / FREE ENTRY / KIDS / MUSEUM

Collections of botany, entomology, mineralogy, palaeontology and zoology plus a fab collection of dinosaur skeletons within a beautifully ornate decor.
South Kensington: Cromwell Rd, SW7 · 10am–5.50pm · www.nhm.ac.uk

Royal Court Theatre
THEATRE

The *NY Times*'s 'most innovative theatre in Europe' has been kicking Sloane Square into touch since 1956, when John Osborne's raw *Look Back in Anger* invented modern British drama. Excellent bookshop and café-bar too.
Chelsea: Sloane Square, SW1 · www.royalcourttheatre.com

Saatchi Gallery
ART / FREE ENTRY / MYTHIC

The man who unleashed the YBAs with 1997's controversial 'Sensation' exhibition now boasts one of the city's most visited galleries, presenting young and international artists whose work has rarely been exhibited in the UK.
Chelsea: Duke of York's HQ, King's Rd, SW3 · 10am–6pm · www.saatchi-gallery.co.uk

Science Museum
FREE ENTRY / KIDS / MUSEUM

Very popular neighbour of the Natural History Museum features crowd-pleasing technological exhibits – the Apollo 10 command module – and, in the Wellcome Wing, traces discoveries in brain science and genetics.
Sth Kensington: Exhibition Rd, SW7 · 10am–6pm · www.sciencemuseum.org.uk

Serpentine Gallery DON'T MISS
ART / BOOKS / FREE ENTRY / WOW

Big-hitting contemporary gallery co-directed by über-curator Hans-Ulrich Obrist also houses a Koenig Books satellite, selling the finest selection of tomes on modern and contemporary art, photography and architecture.
Kensington: Kensington Gardens, W2 · 10am–6pm. Closed Mon · www.serpentinegalleries.org

Serpentine Sackler Gallery
ART / FREE ENTRY / WOW

A second space for London's internationally acclaimed Serpentine Gallery. Designed by Pritzker Architecture Prize laureate Zaha Hadid, it is located just five minutes' walk from the original gallery, inside The Magazine, a former 1805 gunpowder store.
Kensington: West Carriage Drive, Kensington Gardens, W2 · 10am–6pm. Closed Mon · www.serpentinegalleries.org

Tate Britain
ART / FREE ENTRY / MUSEUM

A rejuvenated Tate Britain reopened to the public in 2013 after two years of renovations, with a beautifully restored rotunda, a new restaurant and café, a new staircase and the reopening of the riverside entrance. But go to enjoy the new hang of the permanent collections, dedicated to British art and international modern art.
Millbank: Millbank, SW1 · 10am–6pm · www.tate.org.uk

V&A DON'T MISS
FREE ENTRY / LATES / MUSEUM

Sublime showcase of the decorative arts, including the New British Galleries 1500–1900, which trace the history of UK designers from Morris to Mackintosh. Alongside an extensive programme of talks (there's a great fashion series) Friday Lates offer DJ-fuelled fun after hours.
Sth Kensington: Cromwell Rd, SW7 · 10am–5.45pm (10pm Fri) · www.vam.ac.uk

EAT & COFFEE

202 £££
BREAKFAST / BRUNCH / TERRACE

This glam café is part of Brit designer Nicole Farhi's Westbourne Grove concept store. Brunch is great; enjoy your French toast with maple syrup and bacon on the outdoor tables in summer.
Notting Hill: 202 Westbourne Grove, W11 · 020 7727 2722 · 8.30am (10am Mon)–6pm; Thu–Sat 8.30am–10pm; Sun 10am–5pm · www.202london.com

Casa Brindisa ££
SPANISH / TAKE AWAY / TAPAS

The rustic basement deli, bar and 'Jamoneria' is the elegant sibling of the thriving Southwark Tapas Brindisa. Prices can add up, but you're assured the finest imported Spanish produce.
Sth Kensington: 7–9 Exhibition Rd, SW7 · 020 7590 0008 · 11am (10am Sat)–11.30pm; Sun 10am–10.30pm · www.brindisatapaskitchens.com

Claude's Kitchen ££
BRITISH / BRUNCH / ORGANIC

Claude Compton's rustic, Brit menu features fish fresh in daily from South Cornwall and organic and free-range meat within a relaxed and friendly dining room, tucked away in out-of-the-way Parson's Green.
Parson's Green: 51 Parsons Green Lane, SW6 · 020 7371 8517 · 4pm (noon Sat)–midnight. Sun noon–10.30pm · claudeskitchen.co.uk

Dinner by Heston ££££
BRITISH / WOW

Heston Blumenthal's starry London debut offers a historically-inspired British menu – so think 'meat fruit circa 1500' (chicken liver parfait resembling a mandarin). The room is a marvel in itself, with a theatrical pulley and £70,000 clockwork spitroast.
Knightsbridge: 66 Knightsbridge, SW1 · 020 7201 3833 · Noon–3pm, 6.30–11pm · www.dinnerbyheston.com

Dock Kitchen ££
MODERN EURO

From his open kitchen, chef Stevie Parle serves a daily changing menu of creative fusion food. Located in a converted Victorian Wharf building, the restaurant overlooks the Grand Union Canal and features an exclusive display of the full Tom Dixon furniture and lighting collection (the Tom Dixon shop is downstairs).
Ladbroke Grove: Portobello Docks, 342–344 Ladbroke Grove, W10 · 020 8962 1610 · Noon–3pm, 7–9.30pm (lunch only Sun) · www.dockkitchen.co.uk

Egg Break ££ NEW
BREAKFAST / BRUNCH / MODERN EURO / SMALL PLATES

The wide-ranging menu crisscrosses Europe with all sorts of fresh soups, salads, small plates and burgers, all based around the humble egg, and the drinks list covers everything from Bellinis to organic cold-pressed

juices. Set up by Soho House, its style pedigree is assured.
Notting Hill: 30 Uxbridge St, W8 · No reservations · 7am–6pm. Closed Mon, Tue · www.eggbreak.com

Electric Diner £
AMERICAN / BREAKFAST / BRUNCH / BURGER / TERRACE

The chef behind Chicago's award-winning Au Cheval diner inspired the concept and collaborated on the French-American menu. Expect fun, updated classics including the fried house-made bologna sandwich. There's a cute booth and bar seating, and a specially chosen soundtrack played from the Diner's reel-to-reel machine.
Notting Hill: 191 Portobello Road, W11 · 020 7908 9696 · 8am–midnight (1am Thu–Sat); Sun 8am–11pm · www.electricdiner.com

Gourmet Burger Kitchen £
BUDGET / BURGERS / CHIPS

Wildly popular chain set up by three Kiwis that spares burger fans from the indignities of McDonalds.
Sth Kensington: 107 Old Brompton Rd, SW7 (+ branches) · 0207 581 8942 · 11am–11pm (10pm Sun) · www.gbk.co.uk

Hereford Rd £££
BRITISH

The old butcher's shop has been smartly spruced up and the classic fare from ex St. John Bread & Wine chef Tom Pemberton attracts a relaxed and very appreciative local crowd.
Westbourne Grove: 3 Hereford Rd, W2 · 020 7727 1144 · Noon–3pm (4pm Sun), 6pm–10.30pm (10pm Sun) · www.herefordroad.org

John Doe ££ NEW
BEER / BRITISH

Wild, sustainable and seasonal British ingredients – with a focus on venison – prepared over wood and charcoal for some great smoky flavours. Honouring the historical combination of game and beer (Henry VIII would be proud), craft beer is given the same attention as the artisan wine list.
Notting Hill: 46 Golborne Road, W10 · 020 8969 3280 · Noon–midnight. Closed Sun, Mon · www.johndoerestaurants.com

Kurobuta £££ NEW
JAPANESE

This charismatic, upbeat, new-gen Japanese restaurant serves an East-West fusion of say tea smoked lamb or salmon gravadlax and avocado tartare with dill mayo, rice crunchies and fresh yuzu zest. And now with a 2nd address in Chelsea, at 312 King's Road.
Marble Arch: 17-20 Kendal St, W2 (+ branches) · 020 3475 4158 · Noon–10.30pm daily · www.kurobuta-london.com

Launceston Place £££
BRITISH / ORGANIC

One-Michelin-star modern British exquisiteness with a wine list to match. The 3-course set lunch menu is good value.
Kensington: 1a Launceston Place, W8 · 020 7937 6912 · Noon–2.30pm; 6–10pm. Closed Mon, Tue lunch · www.launcestonplace-restaurant.co.uk

The Ledbury £££
MODERN EURO

Plush two-Michelin-star showcase for rising star Brett Graham's flawless contemporary cuisine. The 4-course set menu at lunch is good value.
Notting Hill: 127 Ledbury Rd, W11 · 020 7792 9090 · Noon–2pm, 6.30pm (7pm Sun)–9.45pm. Closed Mon, Tue lunch. · www.theledbury.com

Lucky Seven Diner ££
AMERICAN / BREAKFAST / BURGERS / KIDS

Tom Conran's fun take on East Coast diner culture features authentic 100% Aberdeen Angus burgers, American breakfasts and XXX thick milkshakes.
Westbourne Grove: 127 Westbourne Park Rd, W2 · No reservations · Noon (9am Sat)–11pm · www.lucky7london.co.uk

Magazine ££
FUSION / WOW

The restaurant inside the curvy, Zaha Hadid designed Serpentine Sackler gallery. New head chef Emmanuel Eger's philosophy of applying simple techniques to create bold yet balanced flavours marries well with the clean and bright interiors.
Kensington: West Carriage Drive, Kensington Gardens, W2 · 020 7298 7552 · 8am (9am Sun)–6pm. Closed Mon · www.magazine-restaurant.co.uk

Mazi ££
GREEK / TERRACE

Innovative, tasty and refined Greek food and an entirely Greek wine list; another plus is their sunny back garden with tables under a grape vine canopy.

Notting Hill: 12-14 Hillgate Street, W8 · 020 7229 3794 · Noon–3pm, 6.30pm–11pm. Closed Mon, Tue lunch · www.mazi.co.uk

Ottolenghi ££ DON'T MISS
BREAKFAST / CAKES / DELI / TAKE AWAY / VEGETARIAN

The best cooked breakfasts in town and extravagant pastries from self-confessed cake geek Yotam Ottolenghi; and the Mediterranean-led salads and vegetable dishes aren't bad either.
Notting Hill: 63 Ledbury Rd, W11 (+ branches) · No reservations · 8am–8pm (7pm Sat); Sun 8.30am–6pm · www.ottolenghi.co.uk

Pizza East Portobello ££
DELI / ITALIAN / PIZZA /

The West London branch of Soho House Group's warehouse-style Shoreditch pizzeria boasts a boho makeover, with blue chairs and expansive views. Expect brunching families enjoying the tempting pizzas and Italian mains.
Notting Hill: 310 Portobello Rd, W10 (+ branches) · 020 8969 4500 · 8am–11.30pm (10.30pm Sun) · www.pizzaeast.com/portobello

Polpo Notting Hill ££ NEW
ITALIAN / SMALL PLATES

The latest outpost of the Venetian *bàcaro* empire gets it right again serving tasty but simple Italian small plates within a cool distressed décor
Notting Hill: 126-128 Notting Hill Gate, W11 (+ branches) · 020 7229 3283 · Noon–11pm (10.30pm Sun) · www.polpo.co.uk

River Café £££ DON'T MISS
BAR / ITALIAN / TERRACE / VIEW

Their cookbooks revolutionised British cooking, bringing seasonal home-style Italian cooking to the fore and inspiring the likes of Jamie Oliver. Made over after a 2008 fire, there's now an open-plan kitchen and cheese room to go with the stunning riverside views.
Hammersmith: Thames Wharf, Rainville Rd, W6 · 020 7386 4200 · 12.30–2.30pm (3pm Sun), 7–11pm. Closed Sun dinner · www.rivercafe.co.uk

 TO LISTEN TO
NICK MULVEY
FIRST MIND
(FICTION RECORDS)

Rosa's ££ NEW
COCKTAILS / THAI / TAKE AWAY

Find all the classics such as pad Thai or green curry at the Chelsea outpost of this popular modern Thai café. And why not a cardamom and grapefruit punch or a sweet basil smash from the bar to compliment your curry?

Chelsea: 246 Fulham Road, SW10 · 020 3773 8384 · 11am–10.30pm (midnight Fri, Sat); Sun noon–10pm · www.rosasthaicafe.com

Royal China Queensway ££
DON'T MISS / CHINESE / DIM SUM

Authentic Hong Kong-style dim sum. With no reservations on the weekends, expect to queue on Sundays.

Bayswater: 13 Queensway, W2 · 020 7221 2535 · Noon–11pm (11.30pm Fri & Sat); Sun 11am–10pm · rcguk.co.uk

Santo ££
MEXICAN

Fabulous Mexican food and margaritas from chef-patron Fernando. On Fridays and Saturdays resident DJ FLex spins Latin beat, salsa & funk.

Notting Hill: 299 Portobello Rd, W10 · 020 8968 4590 · 6pm (noon Fri, Sat)–11pm. Closed Sun & Mon · www.santovillage.com

Tombo £
DELI / JAPANESE

Homely, communal-style restaurant modelled on the delis in Japanese department stores from the founders of London's Tokio clothing boutique.

Sth Kensington: 29 Thurloe Place, SW7 · No reservations · 11.30am–10pm daily · tombodeliandcafe.com

The Troubadour £
BAR / COFFEE / LIVE MUSIC / TERRACE

One of London's last remaining '50s coffee houses with a proud history as a 'low temperature centre of liberty, peace, and bohemian artistic energy.' They also have a lovely garden and a tasty cocktail list. The Troubadour Club in the cellar hosts an eclectic program of live gigs almost nightly.

Earl's Court: 263-265 Old Brompton Rd, SW5 · 020 7370 1434 · 9am–midnight (2am Fri, Sat) · troubadour.co.uk

West Thirty Six ££ NEW
BAR / BREAKFAST / COCKTAILS / MODERN EURO / TERRACE

Located inside a two-storey townhouse, this smart all-day affair offers a variety of rooms and outdoor spaces to eat, drink, work and hang out. The menu spotlights the charcoal grill, and there's an al-fresco bar and BBQ for summer fun.

Notting Hill: 36 Golborne Road, W10 · 020 3752 0530 · 8am–midnight daily · www.w36.co.uk

Wormwood ££ NEW
MEDITERRANEAN / SMALL PLATES

The Algerian born chef/ owner Rabah prepares colourful dishes inspired by Mediterranean mezze culture – from Morocco to Lebanon, Spain to Greece – and executed with French gastronomic flair. Think a pork belly tagine, tomatoes with vanilla, or foie gras with pimiento del piquillo and chocolate.

Notting Hill: 116 All Saints Rd, W11 · 020 7854 1808 · Noon–2pm, 6pm–10pm. Closed Sun & Mon lunch · wormwoodrestaurant.com

Yashin Sushi £££ DON'T MISS
JAPANESE / SUSHI

Known for its anti-soya sauce stance, Yashin does extraordinarily flavoursome sushi (blowtorched for added kick), fresh oysters and excellent tofu. The Japanese teas are cheap, but you'll need to save up for the rest.

Kensington: 1A Argyll Rd, W8 · 020 7938 1536 · Noon–3pm, 6–11pm · www.yashinsushi.com

PARTY

Barts
BAR / COCKTAILS / SSHHH / TERRACE

To find this fun bar you have to walk through a 1930s apartment building until you come to a black door with a lantern and inconspicuous sign. Inside, the place is packed with quirky retro ornaments, plus there's a Cuban-themed Havana garden that's great in summer.

Chelsea: Chelsea Cloisters, 87 Sloane Ave, SW3 · 6pm–midnight (1am Wed–Sat) · www.barts-london.com

Beach Blanket Babylon
BAR / COCKTAILS / TERRACE

This longstanding restaurant and bar pulls in young moneyed locals with its OTT décor, reliable menu and upbeat vibe. Pull up a faux Louis XIV armchair and sip your Porn Star martini by the open fire. Now with a sister site in Shoreditch.

Notting Hill: 45 Ledbury Rd, W11 · Noon (10am Sat, Sun; 6pm Mon)–midnight · www.beachblanket.co.uk

The Blue Bar
COCKTAILS / WOW

Sky-blue armchairs, deep-blue plasterwork and navy-blue menus… the name is not for nothing. This celebrity haunt also features seductive low lighting and cocktails that may be pricey but offer a masterclass in sophistication.

Knightsbridge: The Berkeley, Wilton Place, SW1 · 11am–1am (11pm Sun) · www.the-berkeley.co.uk

Chelsea Arts Club
BAR / LITERARY EVENTS / MEMBERS CLUB / MYTHIC

This long-standing and gloriously eccentric member's club was founded by Whistler and his bohemian chums in 1891. These days leading artists enjoy its weekend lunches and exhibitions, but you'll need to find an arty friend to sign you in.

Chelsea: 143 Old Church St, SW3 · www.chelseaartsclub.com

Churchill Arms
BRITISH / PUB / SUNDAY ROAST / THAI

Brilliant cosy pub riddled with pictures of the cigar-toting British PM. After a few Fuller's ales or a dram of London Porter, you don't even need to move to get a Thai food fix. The knees-up for Winston's birthday (Nov 30) is particularly riotous.

Kensington: 119 Kensington Church St, W8 · 11am–midnight (11pm Mon–Wed); Sun noon–10.30pm · churchillarmskensington.co.uk

The Cow
MODERN EURO / PUB

This friendly gastropub is a Notting Hill institution. Downstairs enjoy a Guinesss or take your pick from the wide selection of beers, then when you're hungry, order a fish stew from the blackboard bar menu, or head upstairs for the finer dining, also with a focus on English seafood.

Notting Hill: 89 Westbourne Park Rd, W2 · Noon–11pm (10.30pm Sun) · thecowlondon.co.uk

Crazy Homies
BAR / COCKTAILS / MEXICAN / TEQUILA

A loud and kitsch Mexican themed bar and canteen next door to Lucky 7 Diner, now with the basement Chamucos Clubhouse downstairs, pimping London's best tequila list.

Westbourne Grove: 125 Westbourne Park Rd, W2 · 6–11pm (midnight Fri); Sat, Sun noon–midnight · www.crazyhomieslondon.co.uk

Dirty Bones
AMERICAN / BAR / COCKTAILS

The hot-dogs are excellent at this posh basement 'dive and dog bar.'
Kensington: 20 Kensington Church St, W8 · 6pm–12.30am (10pm Sun). Closed Mon · dirty-bones.com

Electric Cinema
DON'T MISS / BAR / FILM

London's oldest working cinema whispers luxury with an auditorium bar, leather seats and romantic sofas for two.
Notting Hill: 191 Portobello Rd, W11 · www.electriccinema.co.uk

Evans & Peel Detective Agency
BAR / COCKTAILS / SSHHH

You won't get in to this basement speakeasy for your two-hour 'appointment' without being asked a few questions about the case. Once past the fake bookshelf, bar snacks and cocktails are served amid handsome décor.
Earl's Court: 310c Earl's Court Rd, SW5 · 5pm–midnight (12.30am Fri, Sat). Closed Sun, Mon · www.evansandpeel.com

Notting Hill Arts Club
CLUB / GRUNGY

Pioneering basement club whose genre-defining nights are the best in the area. Creation Records founder (and Oasis guru) Alan McGee's Death Disco provides a haven for indie celebs and punk veterans every Wednesday.
Notting Hill: 19–21 Notting Hill Gate, W11 · 7pm (4pm Sat)–2am; Sun 6pm–1am · www.nottinghillartsclub.com

Portobello Star
BAR / COCKTAILS

This slick Notting HIll bar takes its cocktails seriously.
Notting Hill: 171 Portobello Rd, W11 · 11am–11.30pm (12.30am Fri, Sat) · portobellostarbar.co.uk

Tabernacle
COMEDY / LITERARY EVENTS / LIVE MUSIC

The grade II-listed community arts centre has seen it all over the years, from the Raincoats' debut gig to rehearsals by the Stones. Today it plays host to gigs, talks and comedy.
Notting Hill: 34-35 Powis Square, W11 · www.tabernaclew11.com

The Windsor Castle
PUB / CHIPS / SUNDAY ROAST

This local looks like a film set with its low ceilings and charming maze of rooms. There's decent pub grub too plus a good selection of ales and wine.
Kensington: 114 Campden Hill Rd, W8 · Noon–11pm (10.30pm Sun) · www.thewindsorcastlekensington.co.uk

SHOPPING

Anya Hindmarch
BAGS

This is still the place to buy a handbag that embodies a bit of British wit. This original dedicated bespoke store is home to the full collection, always with acute attention to detail.
Knightsbridge: 15-17 Pont St, SW1 (+ branches) · 10am–6pm. Closed Sun · www.anyahindmarch.com

Conran Shop
DESIGN / INTERIORS

Inside the Art Deco masterpiece the Michelin House building, Terence Conran's brainchild offers everything you need for modern, urban living across furniture, lighting, kitchen and dining ware, from iconic designers to some of the hottest new talent from around the world.
Chelsea: Michelin House, 81 Fulham Rd, SW3 · 10am–6pm (7pm Wed, Thu); Sat 10am–6.30pm; Sun noon–6pm · www.conranshop.co.uk

Couverture & the Garbstore
FASHION / INTERIORS / KIDS / MENS / MULTIBRAND

Two cute stores run by a couple focusing on one-offs and cool international brands. Couverture stocks an eclectic mix of homewares, kids' and womenswear and basement Garbstore offers hip threads for men.
Notting Hill: 188 Kensington Park Rd, W11 · 10am–6pm. Closed Sun · www.couvertureandthegarbstore.com

Cowshed
BEAUTY / SPA

Enjoy a facial or other treatment using something from the Cowshed range of products, made in England using the very best organic, wildcrafted and fairly-traded plant extracts and essential oils at this chic spa, shop and café.
Holland Park: 119 Portland Rd, W11 (+ branches) · 9am–8pm (7pm Sat); Sun 10am–5pm · www.cowshedonline.com

Cutler & Gross DON'T MISS
EYEWEAR / VINTAGE

The landmark London bespoke eyewear company's original 1969 flagship. Check their collabs with designers such as Maison Margiela and Giles Deacon. And don't miss Cutler & Gross Vintage down the street at 7 Knightsbridge Green.
Knightsbridge: 16 Knightsbridge Green, SW1 · 9.30am–7pm; Sun noon–5pm · www.cutlerandgross.com

Daylesford Organic
BRITISH / ORGANIC / TAKE AWAY

'Straight from our farm to your fork' goes the motto. Daylesford Organic has been selling fresh produce from their sustainable farm's market garden, as well as artisan cheese and breads from the creamery and bakery and organic meats from their animals, for over 25 years. The café is a great spot to eat, drink and relax with friends.
Notting Hill: 208-212 Westbourne Grove, W11 (+ branches) · 8am–9.30pm (7pm Mon); Sun 10am–4pm · daylesford.com

Harrods
DEPARTMENT STORE

The lavish 7-floor emporium is an encyclopedia of British luxury. Don't miss the pet department, a novelty.
Knightsbridge: 87-135 Brompton Rd, SW1 · 10am–8pm; Sun 11.30am–6pm · www.harrods.com

Harvey Nichols
DEPARTMENT STORE / DELI

Five floors dedicated to designer and cutting-edge clothing and accessories plus a fine food hall and restaurant. Knightsbridge ladies who lunch simply wouldn't go anywhere else.
Knightsbridge: 109-125 Knightsbridge, SW1 · 10am–8pm; Sun 11.30am–6pm · www.harveynichols.com

Honest Jon's
MYTHIC / VINYL

A tiny gem rammed with reggae, soul and jazz that welcomed Johnny Rotten and Malcolm McLaren in its first incarnation and is now the base of an eponymous world music label in collaboration with Blur's Damon Albarn.
Notting Hill: 278 Portobello Rd, W10 · 10am–6pm; Sun 11am–5pm · www.honestjons.com

Hornet's
MENS / MYTHIC / VINTAGE

Fashion comes and goes but this renowned gentlemen's clothier (with 3 shops in the heart of Kensington) is an eternal fixture offering sartorial elegance across hats, shoes, and suits.
Kensington: 2 & 4 Kensington Church Walk, & 36b Kensington Church St, W8 · 11am–6pm (4pm Sun) · hornetskensington.co.uk

The Idler Academy &
BOOKS / COFFEE / LITERARY EVENTS

Mining an 18th-century coffeehouse vibe, this cerebral West London bookshop dedicated to 'Philosophy, Husbandry and Merriment' is just the place to catch a philosophy lecture (Wednesday evenings) or learn the lost art of calligraphy. Then ponder the bigger picture in the café.
Bayswater: 81 Westbourne Park Rd, W2 · 10am–6pm; Sun 11am–5pm. Closed Mon, Tue · idler.co.uk/academy

Kokon to Zai Notting Hill
FASHION / MENS / MULTIBRAND

Get noticed sporting cutting-edge fashion from radical design duo Marjan Pejoski and Sasha Bezovski. This second location is inside an atmospheric 19th-century butcher shop in Notting Hill.
Notting Hill: 86 Golborne Rd, W10 · 10am–6pm. Closed Sun · www.kokontozai.co.uk

The Library
BOOKS / MENS

Head to this seriously stylish men's boutique for fashion heavyweights and avant garde stars like Dries Van Noten and Carol Christian Poell. They have a rather cool sideline in rare books too.
Sth Kensington: 268 Brompton Rd, SW3 · 10am–6.30pm (7pm Wed); Sun 12.30–5.30pm · www.thelibrary1994.com

Lulu Guinness
BAGS

The Brit handbag designer lives by the extravagant motto 'dare to be different', and her signature piece, the distinctive Dali-esque lips clutch, remains the brand's staple, injecting a touch of the surreal into mainstream fashion.
Chelsea: 3 Ellis St, SW1 · 10am–6pm. Closed Sun · www.luluguinness.com

Manolo Blahnik
SHOES

This Chelsea store has been the cult Spanish designer's flagship since 1972. The artfully adorned stiletto heel is the label's lynchpin and continues to bedazzle fashionistas.
Chelsea: 49-51 Old Church St, SW3 · 10am–5.30pm; Sat 10.30am–5pm. Closed Sun · www.manoloblahnik.com

Matches
FASHION / MULTIBRAND

The well established West London boutique keeps monied Londoners in Lanvin and McQueen, while across the road Matches Spy keeps an eye on trendy labels like Acne. Their My Stylist service is highly recommended.
Notting Hill: 60-64 & 85 Ledbury Rd, W11 · 10am (noon Sun)–6pm · www.matchesfashion.com

Merchant Archive
FASHION / INTERIORS / VINTAGE

A high-end vintage emporium previously limited to designers. These days, housed in an old Lipton general store, the archive spans Art Deco homewares, pristine YSL jumpsuits and one-off Comme des Garçons wallets.
Notting Hill: 19 Kensington Park Rd, W11 · 10am–6.30pm; Sun noon–5pm · www.merchantarchive.com

Music & Goods Exchange
BOOKS / BUDGET / EXCHANGE / MENS / VINTAGE VINYL / SHOES

If you're looking for a bargain these specialist secondhand shops dotted around Notting Hill are an absolute gift. Alongside the book and music/video outlets, stylist favourites Retro Man and Retro Woman are rammed with vintage and designer clothes and an incredible selection of shoes.
Notting Hill: Retro Man & Woman, 34; 32 & 20 Pembridge Rd, W11 (+ branches) · 10am–8pm · www.mgeshops.com

Paul Smith DON'T MISS
BAGS / FASHION / INTERIORS / MENS / SHOES

Paul Smith's 'shop in a house,' dotted with his own art collection, is the perfect encapsulation of his eccentric world. It features all his fashion collections, known for their trademark quirky-classic tailoring, plus the odd piece of furniture.
Notting Hill: 120 Kensington Park Rd, W11 · 10am–6pm (6.30pm Sat); Sun noon–5pm · www.paulsmith.co.uk

Portobello Road Market
DON'T MISS / ANTIQUES / MARKET / VINTAGE

The wildly popular market features antiques at the Notting Hill end and designer and vintage threads under the Westway towards Ladbroke Grove on Fridays and Saturdays. The latter is slightly more manic.
Notting Hill: 9am–5pm (1pm Thu; 6pm Fri, Sat) · Closed Sun · www.portobelloroad.co.uk

Rellik
VINTAGE

The famous Kate Moss favourite is situated at the foot of the iconic Trellick Tower and stocks the most desirable designs, from 1970s Halston dresses to 1980s Vivienne Westwood.
Ladbroke Grove: 8 Golborne Rd, W10 · 10am–6pm. Closed Sun, Mon · relliklondon.co.uk

Rough Trade
CDS / MYTHIC / VINYL

The trailblazing shop launched by Geoff Travis was a key landmark for the punk and reggae scenes, and the eponymous record label has helped launch everyone from The Smiths to The Strokes.
Notting Hill: 130 Talbot Rd, W11 (+ branches) · 10am–6.30pm; Sun 11am–5pm · www.roughtrade.com

The Shop at Bluebird
CONCEPT STORE

Vast lifestyle store founded by Jigsaw co-owner Belle Robinson that is a West London take on Dover Street Market. Beautiful displays showcase luxury labels, interiors and accessories.
Chelsea: 350 Kings Rd, SW3 · 10am–7pm; Sun noon–6pm · www.theshopatbluebird.com

Tom Dixon DON'T MISS
DESIGN / INTERIORS

Curated by the Brit design hero himself, the canal-side shop showcases the full Tom Dixon range of lighting and furniture, plus an exclusive selection of pieces from other brands.
Ladbroke Grove: Wharf Building, Portobello Dock, 344 Ladbroke Grove, W10 · 10am–6pm; Sun 11am–5pm · www.tomdixon.net

Wolf & Badger
CONCEPT STORE / FASHION / INTERIORS / WOW

Ignore the haughty W11 setting and you'll find a genuinely innovative lifestyle boutique that rents space to talented emerging designers across fashion, jewellery and homewares.
Notting Hill: 46 Ledbury Rd, W11 · 10am–6.30pm; Sun 11am–5pm · www.wolfandbadger.com

World's End DON'T MISS
FASHION / MENS / MYTHIC

It has lived many lives since it housed Malcolm McLaren and Vivienne Westwood's punk fetish boutique SEX but it's still a radical paragon. Part Ye Olde Curiosity Shoppe and part 18th-century galleon (check the famous backwards clock), it now plays host to Dame Vivienne's latest collections.
Chelsea: 430 King's Rd, SW1 · 10am–6pm. Closed Sun · worldsendshop.co.uk

Chelsea Physic Garden
PARKS & GARDENS

Given over to apothecaries in the 17th century, this secret garden is frequented by many a West London star in need of repose. Features include a rock garden and alpine plants, and the Tangerine Dream Café is an added boon. Paid entry.
Chelsea: 66 Royal Hospital Rd, SW3 · Open Apr–Oct (Closed Mon, Sat) · chelseaphysicgarden.co.uk

Heritage Routemaster
MYTHIC

The iconic red double-decker buses were withdrawn from service in 2005, but numbers 9 and 15 still carry out shortened versions of their original routes. 9 takes in Kensington, the famous Royal Albert Hall and the luxury sights of Knightsbridge.
Route 9: Royal Albert Hall–Trafalgar Square. Route 15: Trafalgar Square–Tower Hill · 9.30am–6.30pm daily · Every 15 minutes.

Hyde Park
PARKS & GARDENS

A huge swathe of green in the centre of the city where joggers skirt big memorials, romantics row hire boats on the cool stretch of the Serpentine lake and prophets invoke their right to rant at Speakers' Corner.
Sth Kensington: www.royalparks.org.uk

Kyoto Garden
PARKS & GARDENS / WOW

Nestled within the 55-acres of Holland Park, the garden was created for the 1991 Japan Festival of London, and with its koi carp lake and dramatic waterfall it's one of the most idyllic spots in town.

HANGOUTS
Charlotte Olympia Dellal
× × ×

The London shoe designer has imposed her equal parts playful and sexy shoe collections – now covering heels, flats and trainers – onto the world fashion stage; her cute "Kitty Flats" are a fashion phenomenon! Here, the West Londoner lets us in on her fave addresses, explaining "I'm a big online shopper, otherwise I love to browse my own neighbourhood. I live and work at the top of Ladbroke Grove, so I'm close to Portobello and Golborne Road, giving me wonderful access to vintage shops, and the market on weekends."
charlotteolympia.com

Alfie's Antique Market
Has everything from vintage and antique furniture and homeware to clothing, jewellery and accessories.
www.alfiesantiques.com

Circus Antiques
A great selection of antique furniture; I find something whenever I visit.
www.circusantiques.co.uk

The Honey Jam
Great retro toys for boys and girls.
www.honeyjam.co.uk

Assouline
A beautiful book shop in a special setting with impressive high ceilings and including an old-fashioned little cocktail bar.
www.assouline.com

Michael Hoppen Gallery
Shows and sells great photography.
www.michaelhoppengallery.com

Royal Institute of British Architects
A beautiful Deco building with a library and bistro and café for lunch meetings.
www.architecture.com

Natural History Museum
I love this museum almost as much as my boys.
www.nhm.ac.uk

The Tate & Tate Modern
Always make for a good Saturday morning.
www.tate.org.uk

Chelsea Physic Garden
Beautiful to discover in the spring time.
chelseaphysicgarden.co.uk

Dock Kitchen
My favourite restaurant. A delicious menu inspired by countries all over the world; the menu changes every week.
dockkitchen.co.uk

The Gallery at Sketch
A beautiful and feminine room decorated entirely in pink; it makes me want to go there dressed up in shades of the same colour and sip pink cocktails.
sketch.london

The Wolseley
An especially glamorous setting for an old-fashioned brunch.
www.thewolseley.com

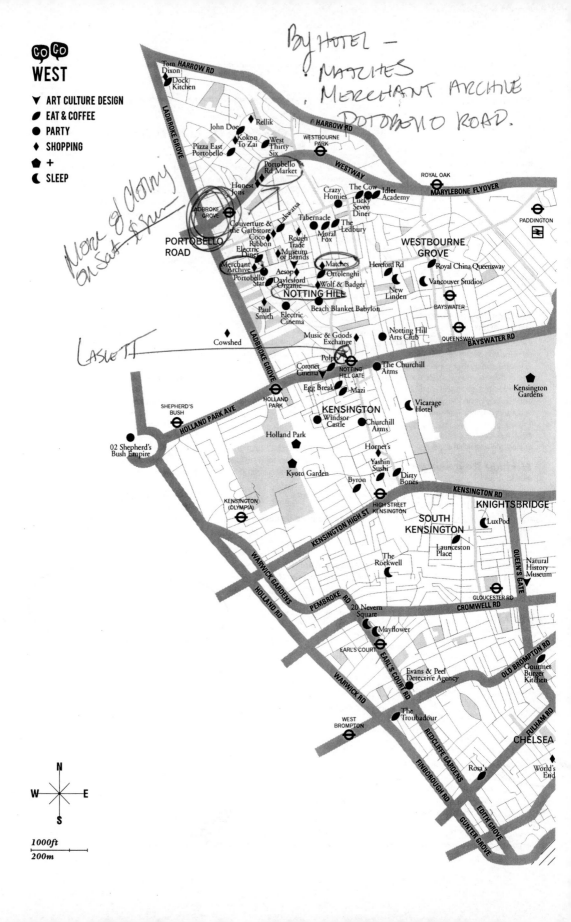

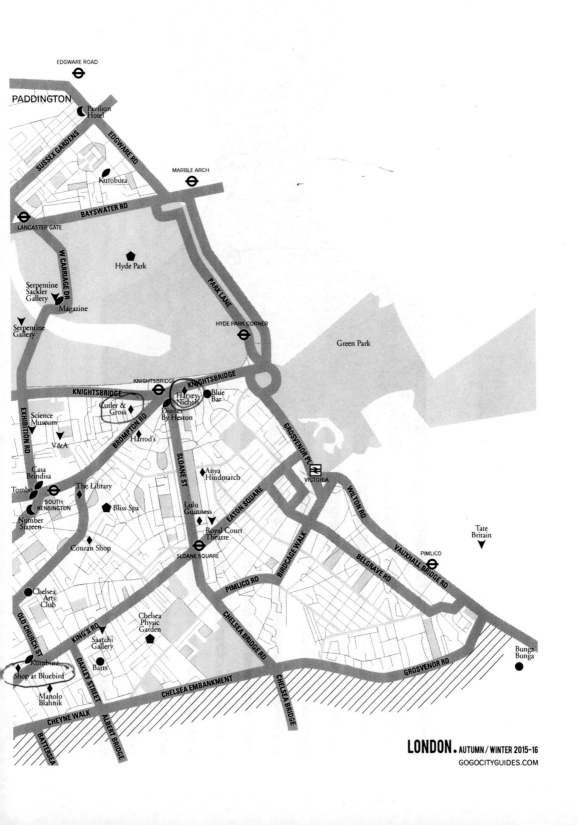

EDGWARE ROAD

PADDINGTON

Pavilion Hotel

SUSSEX GARDENS

EDGWARE RD

Kurobuta

MARBLE ARCH

BAYSWATER RD

LANCASTER GATE

W CARRIAGE DR

Hyde Park

PARK LANE

Serpentine
Sackler
Gallery

Magazine

HYDE PARK CORNER

Serpentine
Gallery

Green Park

KNIGHTSBRIDGE

KNIGHTSBRIDGE

KNIGHTSBRIDGE

Harvey
Nichols

Blue
Bar

Cutler &
Gross

Dinner
By Heston

EXHIBITION RD

Science
Museum

BROMPTON RD

GROSVENOR PL

V&A

Harrod's

VICTORIA

Casa
Brindisa

SLOANE ST

Anya
Hindmarch

WILTON RD

Tombo

The Library

EATON SQUARE

SOUTH
KENSINGTON

Bliss Spa

Lulu
Guinness

Tate
Britain

Number
Sixteen

Royal Court
Theatre

BIRDCAGE WALK

BELGRAVE RD

VAUXHALL BRIDGE RD

PIMLICO

Conran Shop

SLOANE SQUARE

Chelsea
Arts
Club

PIMLICO RD

OLD CHURCH ST

KING'S RD

Chelsea
Physic
Garden

CHELSEA BRIDGE RD

Bunga
Bunga

Saatchi
Gallery

Kurobuta
Shop at Bluebird

Barts

DAKLEY STREET

CHELSEA EMBANKMENT

CHELSEA BRIDGE

GROSVENOR RD

Manolo
Blahnik

CHEYNE WALK

ALBERT BRIDGE

BATTERSEA

LONDON . AUTUMN / WINTER 2015-16
GOGOCITYGUIDES.COM

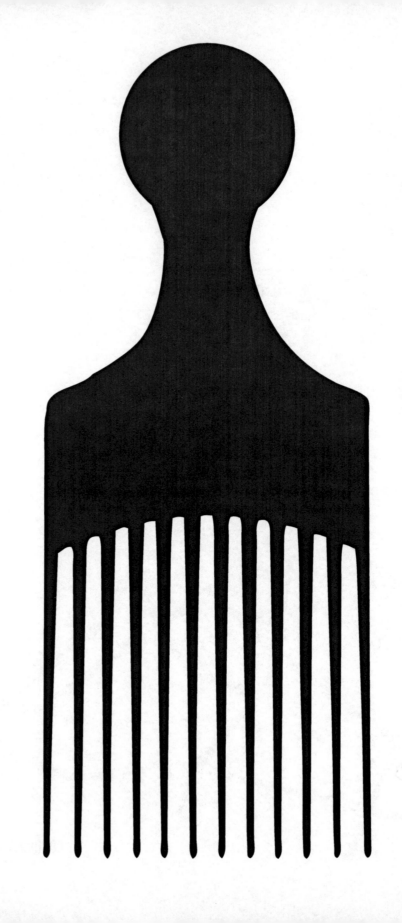

GoGo NORTH

BELSIZE PARK × CAMDEN × HIGHGATE × ISLINGTON × KENTISH TOWN × KING'S CROSS × STOKE NEWINGTON

In the throes of REGENERATION, Eurostar hub King's Cross boasts great RESTAURANTS and CULTURAL SPOTS, from the Gagosian to the British Library. Elegant neighbour Islington can still teach it a thing or two about GENTRIFICATION though: it's all COBBLED streets, Victorian piles and ANTIQUE CHIC. Grungy Camden shelters endless GIG VENUES, pubs and HIPSTER RIFF-RAFF. When they clean up their act, they'll probably move to VILLAGEY Stoke Newington, pram-filled domain of creatives. The well-situated Belsize Park is home to the BRITISH A-LIST, and a short stroll from RURAL Hampstead, the Londoner's Sunday escape for grub and slow gait.

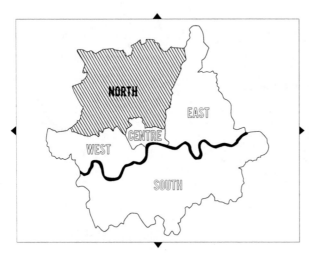

GETTING AROUND

The Northern line will be your ally: **King's Cross**, **Angel**, **Camden** and **Highgate** tubes are the easiest points of access. Areas to check out include **Camden Lock** and **Camden Passage** for quality clobber, and from there wander Upper Street for boutiques and coffee. If your bent runs to daytime drinking, try one of the theatre pubs in **Angel** before taking a trip to the wild and atmospheric Highgate Cemetery. For bars and clubs head to **Stoke Newington's Church Street,** or for a more muted evening, drink and dine down **Camden's Regent's Park Road**.

NEW *The Bull & Gate,
Dishoom, The Dolls House,
Foxlow, Ladies & Gentlemen,
Max's Sandwich Shop,
Oldroyd,Original Sin,
Oui Monsieur, Primeur...*

ART CULTURE DESIGN

Camden Arts Centre DON'T MISS
ART / LATES

With stellar exhibitions, talks and residencies that have welcomed the likes of Martin Creed, this is one of the capital's best contemporary art spaces. The café wins plaudits from locals in its own right.
Camden: Arkwright Rd, NW3 · 10am–6pm (9pm Wed). Closed Mon · www.camdenartscentre.org

Cecil Sharp House
LIVE MUSIC

The arts venue of the English Folk Dance and Song Society hosts concerts, lectures, multi-media events and an array of social dances with the aim of placing the indigenous folk arts of England at the heart of cultural life. Don't miss the sweet little Brit café downstairs.
Camden: 2 Regent's Park Rd, NW1 · www.efdss.org

David Roberts Art Foundation
ART

A massive space for the arts patron featuring more than 1,800 works by over 700 artists originating from his private collection; it seeks to provoke, engage, experiment and share.
Camden: Symes Mews, NW1 · Noon–6pm. Closed Sun–Wed · davidrobertsartfoundation.com

Everyman Cinema
FILM

A famous theatre from the '20s is today a luxury indie cinema and bar; sink into a cushion-clad sofa with your loved one and wait for your food and drinks to be delivered directly to your cinema seat.
Hampstead: 5 Holly Bush Vale, NW3 · Noon–11pm · www.everymancinema.com

The Freud Museum
MUSEUM

The doctor's refuge from Nazi Vienna is a perfect time capsule housing classical antiquities and books alongside the uncanny star exhibit – the very couch on which psychoanalysis was born.
Hampstead: 20 Maresfield Gardens, NW3 · Noon–5pm. Closed Mon, Tue · www.freud.org.uk

Gagosian Gallery
ART

The bigger of two London outposts owned by the gregarious American super-dealer, whose stable ranges from the famous – Jeff Koons – to the even more famous: Andy Warhol.
Camden: 6–24 Britannia St, WC1 · 10am–6pm. Closed Sun, Mon · www.gagosian.com

Grant Museum of Zoology
MUSEUM

London's only remaining university zoological museum is packed full of skeletons, mounted animals and specimens preserved in fluid. Many of the species are now endangered or extinct, including the Tasmanian Tiger, the Quagga and the Dodo.
Camden: Rockefeller Building, University College, 21 University St, WC1 · 1pm–5pm. Closed Sun · www.ucl.ac.uk/museums/zoology

Kings Place
ART / LIVE MUSIC

Assorted concert halls and galleries in the same complex as the *Guardian* and *Observer* newspapers also programme eclectic music and spoken word events.
King's Cross: 90 York Way, N1 · www.kingsplace.co.uk

Lisson Gallery DON'T MISS
ART

Founded in 1967 by Nicholas Logsdail, a champion of conceptual art, Lisson continues to identify and support new generations of artists, each with a radical approach to the artistic possibilities of their times.
St John's Wood: 27 & 52 Bell St, NW1 · 10am–6pm; Sat 11am–5pm. Closed Sun · www.lissongallery.com

Phoenix Cinema
FILM

One of the UK's oldest purpose-built, continuously operating cinemas, the Phoenix has witnessed it all. An independent single-screen cinema, it presents the latest indie and foreign films.
East Finchley: 52 High Rd, N2 · www.phoenixcinema.co.uk

Sadler's Wells
DANCE / MYTHIC

The hallowed international dance house is rated for its edgy collaborations with visual artists and musicians.
Islington: Rosebery Ave, EC1 · www.sadlerswells.com

Shri Swaminarayan Mandir
WOW

Home to one of the largest and most active Hindu organisations within the Indian diaspora, London's first traditional Hindu temple is also the first stone mandir of this scale and intricacy in the western world.
Neasden: 105-119 Brentfield Rd, NW10 · 9am–6pm · londonmandir.baps.org

Wellcome Collection
ART / BOOKS / MUSEUM

Pharmaceutical entrepreneur Sir Henry Wellcome started in the Wild West and died a knight of the British Empire. Here you'll find the world's largest collection of (often gory) medicine-related paraphernalia and fascinating roving exhibitions across life, medicine and art.
Euston: 183 Euston Rd, NW1 · 10am (11am Sun)–6pm (10pm Thu). Closed Mon · www.wellcomecollection.org

♫ TO LISTEN TO
FOXES
ALL I NEED
(SIGN OF THE TIMES / EPIC)

EAT & COFFEE

The Bull & Gate ££ NEW
BRITISH / COCKTAILS / LIVE MUSIC / PUB

The grungy boozer with an extraordinary musical heritage (Blur and Coldplay debuted here) has been relaunched as a trendy gastropub dedicated to seasonal British cuisine. The Boulogne Bar upstairs pimps cocktails, and live jazz on the weekends.

Kentish Town: 389 Kentish Town Rd, NW5 · 020 3437 0905 · 11am–11pm (midnight Thu–Sat); Sun noon–10.30pm · www.bullandgatenw5.co.uk

The Bull & Last ££
BRITISH / PUB

The corner boozer of your dreams singlehandedly makes the word gastropub palatable again with its fine ales and seasonal British classics. Just a stone's throw from Hampstead Heath.

Highgate: 168 Highgate Rd, NW5 · 020 7267 3641 · 11am–11pm (10.30pm Sun) · www.thebullandlast.co.uk

Caravan King's Cross ££
DON'T MISS / BREAKFAST / BRUNCH / COFFEE / SMALL PLATES / TAKE AWAY

Delicious small plates and espresso are favourites at this sprawling counterpart to the original Exmouth Market address. On the canal in a regenerated King's Cross, it's located in a converted 19th-century warehouse, the Granary Building, that also houses Central Saint Martins.

King's Cross: Granary Building, 1 Granary Square, N1 (+ branches) · 020 7101 7661 · 8am–10.30pm (11pm Wed, Thu; midnight Fri); Sat 10am–midnight; Sun 10am–4pm · www.caravankingscross.co.uk

Chin Chin Labs £
COFFEE / ICE CREAM

You'll find lab-coated staff and experimental flavours at Europe's first ever liquid nitrogen ice-cream parlour.

Camden: 49–50 Camden Lock Place, NW1 · Noon–7pm. Closed Mon & Tue · www.chinchinlabs.com

De Beauvoir Deli £
BREAKFAST / DELI / TAKE AWAY

Everything at this local indie grocer-cum-cafe is sourced locally from small independent suppliers to offer the finest in seasonal and artisan produce. Drop in for coffee, breakfast, or lunch, available to eat in or takeaway.

Islington: 98 Southgate Rd, N1 · No reservations · 8am–8pm; Sat 9am–5pm; Sun 10am–4pm · www.thedebeauvoirdeli.co.uk

Delhi Grill £
BUDGET / INDIAN / TAKE AWAY

A rough and ready, but very tasty, Indian 'dhaba', or canteen, on Chapel Market. Dishes change daily.

Islington: 21 Chapel Market, N1 · 020 7278 8100 · Noon–2.45pm, 6pm–10.30pm · www.delhigrill.com

Dirty Burger £
BREAKFAST / BURGERS / TAKEAWAY

Greasy, gimmicky goodness for trendsetters inside a corrugated iron shed. Don't go past the onion rings.

Kentish Town: 79 Highgate Rd, NW5 · No reservations · 7am–midnight (1am Fri); Sat, Sun 9am–1am (11pm Sun) · www.eatdirtyburger.com

Dishoom ££ NEW
BAR / BREAKFAST / COCKTAILS / INDIAN

The third outpost of one of our fave modern Indian tables – inspired by early 20th-century Bombay – is located inside a huge restored Victorian transit shed, next to Granary Square. Expect the same combination of great interiors and a flavourful all-day menu, plus fresh juices, and inventive cocktails in the basement bar, the Permit Room.

King's Cross: 5 Stable Street, N1 · 020 7420 9321 · 8am–11pm (midnight Thu, Fri); Sat 9am–midnight; Sun 9am–11pm · www.dishoom.com

Drink, Shop & Do £
BAR / BREAKFAST / COFFEE / TAKE AWAY

Right near Kings Cross station and surrounded by big chains, this bright indie café transforms into a bar at night and hosts regular dance classes (from twerkshops to swing) and oddball DIY courses ('play with clay Jesus style' for Easter). Drink Shop & Dash next door serves up excellent coffee, fro-yo and other take-aways.

King's Cross: 9–11 Caledonian Rd, N1 · 020 7278 4335 · 9am–midnight (2am Fri, Sat); Sun 10.30am-8pm · www.drinkshopdo.com

Fingers Crossed £
BREAKFAST / BRUNCH / COFFEE / TAKE AWAY

This friendly local café prepares a daily smorgasbord of healthy and delicious meals for breakfast, brunch or lunch using seasonal local produce. Coffee's good too.

Stoke Newington: 247 Amhurst Rd, N16 · No reservations · 7am (8.30am Sat, 10am Sun)-5pm · www.facebook.com/fingerscrossedcafe

Duke of Cambridge ££
BRITISH / ORGANIC / PUB / TERRACE

This fully organic gastropub serves delicious modern British cuisine plus a great range of organic craft beers.

Islington: 30 St Peter's St, N1 · 020 7359 3066 · Noon–11pm; Sun noon–10.30pm · www.dukeorganic.co.uk

The Fish & Chip Shop ££
BRITISH / FISH & CHIPS / TAKE AWAY

Cooking with sustainably sourced fish, this posh, new-gen fish and chippery serves cocktails to go with its long, seafood-centric menu.

Islington: 189 Upper St, N1 · 020 3227 0979 · Noon–midnight; Sat, Sun 10am–11pm · www.thefishandchipshop.uk.com

Folklow ££ NEW
BRUNCH / COCKTAILS / STEAK / SUNDAY ROAST

The Stokie outpost of the "friendly neighbourhood restaurant" concept from the guys behind the Hawksmoor chain, strong on smoky charcoal grilled dishes, and serving a bottomless Bloody Mary for weekend brunch.

Stoke Newington: 71–73 Stoke Newington Church St, N16 · 020 3227 0979 · 10am–3pm, 5–10.30pm; Sat, 10am–10.30pm (10pm Sun) · www.foxlow.co.uk

Ginger & White ££
BREAKFAST / BRUNCH / COFFEE / KIDS / TAKE AWAY / TERRACE

The original address of this kid-friendly coffee shop that serves great artisan espresso coffee (with beans sourced from Square Mile), sandwiches, salads and breakfasts.

Hampstead: 4a-5a Perrin's Court, NW3 (+ branches) · No reservations · 7.30am (8.30am Sat, Sun)–5.30pm · gingerandwhite.com

Grain Store ££
BAR / COCKTAILS / TERRACE / VEGETARIAN

This is the new venture from the Zetter Townhouse team. Located on Granary Square in the heart of a rejuvenated King's Cross, the airy Russell Sage-designed restaurant gives vegetables a starring role on an eclectic menu.

King's Cross: Granary Square, 1-3 Stable St, N1 · 020 7324 4466 · 11am–11.30pm (midnight, Thu–Sat; 4.30pm Sun) · www.grainstore.com

Haché Burger Connoisseurs £
BUDGET / BURGERS / CHIPS

The best of the gourmet burger contingent serves up ciabatta buns packed with the highest quality meat, fish and poultry and accompanied by the elusive perfect chip. It doesn't hurt that the room whispers bistro chic.
Camden: 24 Inverness St, NW1 (+ branches) · 020 7485 9100 · Noon–10.30pm (11pm Fri, Sat; 10pm Sun) · www.hacheburgers.com

Kerb £
BUDGET / MARKET / TAKE AWAY

Feeding the cool cats from nearby St Martins, this lunchtime street food market unites a rotating selection of some of the city's most creative food trucks, by the pretty Regent's Canal on Granary Square.
King's Cross: Granary Square, N1 · No reservations · Noon–2pm · www.kerbfood.com

Marine Ices £
BUDGET / ICE CREAM / KIDS / PIZZA

Ancient family-run institution that serves generous pizzas and pastas in a friendly atmosphere. The thing that gets people lining up, though, is the ice cream: endless sorbets and gelati inside a perfect retro '50s parlour.
Chalk Farm: 8 Haverstock Hill, NW3 · 020 7482 9000 · Noon–3pm, 6–11pm; Sat, Sun noon–11pm (10pm Sun). Closed Mon · www.marineices.co.uk

Odette's £££
BRITISH

One of London's original dining rooms now has Welsh chef-owner Bryn Williams in the kitchen, serving serious modern Brit cuisine in a 'contemporary snob' kind of décor. The walled garden or pavement tables are a great spot to eat in summer.
Primrose Hill: 130 Regents Park Rd, NW1 · 020 7586 8569 · Lunch & dinner daily · www.odettesprimrosehill.com

Oldroyd ££ NEW / DON'T MISS
MODERN EURO

Relaxed service, elegant 2-floor digs, and a delicious daily changing menu built around the best seasonal British ingredients from chef Tom Oldroyd.
Islington: 344 Upper Street, N1 · 020 8617 9010 ·Noon–11pm (midnight Fri); Sat 10am–midnight (10pm Sun) · www.oldroydlondon.com

Ottolenghi ££ DON'T MISS
BRUNCH / CAKES / VEGETARIAN

His cookery books have revolutionised middle-class London dinner parties, but it's less hard work to sample his fare at the original London HQ. Turn up early for the lunchtime salad buffet and creative Middle Eastern mains.
Islington: 287 Upper St, N1 · 020 7288 1454 · 8am–10.30pm; Sun 9am–7pm · www.ottolenghi.co.uk

Oui Monsieur ££ NEW
COCKTAILS / FRENCH / SMALL PLATES

A moody, mini, hipster French bistro with a daily changing menu and a party room in the basement.
Stoke Newington: 182 Stoke Newington Rd, N16 · 020 3674 2967 · 6pm–midnight (1am Thu; 2am Fri, Sat). Sun 1–10pm · ouimonsieur.co.uk

Max's Sandwich Shop £ NEW
DON'T MISS / BRUNCH / TAKE AWAY

A hot sandwich shop, with seats and booze, that's open really late. Everything is made on site, from the focaccia, to the generous fillings, think braised beef short rib, kimchi, gravy mayo with deep-fried broccoli, or why not ham hock, parsley, fried duck egg, shoestring fries, piccalilli and mustard mayo for brunch on the weekend.
Finsbury Park: 19 Crouch Hill, N4 · No reservations · 5pm–11pm (midnight Fri); Sat 11am–midnight (6pm Sun). Closed Mon, Tue

Pig & Butcher ££
BRITISH / PUB / SUNDAY ROAST

Excellent produce at this Islington gastropub: meat is straight from the farm, fish straight off the boat, and the fresh vegetables are shipped in from Kent. In summer expect grilled dishes, and in winter they brine, cure, smoke and braise.
Islington: 80 Liverpool Rd, N1 · 5pm–11pm (midnight Thu); Fri–Sun noon–1am (11pm Sun) · www.thepigandbutcher.co.uk

Primeur ££ NEW / DON'T MISS
MODERN EURO / SMALL PLATES

A daily changing food and wine menu served at communal tables inside a former garage at this new chef-driven affair that celebrates simplicity, honesty & conviviality. Expect dishes like duck rillette with pickled cucumber, fish stew, and rump steak with snails & garlic.

Stoke Newington: 116 Petherton Rd, N5 · No reservations · 5pm (noon Fri, Sat)–10.30pm; Sun noon–5pm Closed Mon · www.primeurn5.co.uk

Ruby Dock £
BREAKFAST / COFFEE / TAKE AWAY

Inside the increasingly foodie Camden Lock Market is this little oasis of Antipodean coffee culture serving sensational artisan coffee and tea, plus healthy home-made fare at breakfast and lunch.
Camden Lock: 45-46 Camden Lock Place, NW1 · No reservations · 9am–5.30pm · www.rubydockcafe.co.uk

Smokehouse ££ DON'T MISS
BEER / MODERN EURO / PUB /

A gastropub from the talented crew behind the Princess of Shoreditch has chef and BBQ expert Neil Rankin in the kitchen turning out excellent grilled meat and seafood. There's a nice line in craft beer too.
Islington: 63-69 Canonbury Rd, N1 · 020 7354 1144 · 5pm–11pm (midnight Thu, Fri); Sat 11am–midnight; Sun noon–10.30pm · www.smokehouseislington.co.uk

St Pancras Grand ££
BAR / BRITISH / BRUNCH / LATE / OYSTERS / TAKE AWAY / WOW

This European-style brasserie is the perfect setting for a brief encounter. For the menu, think British classics like afternoon tea and all-day brunch.
St. Pancras: St Pancras Station, Upper Concourse, Euston Rd, N1 · 020 7870 9900 · 7am–11pm; Sun 8am–late · www.searcys.co.uk/stpancrasgrand

Towpath £
BUDGET / BREAKFAST / COFFEE / TERRACE / VIEW

A venture from the improbably named food writer Lori de Mori nestled on the Regent's Canal. The menu is far more ambitious than you'd expect, and the location pleasingly surreal.
Regent's Canal: 42 De Beauvoir Crescent, N1 · No reservations · 8am–dusk (5pm Tue, Wed). Closed Mon.

Trangallan ££
BAR / SPANISH / TAPAS

Fresh, local ingredients draw on culinary adventures in Toscana, Catalunya and Provence. In the basement are weekly gigs, anything from burlesque to film screenings. (Btw, all the vintage furniture you see here is for sale.)

Stoke Newington: 61 Newington Green, N16 · 020 7359 4988 · Noon (11am Sat, Sun)–3pm, 5.30–11.30pm. Closed Mon · www.trangallan.com

York & Albany ££
BREAKFAST / BRITISH / COCKTAILS / PIZZA / SUNDAY ROAST / TAKE AWAY

A genial Ramsay-affiliated boutique hotel and restaurant overlooking Regent's Park with a serious menu overseen by capable protégée Angela Hartnett. Don't miss the wood-fired pizza kitchen in the old stables.
Camden: 127–129 Parkway, NW1 · 020 7388 3344 · 7am–11pm · www.gordonramsay.com/yorkandalbany

PARTY

69 Colebrooke Row DON'T MISS
BAR / COCKTAILS / SSHHH

The brainchild of cocktail guru Tony Conigliaro, this small and romantic 'bar with no name' is a real find, tucked just off Islington Green. Cocktails, served by bow-tied staff, take in liquorice whisky sours and El Presidentes.
Islington: 69 Colebrooke Row, N1 · 5pm–late · 69colebrookerow.com

Bar Pepito
BAR / SHERRY / TAPAS

Nestled in a courtyard, this rustic Iberian *bodega* combines authentic tapas with a classy list of recommended sherry accompaniments.
King's Cross: 3 Varnishers Yard, The Regent Quarter, N1 · 5pm–midnight. Closed Sun–Tue · barpepito.co.uk

Camden Town Brewery
BAR / BEER

Come right to the source of one of London's most popular craft brewers. This bar serves their six permanent brews: Hells Lager, USA Hells Lager, Unfiltered Hells, Pale Ale, Gentleman's Wit, and Camden Ink, plus a few limited edition beers. Food is provided by a changing roster of food trucks, parked out the front.
Kentish Town: 55-59 Wilkin St Mews, NW5 · Noon–11pm Thu–Sat · www.camdentownbrewery.com

The Dolls House NEW
BAR / BRITISH / COCKTAILS / LIVE MUSIC / MEMBERS CLUB / SUNDAY ROAST

The Hoxton nightlife hub has moved north. Decorated by Adam Towner and Katy Gray Rosewarne in the same intricate marker-pen detail, the place fills three floors of a Victorian building. There's live jazz and swing on Thursdays and Sundays and resident DJs get the place jumping on Fridays and Saturdays.
Islington: 181 Upper St, N1 · 6pm–4am. Closed Mon–Wed · www.thedeaddollsclub.com

Hawley Arms
PUB / SUNDAY ROAST / TERRACE

A local institution, this low-key pub was shot to fame by doomed Camden celeb Amy Winehouse's antics. The roof terrace is great in summer.
Camden: 2 Castlehaven Rd, NW1 · Noon–midnight (1am Fri, Sat) · www.thehawleyarms.co.uk

The Holly Bush
PUB / SUNDAY ROAST

A perfectly cosy and antiquated pub popular with locals for its Sunday roast and impressive selection of real ales.
Hampstead: 22 Hollymount, NW3 · Noon–midnight (10.30pm Sun) · hollybushhampstead.co.uk

Hoxley & Porter DON'T MISS
BAR / COCKTAILS

This lush cocktail bar & restaurant serves fine English-inspired fare and more far-flung cocktails inside a unique decor inspired by the glories of 19th-century train travel.
Islington: 153 Upper St, N1 · Noon–midnight (1am Thu; 2.30am Fri, Sat; 11am Sun) · www.hoxleyandporter.co.uk

KOKO
CLUB / LIVE MUSIC

The Camden staple is a part of rock history, having hosted the likes of The Sex Pistols and The Clash before reincarnation by Visage's Steve Strange as the Camden Palace. These days it hosts big-hitting indie gigs and Friday's popular Club NME.
Camden: 1a Camden High St, NW1 · 0870 432 5527 · 7–11pm; Sat, Sun 9pm–4am · www.koko.uk.com

Ladies & Gentlemen NEW
DON'T MISS / BAR / COCKTAILS

Trend alert! Another London bar set up within condemned public toilets.

Take the stairs down below and enjoy a martini prepared with house distilled gin, plus there's great bar snacks including homemade sausage rolls.
Kentish Town: 2 Highgate Road, NW5 · 5pm-12.30am. Closed Sun, Mon · ladiesandgents.co

The Lexington
LIVE MUSIC / PUB / QUIZ NIGHTS

American whiskies in a bordello baroque setting downstairs, and progressive alternative gigs upstairs. Hosts the very amusing Rough Trade Records quiz night every Monday.
Islington: 96–98 Pentonville Rd, N1 · Noon–2am (3am Thu; 4am Fri, Sat) · www.thelexington.co.uk

Original Sin NEW / DON'T MISS
BAR / COCKTAILS

One of Hackney's best bars Happiness Forgets has opened this big new address in Stoke Newington. An all-girl bar crew prepare 8£ cocktails favouring spirits such as white rye, Kamm & Sons and mezcal. There's a free pool table down the back, and upstairs you'll find cool new burger restaurant Stokey Bears.
Stoke Newington: 129 Stoke Newington High St, N16 · 6pm–1.30am (midnight Tue, Wed); Sun 6–11pm. Closed Mon) · www.originalsin.bar

Proud
BAR / CLUB / LIVE MUSIC / PHOTO

By day the huge former Horse Hospital hosts exhibitions of popular contemporary photography. By night, the rock royalty on the walls comes to life, with gigs by North London indie bands as well as diverse club nights.
Camden: Stables Market, NW1 · 10am–1.30am (2.30am Thu–Sat, 12.30am Sun) · www.proudcamden.com

The Roundhouse
COMEDY / LIVE MUSIC / THEATRE / WOW

Re-opened in 2006, this impressive vaulted (and yes, round) venue has regained the edge it was known for in its '60s heyday. Hosting theatre and comedy, it's mainly an atmospheric place to catch superior gigs.
Camden: Chalk Farm Rd, NW1 · 10am–11pm · www.roundhouse.org.uk

Simmons
BAR / COCKTAILS

Just opposite KOKO is this outpost of the eccentric King's Cross bar,

decorated with retro-chic bric-à-brac including 'the worlds largest skull mirror ball' and a SNES console (with Mario Kart, obviously). Your cocktail might be served in a teacup, and there's a 5-hour happy hour from 4pm on weekdays.
Camden: 7 Camden High St, NW · 4–11.30pm (midnight Fri, Sat) · www.simmonsbar.co.uk

The Waiting Room
JAZZ / LIVE MUSIC / PUB / QUIZ NIGHTS

Managed by the team behind the Lock Tavern and Shacklewell Arms, this basement venue beneath a pub is equally loved for its vintage tube-style tiling, cool club nights and 4am weekend licence.
Stoke Newington: 175 Stoke Newington High St, N16 · 4pm–midnight (2am Thu; 4am Fri, Sat) · www.waitingroomn16.com

The Wenlock Arms
JAZZ / LIVE MUSIC / PUB / QUIZ NIGHTS

The perfect local just off the Regent's Canal, where art students, real-ale enthusiasts and loquacious regulars bond over a decent pint. It's best on Fridays and Saturdays, when frail-looking jazz veterans suddenly break out in riotous sessions.
Islington: 26 Wenlock Rd, N1 · Noon–11pm (midnight Thu; 1am Fri, Sat) · wenlockarms.com

SHOPPING

Albam
MENS

This British indie menswear label designs and makes their own denim, jeans, chinos, shirts, T shirts, sweatshirts, tailoring and suits, handmade shoes (in collaboration with Grenson), in excellent factories in the British Isles and Portugal. You'll find some carefully selected homewares, gifts and accessories alongside the clothes.
Islington: 286 Upper St, N1 (+ branches) · 11am–7pm; 11.30am–5.30pm · www.albamclothing.com

Camden Passage Antiques Market
ANTIQUES / JEWELLERY / MARKET / VINTAGE

Mingle with interior designers, stylists and collectors in the bijou shops that line this atmospheric passage. On Wed and Sat the market boasts excellent vintage jewellery and clothes; don't miss stalls by Julie and Sarah.

Islington: 11am (9am Wed, Sat)–6pm · www.camdenpassageislington.co.uk

Diverse
FASHION / MENS / MULTIBRAND

This much-loved store has been inspiring generations of fashion-lovers since 1986 with its selection of international designers for men and women, including Helmut Lang, Alexander McQueen and Opening Ceremony.
Islington: 294 Upper St, N1 · 10.30am–6.30pm (7pm Thu); Sun 11.30am–5.30pm · www.diverseclothing.com

Hub Men
MENS / MULTIBRAND

Down the street from Hub Women (see below), the menswear store stocks pieces from fine international brands including Brit icons Barbour, Sunspel or Folk.
Stoke Newington: 88 Stoke Newington Church St, N16 · 10.30am–6pm; Sun 11am–5pm · hubshop.co.uk

Hub Women DON'T MISS
FASHION / MULTIBRAND

This is where it all started for the great North London multibrand. Hub makes its reputation stocking the best pieces from designers including Sessun, Acne and H by Hudson.
Stoke Newington: 49 Stoke Newington Church St, N16 · 10.30am–6pm; Sun 11am–5pm · hubshop.co.uk

Olive Loves Alfie
BOOKS / FASHION / KIDS / SHOES

Stoke Newington's yummy mummies adore this adorable independent boutique, stocking kids' shoes, hip labels like Mini Rodini and iconic children's books. They also have a small range of womenswear.
Stoke Newington:
84 Stoke Newington Church St, N16 · 10am–6pm; Sun 11am–5pm · www.olivelovesalfie.co.uk

Paul A Young Fine Chocolates
CAKES / CHOCOLATE

This pretty boutique on Camden Passage showcases the groundbreaking flavour combinations of top chocolatier Paul A Young. It's worth checking the website for frequent classes and demonstrations by the master.
Islington: 33 Camden Passage, N1 (+ branches) · 10am–6.30pm (7pm Fri); Sun 11am–6pm. Closed Mon · www.paulayoung.co.uk

Stables Market
INTERIORS / MARKET / TAKE AWAY / VINTAGE

Since regeneration in 2009, this endless catacomb of stalls and shops nestled beneath railway arches has lost its subversive grunge but gained in appeal. After plundering the threads, pause for some world food before settling down on the banks of Camden Lock.
Camden: Chalk Farm Rd, NW1 · 10.30am (10am Sat, Sun)–6pm · www.stablesmarket.com

Strut
FASHION / MENS / VINTAGE

Ex-models and muses tend to deposit their old Rive Gauche pieces in this popular Stoke Newington vintage shop. There's also a new branch on Broadway Market.
Stoke Newington: 182 Stoke Newington Church St, N16 (+ branches) · 11am–6pm daily · www.strutlondon.com

Hampstead Heath Swimming Ponds
PARKS & GARDENS / SWIMMING

Amid the bucolic delights of the ancient Heath, three ponds (for women, men and mixed groups) entice hardy city dwellers to return to nature before heading to work.
Hampstead: off Millfield Lane, Hampstead Heath · 7am–dusk

Highgate Cemetery
CEMETERY / MYTHIC

Pay your respects to the ghosts of luminaries from George Eliot to Karl Marx in this ivy-clad Victorian maze. The catacombs of the majestic West Cemetery are only accessible by booking the organised tour.
Highgate: Swain's Lane, N6 · 10am (11am Sat, Sun)–5pm (4pm Nov–Feb) · www.highgate-cemetery.org

London Zoo
ZOO

The world's oldest scientific zoo opened to the public in 1847. Don't miss the latest enclosure Tiger Territory showcasing the Sumatran tiger.
Regent's Park: Outer Circle, Regent's Park, NW1 · 10am–5.30pm · www.zsl.org

Regent's Canal Walk

It may not be pretty, but there is something defiantly romantic about a walk along the canal – and it's practical too. Start at Camden and skirt King's Cross, Angel and the City Basin before arriving in Dalston. Broadway Market and Victoria Park lie to the east.
Start: Camden Lock.
End: Dalston Kingsland Rd.

Regent's Park
KIDS / PARKS & GARDENS / ZOO

Landscaped by visionary architect John Nash, this fragrant stretch encompasses a truly romantic rose garden, the famous London Zoo and, to the north, remarkable views from Primrose Hill.

NOTES

HANGOUTS
Heidi Knudsen
×××

*Heidi is head wine buyer for **Nopi** and **Ottolenghi** and General Manager at Nopi. She puts together the wine lists – featuring loads of organic and biodynamic picks – for all Yotam Ottolenghi's locations, including his newest deli in Spitalfields, open since March.*
www.ottolenghi.co.uk

40 Maltby Street

Crossing the Thames at night is pretty magical, especially if you are heading south to 40 Maltby Street. A wonderful restaurant and wine warehouse situated in an old railway arch, it serves delicious, seasonal food and interesting wines. Bring a bag to carry home the extra bottles you'll most certainly end up purchasing.
www.40maltbystreet.com

Trangallan

If you are interested in visiting a small neighbourhood restaurant away from the glitz of Soho and the West End, visit Trangallan in Hackney. The menu is full of traditional Galician dishes with a modern twist and features a wonderful sherry list. The décor is beautiful, and there's a cute little bottle shop as well.
www.trangallan.com

Ombra

On a hot summer's day, there's no place I'd rather be than Ombra on Vyner Street in Hackney – sitting on the terrace, sipping Aperol Spritz and snacking on Venetian cicchetti, to be exact!y.
ombrabar.com

Brilliant Corners

If you feel in the mood for dancing (or watching cool young things groove around), go to Brilliant Corners on Kingsland Road in the ever hip Dalston area. Expect delicious Japanese food, some of the best wines around at very friendly prices and jazz blaring out of the sound system.
brilliantcornerslondon.co.uk

Bodega 50

If you are keen on caffeine, Bodega 50 in Stoke Newington offers great coffee and lots of yummy gluten-free snacks and fresh salads. Bruce, the cafe dog, is a local celebrity.
50 Allen Rd, N16.

Coram's Fields

A lovely break from shopping and busy streets, this little gem near King's Cross has a range of outdoor activities for kids of all ages, plus a small city farm.
coramsfields.org

V&A Museum of Childhood

On a rainy day there's no better place to go with your little ones. The permanent collection is fun and inspiring – you'll always walk away having learned something new!
www.vam.ac.uk/moc

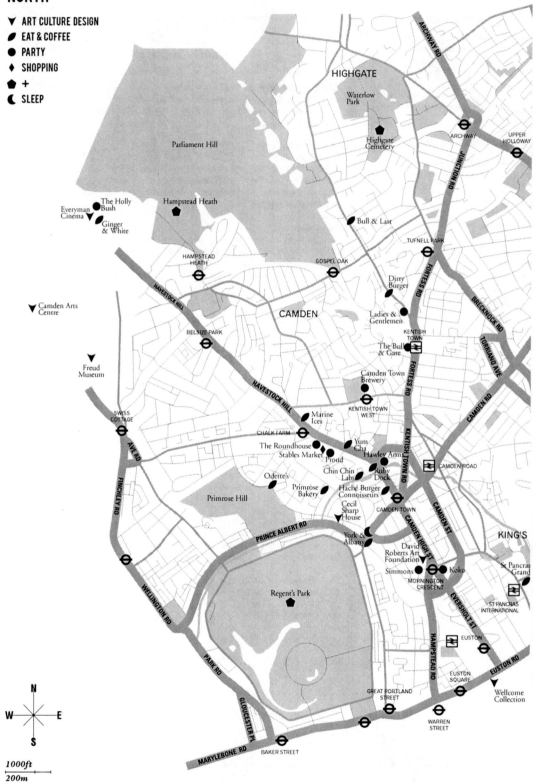

GOGO NORTH

- ▼ ART CULTURE DESIGN
- ◖ EAT & COFFEE
- ● PARTY
- ◆ SHOPPING
- ⬠ +
- ☾ SLEEP

HIGHGATE

Waterlow Park

Parliament Hill

Highgate Cemetery

ARCHWAY RD

ARCHWAY

UPPER HOLLOWAY

Hampstead Heath

The Holly Bush
Everyman Cinema
Ginger & White

Bull & Last

TUFNELL PARK

HAMPSTEAD HEATH

GOSPEL OAK

CAMDEN

Dirty Burger

Ladies & Gentlemen

FORTESS RD

BRECKNOCK RD

TORRIANO AVE

Camden Arts Centre

BELSIZE PARK

KENTISH TOWN

The Bull & Gate

CAMDEN RD

Freud Museum

HAVESTOCK HILL

Camden Town Brewery

KENTISH TOWN WEST

SWISS COTTAGE

AVE RD

Marine Ices

CHALK FARM

Yum Cha

Hawley Arms

KENTISH TOWN RD

CAMDEN ROAD

FINCHLEY RD

The Roundhouse
Stables Market

Proud

Chin Chin Labs

Ruby Dock

Odette's

Primrose Bakery

Haché Burger Connoisseurs

Cecil Sharp House

CAMDEN TOWN

KING'S

Primrose Hill

York & Albany

David Roberts Art Foundation

St Pancras Grand

WELLINGTON RD

PRINCE ALBERT RD

Simmons

Koko

CAMDEN HIGH ST

CAMDEN ST

MORNINGTON CRESCENT

St Pancras International

Regent's Park

PARK RD

EVERSHOLT ST

EUSTON RD

HAMPSTEAD RD

EUSTON

GREAT PORTLAND STREET

EUSTON SQUARE

Wellcome Collection

GLOUCESTER PL

WARREN STREET

N
W   E
S

MARYLEBONE RD

BAKER STREET

1000ft
200m

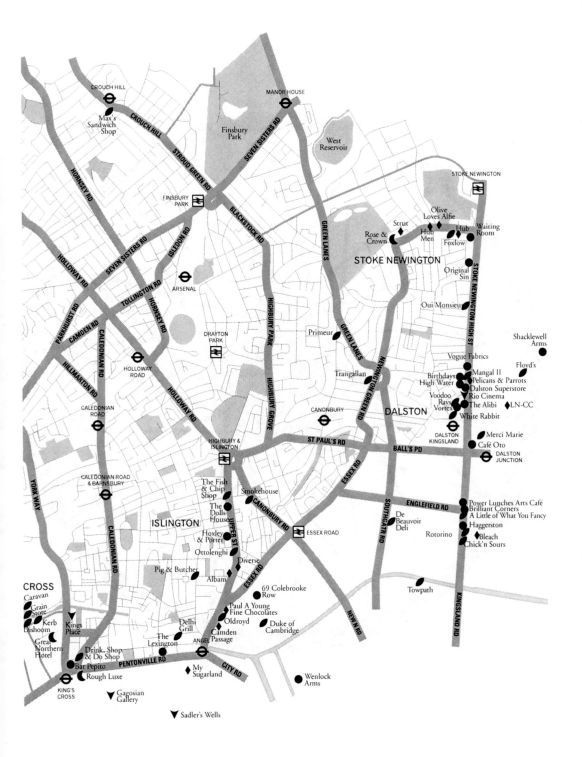

CROUCH HILL

Max's
Sandwich
Shop

CROUCH HILL

STROUD GREEN RD

SEVEN SISTERS RD

MANOR HOUSE

Finsbury
Park

West
Reservoir

STOKE NEWINGTON

HORNSEY RD

FINSBURY
PARK

BLACKSTOCK RD

GREEN LANES

Olive
Loves Alfie
Strut   Hub   Hub   Waiting
Rose &   Men   Foxlow   Room
Crown

STOKE NEWINGTON

Original
Sin

Oui Monsieur

STOKE NEWINGTON HIGH ST

HOLLOWAY RD

SEVEN SISTERS RD

ISLEDON RD

ARSENAL

TOLLINGTON RD

HORNSEY RD

Primeur

Shacklewell
Arms

PARKHURST RD

CAMDEN RD

DRAYTON
PARK

HIGHBURY PARK

GREEN LANES

Vogue Fabrics
Floyd's

Trangallan

Mangal 11
Birthdays   Pelicans & Parrots
High Water Dalston Superstore
Voodoo   Rio Cinema
Rays   The Alibi   LN-CC
Vortex   White Rabbit

HILLMARTON RD

CALEDONIAN RD

HOLLOWAY
ROAD

HOLLOWAY RD

CANONBURY

DALSTON

CALEDONIAN
ROAD

HIGHBURY GROVE

NEWINGTON GREEN RD

DALSTON
KINGSLAND

Merci Marie
Café Oto

YORK WAY

CALEDONIAN ROAD
& BARNSBURY

HIGHBURY &
ISLINGTON

ST PAUL'S RD

BALL'S PO

DALSTON
JUNCTION

ESSEX RD

The Fish
& Chip
Shop
Smokehouse

ENGLEFIELD RD

Power Lunches Arts Café
Brilliant Corners
A Little of What You Fancy

CALEDONIAN RD

ISLINGTON

The
Dolls
House

CANONBURY RD

UPPER ST

SOUTHGATE RD

De
Beauvoir
Deli

Haggerston

Hoxley
& Porter

ESSEX ROAD

Rotorino

Ottolenghi

Diverse

ESSEX RD

Bleach
Chick'n Sours

Pig & Butcher

Albam

69 Colebrooke
Row

KINGSLAND RD

Towpath

CROSS
Caravan
Grain
Store
Kerb
Dishoom
Kings
Place

Paul A Young
Fine Chocolates
Oldroyd
Delhi   Camden
Grill   Passage

Duke of
Cambridge

NEW RD

Great
Northern
Hotel

Drink, Shop
& Do Shop

The
Lexington

ANGEL

Bar Pepito
Rough Luxe

PENTONVILLE RD

CITY RD

KING'S
CROSS

My
Sugarland

Wenlock
Arms

Gagosian
Gallery

Sadler's Wells

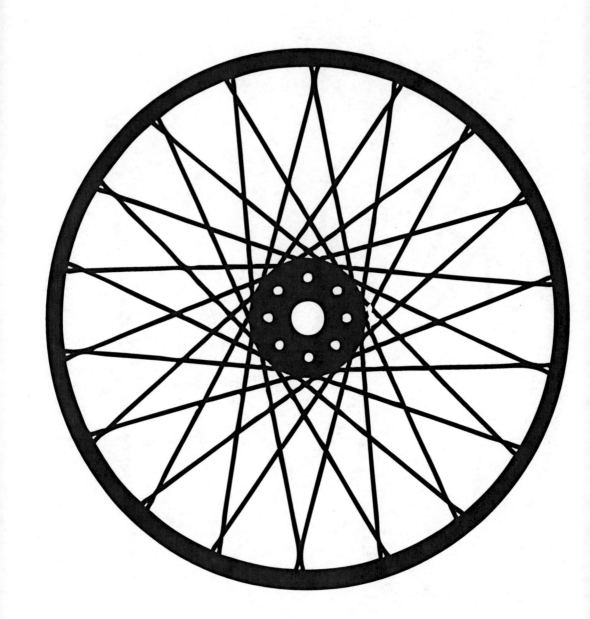

GoGo EAST

BETHNAL GREEN × BRICK LANE × DALSTON
HACKNEY × SHOREDITCH × SPITALFIELDS × WHITECHAPEL

Spitalfields' thriving covered MARKET, heritage DELIS and smart new RESTAURANTS trace the edge of the City, but by buzzing Dray Walk (home to the popular Rough Trade East) endless BARS, CURRY HOUSES and vintage EMPORIUMS, backdropped by the iconic Old Truman Brewery, mark a shift into the GRITTIER Brick Lane. Nearby Whitechapel is resurgent after a revamp of the famous gallery, while to the north Shoreditch continues to tempt the CREATIVES down from their Hackney lofts with its lively selection of BARS & CLUBS. Dalston is best seen at NIGHT and is where you will inevitably find yourself, in one of its edgy but ULTRA-HIP NIGHTSPOTS.

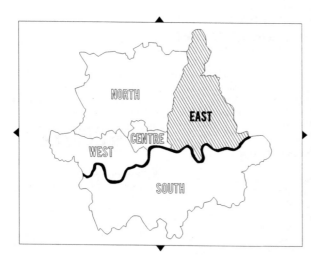

GETTING AROUND

Get out at **Liverpool St** for a shopping tour of **Spitalfields** and, via Dray Walk, **Brick Lane**. The vintage and homewares on **Cheshire St** are a short stroll north along here, while happening **Redchurch St** takes you on into **Shoreditch** proper. For Shoreditch's bars, shops and galleries, get out at **Old St** tube and slowly wend your way east via **Hoxton Square**, stopping for refreshments on **Columbia Rd**. From there take a 55 or 26 bus to **Broadway Market** and then continue northwards to **Dalston** for a full-night's entertainment.

NEW *Bad Egg, Berber & Q, Blixen, Chick'n Sours, The Glory, High Water, Jago, Marksman Public House, Oslo, Paradise Garage, Peg + Patriot, The Richmond, Rotorino, Taberno Do Mercado, Tonkotsu East, Typing Room, Viktor Wynd Museum of Curiosities...*

ART CULTURE DESIGN

The Approach
ART

One of the East End's pioneering contemporary galleries, located above a nice pub.
Bethnal Green: 1st Floor, 47 Approach Rd, E2 · Noon–6pm. Closed Mon, Tue · www.theapproach.co.uk

Hackney Picture House
BAR / FILM

A four-screen, three-bar arthouse cinema in the heart of Hackney.
Hackney: 270 Mare St, E8. www.picturehouses.co.uk

Herald St
ART

A young gallery with a taste for nicely twisted artists like Oliver Payne and Nick Relph, Peter Coffin, Klaus Weber... What's more, Donlon Books has opened a corner there specialising in art, photography and fashion titles.
Bethnal Green: 2 Herald St, E2 · 11am (noon Sat, Sun)–6pm. Closed Mon, Tue · www.heraldst.com

Kate MacGarry
ART

This East End gallery imposed itself on the contemporary scene accompanying artists on the rise, such as Goshka Machuga, Francis Upritchard and Peter McDonald.
Bethnal Green: 27 Old Nichol St, E2 · Noon–6pm. Closed Sun–Tue · www.katemacgarry.com

Maureen Paley DON'T MISS
ART

Twenty years after pioneering the East End art scene from her Hackney home, Paley continues to show former Turner prizewinners (Wolfgang Tillmans, Gillian Wearing) alongside current nominees.
Bethnal Green: 21 Herald St, E2 · 11am–6pm. Closed Mon, Tue · www.maureenpaley.com

Rich Mix
BAR / LIVE MUSIC

Five floors of vibrant creativity offering live music, film, dance, theatre, comedy, spoken word and a range of creative activities for people of all ages and all cultures. All profits go back to support education, arts and community activities which nurture new and local talent.
Shoreditch: 35-47 Bethnal Green Rd, E1 · Café open 9am–9pm, daily · www.richmix.org.uk

Rio Cinema
FILM / KIDS

All the other cinemas in Hackney have long since morphed into pool halls, but the velvet seats of the Rio continue to beckon locals. World film festivals and parent and baby matinées make it family-friendly.
Dalston: 107 Kingsland High St, E8 · www.riocinema.org.uk

Space
ART

Charitable network of artists' studio spaces co-founded by Bridget Riley in 1968. The buoyant gallery programme has revived under the appointment of curator Paul Pieroni.
Hackney: 129–131 Mare St, E8 · 10am–5pm; Sat, Sun 12–6pm · www.spacestudios.org.uk

V&A Museum of Childhood
DON'T MISS / FREE ENTRY / MUSEUM

This charming museum houses the V&A's collection of childhood-related objects and artefacts, spanning the 1600s to the present day.
Bethnal Green: Cambridge Heath Rd, E2 · 10am–5.45pm · www.museumofchildhood.org.uk

Victoria Miro
ART

Located in a former Victorian furniture factory with a landscaped garden, Victoria Miro's vast East End HQ is always worth a look. Among the starry artists she represents are Turner Prize winners Grayson Perry and Chris Ofili.
Hoxton: 16 Wharf Rd, N1 · 10am–6pm. Closed Sun, Mon · www.victoria-miro.com

Viktor Wynd Museum of Curiosities NEW
BAR / MUSEUM

The inimitable East-End artist, impresario and collector has converted his old shop into a museum, presenting an eccentric and seemingly random collection of objects – everything from shrunken heads to narwhal tusks. This museum seeks not to educate but to subvert, to show the world not in a grain of sand, but in a Hackney basement.
Hackney: 11 Mare St, E8 · 11am–10pm. Closed Mon, Tue · thelasttuesdaysociety.org

Vilma Gold
ART

Longstanding and adventurous gallery with an aggressively international stable of artists including Mark Titchner and renowned video artist Charles Atlas.
Bethnal Green: 6 Minerva St, E2 · 11am–6pm. Closed Sun, Mon · vilmagold.com

Whitechapel Gallery DON'T MISS
ART / FREE ENTRY

Overhauled in 2009 and featuring a new café and dining room, the original East End gallery showcases world-class contemporary exhibitions and remains free to visit.
Whitechapel: 77-82 Whitechapel High St, E1 · 11am–6pm (9pm Thu). Closed Mon · www.whitechapelgallery.org

Wilkinson Gallery
ART

Vyner Street once housed more galleries per square foot than anywhere else in London. Although some of the more edgy players have moved on, the ritzy wine-fuelled openings continue to attract parades of arty locals.
Hackney: 50–58 Vyner St, E2 · 11am (noon Sun)–6pm. Closed Mon, Tue · www.wilkinsongallery.com

EAT & COFFEE

8 Hoxton Square ££
BREAKFAST / MODERN EURO / SMALL PLATES / TERRACE

All the critics agree, this rowdy, unpretentious place on Hoxton Square is serving some of the best value and delicious food in all London.
Hoxton: 8 Hoxton Square, N1 · 020 7729 4232 · Noon (10am Sat)–11pm; Sun 10am-5pm · www.8hoxtonsquare.com

A Little of What You Fancy £
DON'T MISS / BRITISH

Dalston may be hip, but until this living-room-style café restaurant opened, eating out meant Turkish kebabs or Vietnamese. Here you'll find a friendly vibe alongside generous portions of seasonal British classics (think Stoke Newington smoked salmon).

Dalston: 464 Kingsland Rd, E8 · 020 7275 0060 · 9am (10am Sun, 10.30am Tue–Wed, 6.30pm Mon)–10pm · www.alittleofwhatyoufancy.info

Albion £
BREAD / BREAKFAST / BRITISH / CAKES / TERRACE

Terence Conran's airy ground-floor café and bakery is ideal for meetings and people-watching, and serves a good-value nostalgic Brit menu. Head downstairs for the smarter Boundary restaurant.

Shoreditch: 2-4 Boundary St, E2 · No reservations · 8am–11pm · www.albioncaff.co.uk

Allpress Espresso £
BREAKFAST / BUDGET / CAKES / COFFEE

Steal a look at the Petroncini roaster by the entrance, and you'll see how seriously this communal-style Shoreditch coffee shop takes its beans. Cake, sandwiches and breakfasts (think salmon on toast) are an added boon.

Shoreditch: 58 Redchurch St, E2 · No reservations · 8am (9am Sat, Sun)–5pm · nz.allpressespresso.com

Bad Egg £ NEW
BAR / BREAKFAST / BRUNCH / TAKE AWAY

After the success of The Smokehouse, Neil Rankin has opened this casual walk-in spot focusing on that ultimate fast food, the egg: baked eggs, hash, burgers, tacos plus sides including shitake, kale and chilli. Wash it all down with a house-made peach and curry cocktail.

Moorgate: City Point, Unit 1b, 1 Ropemaker Street, EC2 · No reservations · 8am–11pm; Sat 9am–10pm. Closed Sun · badegg.london

Beagle ££ DON'T MISS
BAR / BRITISH / COCKTAILS / COFFEE / TAKE AWAY / TERRACE

A restaurant, bar and coffee shop set in three beautifully restored railway arches in Hoxton with chef James Ferguson (formerly at Rochelle Canteen) devising daily changing and seasonal menus of contemporary British grub, often cooked over a traditional wood grill.

Hoxton: 397-400 Geffrye St, E2 · 020 7613 2967 · 4pm (noon weekends)–midnight · www.beaglelondon.co.uk

Berber & Q ££ NEW
COCKTAILS / MEDITERRANEAN

A funked-up East London grill house taking eclectic inspiration from the Middle East and North Africa via Brooklyn, New York. If the mezze's from the East, the electro soundtrack is from the West.

Haggerston: Arch 338, Action Mews, E8 · No reservations · 6–11pm. Closed Mon · berberandq.com

Bistrothèque ££ DON'T MISS
BRUNCH / CABARET / COCKTAILS / FRENCH

Fashion-friendly warehouse-style spot famed for its camp cabaret, beautiful staff and piano-backdropped weekend brunch.

Hackney: 27 Wadeson St, E2 · 020 8983 7900 · 5.30pm (11am Sat, Sun)–midnight · www.bistrotheque.com

Blixen ££ NEW
BREAKFAST / COCKTAILS / MODERN EURO / TERRACE

A relaxed new all-day affair, spanning everything from almond milk porridge in the morning to nighttime cocktails, inside a big old bank in Spitalfields.

Spitalfields: 65A Brushfield St, E1 · 8am (9am Sat)–11pm; 9am–10pm Sun · www.bllxen.co.uk

Brawn ££
FRENCH / WINE BAR

An offshoot of the successful wine bar Terroirs, this robust eatery devotes a whole section of the menu to 'pig,' while the biodynamic wine and wild sourdough bread reflect a similarly foodie-friendly ethos.

Shoreditch: 49 Columbia Rd, E2 · 020 7729 5692 · Noon–3pm, 6–10.30pm (11pm Fri, Sat). Closed Sun dinner · www.brawn.co

Breakfast Club £
BREAKFAST / BRUNCH / BUDGET / COCKTAILS / LATE

As befits the name, the walls of this inviting chain, situated just off Hoxton Square, are covered in '80s memorabilia. The menu screams comfort food: maple syrup pancakes and a full English, with cocktails and burgers by night.

Shoreditch: 2-4 Rufus St, N1 (+ branches) · 020 7729 5252 · 8am–11pm (midnight Thu, Fri, Sat; 10pm Sun) · www.thebreakfastclubcafes.com

Brick Lane Beigel Bake £
BUDGET / LATE / MYTHIC / TAKE AWAY

All life ends up in this tiny shop and you're as likely to see builders as clubbers queueing up for a fix of bagels and platzels in the early hours.

Brick Lane: 159 Brick Lane, E1 · No reservations · Open 24/7.

Brilliant Corners £
JAPANESE / LIVE MUSIC / WINE BAR

An exciting combination of a hardcore sound system – 4 massive Klipsch speakers, a rack of valve amps, custom decks and sound-absorbing wall panels – with great Japanese food and natural wines.

Dalston: 470 Kingsland Rd, E8 · No reservations · 5.30pm–midnight (1.30am Fri, Sat); Sun 4pm–midnight. Closed Mon · brilliantcornerslondon.co.uk

Cây Tre ££
VIETNAMESE

This Hoxton restaurant offers a slicker alternative to the Vietnamese sprawl on nearby Kingsland Road. By day, it's worth heading over the road to its sister venue, the Kêu! Café, which serves moreish Banh Mi baguettes.

Hoxton: 301 Old St, EC1 (+ branches) · 020 7729 8662 · 11am–11pm (10.30pm Sun) · caytre.co.uk

Chick'n Sours £ NEW
BRUNCH / COCKTAILS / FUSION / ORGANIC

Fried chicken with an Asian twist paired with sour cocktails, local beers & soft serve ice cream creations. The free-range, herb-fed chickens come from Pilmoore Grange Farm in Yorkshire and the tasty vegetables from Keveral Farm, an organic farm community in Cornwall.

Haggerston: 390 Kingsland Road, E8 · Reserve online · 6–10pm (10.30pm Fri); Sat, Sun Noon–3.30pm, 6–10.30pm (9.30pm Sun). Closed Mon · chicknsours.co.uk

Climpson & Sons £
BREAKFAST / COFFEE / BUDGET / TAKE AWAY

A key name in London's coffee revolution. Climpson & Sons run a busy Broadway Market café and Saturday market stall. Buy one of their intense and fruity espresso blends to take away and they'll grind the beans while you wait.

Hackney: 67 Broadway Market, E8 · No reservations · 7.30am (8.30am Sat, 9am Sun)–5pm · www.climpsonandsons.com

The Clove Club £££ DON'T MISS
BAR / BRITISH

One of the most exciting dining addresses
in London right now. After a string of
hyped pop-ups, the three friends Daniel
Willis, Johnny Smith and chef Isaac
McHale now have a permanent address
inside an impressive 2-room Edwardian
space. The ambitious 5-course dining
menu features often overlooked British
ingredients and produce.
Shoreditch: **Shoreditch Town Hall,
380 Old St, EC1** · 020 7729 6496 ·
noon–4pm, 6pm–midnight. Closed Mon
lunch and Sun · thecloveclub.com

Cooper & Wolf ££
COFFEE / SCANDINAVIAN

This super cool Swedish café is great for
families. Enjoy the moreish 'Kanelbulle,'
freshly baked cinnamon buns (great
with the Caravan coffee) or 'Köttbullar,'
homemade Swedish meatballs.
Clapton: **145 Chatsworth Rd, E5** ·
No reservations · 9am (10am Sat,
Sun)–5.30pm (6pm Fri–Sun) ·
www.cooperandwolf.co.uk

Crate Brewery £
BAR / BEER / PIZZA / TERRACE

A craft brewery and pizzeria, situated
canal-side in a former print factory.
All beers are brewed on-site,
and what better to accompany a pint
than a delicious stone-baked pizza?
Hackney Wick: **White Building, E9** ·
078 3427 5687 ·
Noon–11pm (midnight Fri, Sat) ·
www.cratebrewery.com

The Diner £
AMERICAN / BREAKFAST / BUDGET / BURGERS

Small and fashionable chain run by
the crew behind the Hoxton Bar
and Kitchen. Grab a milkshake
and fries and settle down in one of
the appealing leather booths.
Shoreditch: **128–130 Curtain Rd, EC2** ·
020 7729 4452 · 9am–11.30pm (midnight
Thu–Sat) · www.goodlifediner.com

Dishoom ££
AFTERNOON TEA / BREAKFAST / COCKTAILS /
INDIAN

Reliable, all-day Bombay-style café serves
up tasty fare in a chic, East London take
on an Indian diner. Don't miss afternoon
chai with a freshly baked Nankhatai
cookie from the house bakery.
Shoreditch: **7 Boundary St, E2**
(+ branches) · 020 7420 9320 ·
8am (9am Sat, Sun)–11pm (midnight
Thu–Sat) · www.dishoom.com

E Pellicci £
BREAKFAST / BUDGET / CHIPS / COFFEE /
ITALIAN / MYTHIC

An East End institution replete with
Formica tables and an antique till,
the magical E Pellicci draws a mixed
crowd of market traders and hungover
hipsters. You could opt for a healthy
breakfast, but it only really makes sense
to get the full English, or Italian classics
like spaghetti Bolognese and lasagne.
Shoreditch: **332 Bethnal Green Rd, E2** ·
No reservations · 7am–4pm. Closed Sun.

Floyd's ££
BREAKFAST / COCKTAILS / MODERN EURO /PIZZA

Great vibe at this restaurant/bar serving
a fresh and inspired menu: how about
home-cured gravlax using line-caught wild
salmon with a fresh dill sauce, or roast
pork belly with apple pizza?
Dalston: **89 Shacklewell Lane, E8** ·
020 7923 7714 · 10am–11pm (6pm Sun) ·
www.facebook.com/friendsoffloyds

Hawksmoor £££
BRUNCH / COCKTAILS / STEAK

Come here for the brilliant and
generously portioned steak and the
supremely crafted cocktails.
Spitalfields: **157a Commercial St, E1** ·
020 7247 7392 ·
Noon–10.30pm (4.30pm Sun) ·
thehawksmoor.co.uk

Hix City ££
BAR / BRITISH / COCKTAILS

The seasonal menu celebrates great
British produce: oysters and seafood
from the British Isles, locally produced
meats and steaks, and often foraged
ingredients. In the basement is a
second Mark's Bar, championing
British drinks, incorporated into
seasonal and foraged infusions
(Mon-Fri, noon–2.30am).
Bishopsgate: **9a Devonshire Square, EC2** ·
020 7220 9498 · 11.30pm–midnight ·
www.hixcity.co.uk

Hoi Polloi ££ DON'T MISS
BAR / BREAKFAST / COCKTAILS / MODERN EURO

The hip restaurant/bar belonging
to London's Ace Hotel is an all-day
modernist brasserie for the Shoreditch
set, open daily from 7am. Enter through
the hotel's charming flower shop
and take breakfast, elevenses, lunch,
afternoon tea, aperitif, dinner, late
supper or a nightcap!
Shoreditch: **100 Shoreditch High St, E1** ·
020 8880 6100 · 7am–midnight, daily ·
www.hoi-polloi.co.uk

Jago ££ NEW
MEDITERRANEAN / SMALL PLATES

A Jewish diaspora menu from the
former Ottolenghi chef, Louis Solley. Try
the salt beef & chrain beigel; the veal
cheek goulash, orzo & sour cream; or
pickled herring, beetroot, yoghurt & dill.
The café is located inside quirky start-
up 'workspace hub' Second Home,
designed by Spanish architect duo
SelgasCano (also chosen to design
the 2015 Serpentine Pavilion).
Spitalfields: **68–80 Hanbury St, E1** ·
020 3818 3241 · 8am (10am Sat)–10.30pm.
Closed Sun · www.jagorestaurant.com

L'Atelier Dalston £
COFFEE / INTERIORS / VINTAGE

There's a focus on artisanal quality
at this hybrid furniture shop/café,
that invites lingering, perusing, sipping.
Dalston: **31 Stoke Newington Rd, N16** ·
020 7254 3238 ·
7.30am (10am Sat, Sun)–11pm ·
www.facebook.com/LatelierDalston

L'Entrepôt £
WINE BAR

A combination of off-licence, wine
bar and café set up by trendy
winemerchants Borough Wines.
Walk past the bottles and barrels to
the small open kitchen at the back to
sample delicious small plates and over
30 different vintages sold by the glass.
Hackney: **230 Dalston Lane, E8** ·
020 7249 1176 · Noon–11pm; Sat, Sun
11am–3pm, 6–11pm · boroughwines.co.uk

L'Eau à la Bouche £
BREAD / BREAKFAST / CAKES / COFFEE / DELI /
FRENCH / TAKE AWAY / TERRACE

Foodies and hipsters fight for pavement
space outside this bijou Broadway
Market staple.
Hackney: **35–37 Broadway Market, E8** ·
No reservations ·
Sat 8.30am–5pm; Sun 9am–5pm ·
www.labouche.co.uk

Lardo £
ITALIAN / PIZZA

This fine pizzeria based in Hackney's
Arthaus complex uses exceptional
ingredients. (The wood-fired pizza oven
is worth a look too.)
Hackney: **197-205 Richmond Rd, E8** ·
020 8985 2683 · 11am–11pm (10pm Sun) ·
www.lardo.co.uk

Leila's Shop £ DON'T MISS
BREAD / BREAKFAST / CAKES / COFFEE / DELI / ORGANIC / TERRACE

Absolute local gem in a cute mismatched room that spills out onto the pavement. The eggs and sage served in the frying pan are not be missed.

Shoreditch: 17 Calvert Ave, E2 · No reservations · 10am–6pm. Closed Mon, Tue ·

Les 3 Garçons £££
FRENCH / WOW

It's hard to see beyond the maximalist temple's décor – costume jewellery, handbags and chandeliers hanging from the walls – but the rich French cuisine is pretty special too. An ideal spot for romance. (And now with a more casual café and shop Maison 3 Garçons around the corner at 45 Redchurch Street!)

Shoreditch: 1 Club Row, E1 · 020 7613 1924 · 6–9.30pm (10.30pm Fri, Sat). Closed Sun · www.lestroisgarcons.com

Little Georgia £
RUSSIAN / TERRACE

This small and charming Hackney café serves homely Georgian fare like borscht and soft cheese blini. The pavement tables tend to catch the sun and are great for people-watching.

Hackney: 87 Goldsmiths Row, E2 · 020 7739 8154 · 10am–11pm (5pm Mon) · www.littlegeorgia.co.uk

Lyle's ££ DON'T MISS
BREAKFAST / BRITISH

The chef of the hyped 'Young Turk' trio James Lowe's first solo venture, inside Shoreditch's iconic Tea Building. With light streaming in through the large windows, and with an open kitchen, the restaurant starts with breakfast in the morning and runs through to an inventive 7-course tasting menu in the evening.

Shoreditch: Tea Building, 56 Shoreditch High St, E1 · 020 3011 5911 · 8am (6pm Sat)–11pm. Closed Sun · www.lyleslondon.com

Mangal II £
BUDGET / LATE / TURKISH

Best known for its longtime diners-in-residence, the artists Gilbert & George, this Dalston icon does fantastic meze – expert barbecued meats and plentiful salads.

Hackney: 4 Stoke Newington Rd, N16 · 020 7254 7888 · Noon–1am (midnight Sun) · www.mangal2.com

Marksman Public House ££
NEW / DON'T MISS / MODERN EURO / PUB / SUNDAY ROAST

A proper 'London boozer' now with two stylish St John alumni Tom Harris and Jon Rotheram at the helm. Pop in for a pint, stay for an excellent dinner. .

Bethnal Green: 254 Hackney Road, E2 · 020 7739 7393 · 11am–midnight; Sun 10am–11pm · www.marksmanpublichouse.com

Merci Marie £
BREAKFAST / BYO / COFFEE / FRENCH / ORGANIC / SSHHH / TAKE AWAY / VEGETARIAN

On the ground floor of Fitzroy House, this hidden-away Dalston café uses organic dairy products, local and seasonal vegetables and sustainable meat and fish. On Friday night, the pop-up dining club allows French chef Marie Gonfond to get more creative.

Dalston: Fitzroy House, 3 Abbot St, E8 · 020 7254 2456 · 9am–3pm, 7pm–midnight. Closed Sat, Sun · www.merci-marie.com

Old Shoreditch Station £
BAR / COFFEE

This hybrid bar / café / shop provides another stomping ground for the Shoreditch style set from the people behind neighbouring DreamBagsJaguarShoes. And now it's also the historic home to the UK's first Bitcoin ATM.

Shoreditch: 1 Kingsland Rd, E2 · No reservations · 8am (10am Sat, Sun)–1am (11pm Sun–Tue) · www.jaguarshoes.com

Ombra ££
BAR / ITALIAN / TAPAS

This authentic Venetian *bacaro* right next to Regent's Canal serves Aperol spritzer and fine Italian bottles to go with their '*cicchetti*,' or Venetian-style tapas.

Bethnal Green: 1 Vyner St, E2 · 020 8981 5150 · 9am (10am Sat, 11am Sun)–11pm. Closed Mon · ombrabar.com

Pacific Social Club £
BREAKFAST / COFFEE

Amazing sandwiches and atmosphere at this tiki café pushing 'nice coffee, ice coffee, ice tea, self-help books, exotic sandwiches, coconuts, Nigerian soft drinks...'

Hackney: 8 Clarence Rd, E5 · No reservations · 8am–6pm; Sat, Sun 9.30am–5pm · www.facebook.com/pacificsocial

Paradise Garage ££ NEW
DON'T MISS / BRITISH

A hot new table serving contemporary British cuisine – say, cured mackerel, damsons, hazelnuts & smoked buttermilk – inside a distressed space under railway arches in Bethnal Green, from the winning team behind The Dairy & The Manor.

Bethnal Green: 254 Paradise Row, E2 · 020 7613 1502 · Open lunch & dinner Wed–Sat; Sun lunch only; Tue dinner only. Closed Mon · www.paradise254.com

Pizza East ££
ITALIAN / LATE / PIZZA

Sharing the same building and owners as Shoreditch House, this vast factory-style space is permanently buzzing with crowds savouring the substantial antipasti and reliably flavoursome pizza.

Shoreditch: 56 Shoreditch High St, E1 · 020 7729 1888 · Noon–midnight (1am Thu, 2am Fri); Sat 10am–2am; Sun 11am–midnight · www.pizzaeast.com

Poppies Fish & Chips £
BRITISH / FISH & CHIPS / TAKE AWAY

A real piece of the old East End. Enjoy great fish and chips the way it should be, served in newspaper of course.

Spitalfields: 6-8 Hanbury St, E1 · 020 7247 0892 · 11am–11pm (11.30pm Fri, Sat; 10.30pm Sun) · poppiesfishandchips.co.uk

Rawduck £
BREAKFAST / MODERN EURO

After their restaurant fell down! Hackney's wonderful Rawduck reopened in new premises, with interiors by Seng Watson. Ducksoup's sister restaurant touts an all-day seasonal menu, and they make all their own pickles, ferments, jams and drinks in-house and smoke their own salmon, trout and bacon too.

Hackney: 197 Richmond Rd, E8 · 020 8986 6534 · 10am (6pm Mon)–10.30pm · www.rawduckhackney.co.uk

The Richmond ££ NEW
BAR / MODERN EURO / OYSTERS

Natural wines, classic cocktails and locally sourced 'comfort food' at Brett Redman (of Brett's of Borough Market fame) and stylist Margaret Crow's relaxed bar and restaurant. The eatery includes East London's first and only raw seafood bar serving UK oyster varieties from Essex, Scotland, Wales, and Ireland.

Hackney: 316 Queensbridge Rd, E8 ·
020 7241 1638 · 5pm–midnight; Sat noon–
3pm, 5pm–midnight; Sun noon–8pm ·
www.therichmondhackney.com

Rita's Bar & Dining £
AMERICAN / BAR / BRUNCH / COCKTAILS / TAKE AWAY

What started life as a pop-up in East
London founded by four friends who
share a love for great food and drink,
music and good times is now a
permanent 'Hackney neighbourhood
restaurant,' where Rita and her team
are serving the same fried chicken
and other new-gen junk food we've all
come to know and love.

Hackney: 175 Mare St, E8 ·
020 3096 1530 · Noon–3pm (4pm Sat, Sun),
6–11pm. Closed Tue lunch, Sun dinner
& Mon · ritasbaranddining.com

Rivington Bar & Grill ££
BREAKFAST / BRITISH / BRUNCH / VEGETARIAN

Classic comfort food (fish fingers
and mushy peas) in a sophisticated
room adorned with artworks by local
luminaries like Tracey Emin.

Shoreditch: 28-30 Rivington St, EC2 ·
020 7729 7053 · 8am–12.30am; Sat, Sun
11am–midnight ·
www.rivingtonshoreditch.co.uk

Rochelle Canteen ££
BREAKFAST / BRITISH / SSSHH / TERRACE

A buzzer on the door of the old school's
wall gains you access to the perfect
arty spot for lunch. The menu is a
relaxed take on St. John (owner Margot
is married to Fergus Henderson.)

Shoreditch: Arnold Circus, E2 ·
020 7729 5677 · 9am–4.30pm.
Closed Sat, Sun ·
www.arnoldandhenderson.com

Rotorino ££ NEW
ITALIAN / SMALL PLATES

A hyped second address from young
chef Stevie Parle, of Dock Kitchen (and
before that of the River Café). Next
door to the landmark Haggerston pub,
this grown-up table looks like it has
been teleported out of elegant Soho
to grungy Dalston. The modern Italian
menu proposes all sorts of delicious
small plates to share.

Dalston: 434 Kingsland Rd, E8 ·
020 7249 9081 · 6pm–midnight daily;
Noon–3pm Sat, Sun · www.rotorino.com

Shoreditch Grind £
BREAKFAST / COCKTAILS / COFFEE

The first of the Grinds, this popular
espresso bar on the busy Old
Street roundabout has spawned an

empire. Coffee bar by day, cocktail
bar by night, plus an all-day café
menu covering porridge, focaccia
sandwiches and piadinas, to a soup of
the day. The upstairs recording studio
adds a rock'n'roll vibe.

Shoreditch: 213 Old St, EC1 ·
No reservations · 7am (Sat 8am)–11pm
(Fri 1am). Sun 9am–7pm ·
www.shoreditchgrind.com

St John Bread & Wine ££
DON'T MISS / BREAKFAST / BRITISH

Located across the street from
Spitalfields Market, it's easier to get
a table without booking here than
at the bigger, sister restaurant, and
it's just as good! Slightly less formal,
guests are encouraged to share dishes
as they're ready from the kitchen.

Spitalfields: 94-96 Commercial St, E1 ·
020 7251 0848 · 9am–11pm daily ·
www.stjohngroup.uk.com/spitalfields

Story Deli £
ITALIAN / ORGANIC / PIZZA / TAKE AWAY

The latest address for Story Deli is an
elegant, lo-fi affair, but pizza is the star
attraction – wafer thin, wood-fired and
piled high with delicious organic toppings.

Shoreditch: 123 Bethnal Green Rd, E2 ·
No reservations · Noon–10.30pm ·
www.storydeli.com

Taberno Do Mercado ££
NEW / PORTUGUESE / SMALL PLATES

Chef Nuno Mendes, of Chiltern
Firehouse fame, has opened this casual
all-day taverna inside busy Spitalfields
Market serving the food and wine from
his native Portugal.

Spitalfields: Old Spitalfields Market, 107b
Commercial St, E1 · No reservations ·
11am–11pm daily ·
www.tabernamercado.co.uk

Tayyabs £ DON'T MISS
BYO / INDIAN

East London's landmark Indian
restaurant has been serving 'the finest
in Punjabi cuisine' to grateful locals
since 1972 and remains family run.
A no-charge BYO policy only sweetens
the deal. Book.

Whitechapel: 83-89 Fieldgate St, E1 ·
079 7247 6400 · Noon–midnight ·
tayyabs.co.uk

Tonkotsu East £ NEW
BAR / COCKTAILS / JAPANESE / WHISKY

On top of the home-made tonkotsu
and Tokyo ramens, gyoza and chicken
karaage, the mini chain's fourth address

features a couple of exclusive recipes
including the seafood ramen bursting
with king prawns, squid and clams, and
all with added kick from their famous
Eat the Bits chilli oil. Put out the fire with
a Japanese whisky from the bar.

Hackney: 382 Mare Street, E8 ·
079 8533 1840 · Noon–3pm, 5–10.30pm
(11pm Fri). Sat, Sun Noon–10.30pm ·
www.tonkotsu.co.uk

Tramshed ££
STEAK / TAKE AWAY

Mark Hix has transformed a vast old
tramshed into a chic spot dedicated
to chicken and steak; it even flaunts
a specially commissioned artwork by
Damien Hirst.

Shoreditch: 32 Rivington St, EC2 ·
020 7749 0478 · 11am–midnight
(10pm Sun; 11pm Mon, Tue) ·
www.chickenandsteak.co.uk

Typing Room ££ NEW
BRITISH

Jason Atherton protégé Lee Westcott
has taken over the restaurant at the
Town Hall Hotel (after Nuno Mendes
decamped to the Chiltern Firehouse).
From an open kitchen, Westcott offers a
refined showcase of the British seasons
and produce, such as mackerel, burnt
cucumber & dill, smoked pigeon,
celeriac, lovage or hazelnut.

Bethnal Green: Town Hall Hotel,
Patriot Square, E2 · 020 7871 0461 ·
Noon–2.30pm, 6–10.30pm. Closed Sun,
Mon, Tue lunch · typingroom.com

Verde & Company £
CHOCOLATE / COFFEE / DELI

Great little Dickensian deli owned by the
writer Jeanette Winterson. The gourmet
sandwiches and Pierre Marcolini
chocolates are especially moreish.

Spitalfields: 40 Brushfield St, E1 ·
No reservations ·
8.30am (10am Sat, Sun)–6pm ·
verdeandco.co.uk

Voodoo Ray's £
LATE / PIZZA

Late-night pizza by the slice plus frozen
margaritas from the Dalston Superstore
crew. Oh, and there's something
downstairs called Dance Tunnel…

Dalston: 95 Kingsland High St, E8 ·
No reservations · 5pm–midnight
(1am Thu, 3am Fri); Sat noon–3am ·
www.voodoorays.co.uk

White Rabbit ££
BRITISH / BRUNCH

Dalston's first Modern Brit restaurant is a modish affair serving an imaginative menu of fresh and seasonal dishes designed for sharing.
Dalston: 15-16 Bradbury St, N16 · 020 7682 0163 · 6pm–midnight; Sat, Sun 11am–4pm, 6pm–midnight · www.whiterabbitdalston.com

Wilton Way Café £
BREAKFAST / BRITISH / BRUNCH / BUDGET / COFFEE

Wilton's is a firm favourite of Hackney hipsters, and not just because London Fields Radio broadcasts from the doorstep. Food (avocado on toast, bacon baps) benefits from the finest artisanal produce in town – like cheese from Neal's Yard.
Hackney: 63 Wilton Way, E8 · No reservations · 8am (9am Sun)–5pm (6pm Sat, Sun) · www.facebook.com/wiltonwaycafe

Wright Brothers Spitalfields ££
OYSTERS / SEAFOOD / TERRACE

Located inside the historic Old Spitalfields Market, this 'sea-to-plate' dining address from the Wright Brothers allows you to choose your live crab, lobster or oysters from seawater tanks, then pair them with a gin cocktail, craft ale or cider at the Carrara marble bar, on a banquette, or at the stylish market terrace.
Spitalfields: 8/9 Lamb St, Old Spitalfields Market, E1 · 020 7377 8706 · Noon–midnight (10pm Sun) · www.thewrightbrothers.co.uk

PARTY

93 Feet East
BUDGET / CLUB / GRUNGY / LIVE MUSIC

Pumping place by the Truman Brewery that encapsulates the indie-grunge feel of Brick Lane.
Brick Lane: The Old Truman Brewery, 150 Brick Lane, E1 · Thu 5–11pm; Fri, Sat 5–1am; Sun 2–10.30pm · www.93feeteast.co.uk

♫ TO LISTEN TO

KWABS
LOVE + WAR
(ATLANTIC RECORDS)

The Alibi DON'T MISS
BAR / CLUB / GRUNGY

Edgy, raw – the scent of MDF permanently in the air – this is one of Dalston's hippest destinations. Musically, the basement club is totally on the money, with nights spanning Italo, indie, electronica and grime.
Dalston: 91 Kingsland High St, E8 · 8pm–2am (3am Thu–Sat) · www.thealibilondon.co.uk

Bethnal Green Working Men's Club DON'T MISS
BAR / CLUB

The place to be since 1953! Today it's an avant-garde playground for local creatives, hosting sometimes racy, sometimes cultural and refined – but mostly wild, unhinged – good-times. PS You can also nosh on British fodder with an East End twist in the upstairs dining room (Thu–Sun).
Shoreditch: 42-46 Pollard St, E2 · Opening days and times vary, check the website · www.workersplaytime.net

Birthdays
BAR / CLUB / LIVE MUSIC

A two-floor fun factory: on the ground floor is a bar with cocktails and in the basement a gig room with a massive sound system, a stage and pretty lights.
Dalston: 33-35 Stoke Newington Rd, N16 · 4pm (noon Sat, 11am Sun)–midnight (3am Fri, Sat) · birthdaysdalston.com

The Book Club
BREAKFAST / COCKTAILS / LIVE MUSIC / LITERARY EVENTS

Boozing meets brain power in this appealing venture from the team behind the grungier Queen of Hoxton. The eclectic programme spans talks, evening classes & cross-platform club nights.
Shoreditch: 100 Leonard St, EC2 · 8am (10am Sat, Sun)–midnight (2am Thu–Sat) · www.wearetbc.com

Café Oto DON'T MISS
BAR / BUDGET / JAPANESE / LIVE MUSIC

Intriguing café-cum-experimental platform for left-field music, literary and film events. Think Sun Ra and author Ian Sinclair getting down over a few Japanese cocktails. Check the programme online.
Dalston: 18–22 Ashwin St, E8 · café: 8.30am (9.30am Sat; 10.30am Sun)–5.30pm · www.cafeoto.co.uk

Cat & Mutton
PUB

This landmark 300-year-old pub, located on a huge corner site on Broadway Market, has had a refurb. Today with a trendy food and cocktail menu, it's a massively popular and chaotic affair, at times victim of its (well-deserved) success.
Hackney: 76 Broadway Market, E8 · Noon–midnight (11.30pm Mon, 1am Fri, 11pm Sun); 11am–1am Sat · www.catandmutton.com

Catch
CLUB / LIVE MUSIC

Most East End hipsters have collapsed in the intimate wooden booths downstairs at some point, or danced away the night at one of the edgy club nights upstairs. After 11pm it's rammed, and flirting steps up a gear.
Shoreditch: 22 Kingsland Rd, E2 · Noon–midnight (2am Thu–Sat, 1am Sun) · thecatchbar.com

Dalston Superstore
BRUNCH / CLUB

Self-consciously hip and joyfully camp, this two-tier temple to industrial chic has been lording it over Dalston rivals ever since it opened. On weekends the downstairs space is the quintessence of hedonistic.
Dalston: 117 Kingsland High St, E8 · 11.45am–late daily · dalstonsuperstore.com

The Dove
CHIPS / PUB / SUNDAY ROAST

Consistently packed with young locals who come for the definitive Belgian beer selection, superior pub lunches and unbeatable chips.
Hackney: 24–28 Broadway Market, E8 · Noon (11am Sat)–11pm · dovepubs.com

Dream Bags Jaguar Shoes
BAR / COCKTAILS / PIZZA

It may be accused of being pretentious, but one of Shoreditch's pioneering hangouts (open since 2002) continues to thrive. Come to throw back some cheap drinks with local hipsters, talk about the exhibition on the walls, and order in delicious stone-baked pizzas from next-door Amici Miei2Go.
Shoreditch: 32-34 Kingsland Rd, E2 · Noon–1am · www.jaguarshoes.com

Dukes Brew & Que
BEER / BRUNCH / BURGERS / TEQUILA

In Hackney's De Beauvoir town, this 'brewpub' includes its own artisan microbrewery on site, brewing both cask and bottle-conditioned beers by hand. The 'Que' side of things is a rib-sticking American-style BBQ menu of slow-smoked dishes, including their famous ribs.

Hackney: 33 Downham Road, N1 · 4pm–11pm (11.30pm Thu, Fri); Sat, Sun 11am–11pm (11.30pm Sat) · dukesbrewandque.com

East London Liquor Company
BAR / COCKTAILS

Bringing spirits production back to London's East End after more than a century, this craft spirits producer distills gins, vodka, rum and whisky from an old glue factory in Bow Wharf. The bar prepares cocktails featuring their own spirits but also dips into the rich heritage of gin production worldwide. Plus there's a rotating selection of draught and bottled craft beers.

Bow: Unit GF1, Bow Wharf, Grove Road, E3 · Noon–11.30pm (midnight Fri, Sat) · www.eastlondonliquorcompany.com

The George & Dragon
PUB / GRUNGY / MYTHIC

Kitsch and gay-friendly East End institution that's ideally placed for a drink. Standing room only on weekends.

Shoreditch: 2 Hackney Rd, E2 · 6pm–midnight ·

The Glory NEW
BAR / LIVE MUSIC

East London drag queen and star of Gay Bingo Jonny Woo has set up an alternative 'super-pub,' performance venue and late-night disco haunt in Haggerston (or is that Faggerston?), that's set to become the new epicentre of East London's thriving alt nightlife scene. And it's open 7 nights a week!

Haggerston: 281 Kingsland Rd, E2 · 5pm–midnight daily · www.theglory.co

Haggerston
GRUNGY / JAZZ / LATE / LIVE MUSIC / PUB

A late-night dive that's always packed with Dalstonites getting happily drunk before heading on to one of the clubs nearby. On Sunday nights there are jazz sessions led by guitarist Alan Weekes.

Dalston: 438 Kingsland Rd, E8 · 11am–1am (3am Fri–Sun) · www.thehaggerstonpub.com

Happiness Forgets DON'T MISS
BAR / COCKTAILS

This tiny, dimly lit bar serves inventive cocktails for grown-ups.

Hoxton: 8-9 Hoxton Square, N1 · 5.30–11pm · www.happinessforgets.com

High Water NEW
BAR / COCKTAILS

World class cocktails, craft beer and whisky, and a sophisticated atmosphere, in the grimy heart of Dalston.

Dalston: 23 Stoke Newington Rd, N16 · 6pm–late daily · www.highwaterlondon.com

Hoxton Square Bar & Kitchen
BAR / BURGERS / LIVE MUSIC / TERRACE

A Hoxton classic with a long and lively main bar, upmarket diner-style food and an edgy but crowd-pleasing programme of live music from bands often on the cusp of great things.

Hoxton: 2–4 Hoxton Square, N1 · Noon–1am (2am Fri, Sat) · mamacolive.com/hoxton

The King's Head DON'T MISS
MEMBERS CLUB / SSHHH

Riffing off East London's creative energy, this members club hides five wild floors dedicated to art, film, music and performance behind a low-key façade. Plus there's a restaurant and basement club. Now you just have to find someone to get you in!

Shoreditch: 257 Kingsland Rd, E2 · 7am–3.30am · www.thekingshead-london.com

Lounge Bohemia DON'T MISS
BAR / COCKTAILS / SSHHH

A nondescript doorway between a kebab shop and newsagent leads down to this romantic basement cocktail bar, mining a '60s bohemian vibe. Don't miss the sumptuous Czech canapés and bohemian iced tea for two. Reserve on weekends.

Shoreditch: 1E Great Eastern St, EC2 · 6pm–midnight (11pm Sun) · loungebohemia.com

Loungelover
BAR / COCKTAILS

Owned by the team behind neighbouring restaurant Les Trois Garçons, this ultra kitsch and opulent cocktail bar is something for a special night out. Cocktails are top-notch, and there's plenty of yummy Asian snacking to be had on the side.

Shoreditch: 1 Whitby St, E1 · 6pm–midnight (11pm Sun, Mon); Fri, Sat 5pm–1am · www.loungelover.uk.com

The Macbeth
LIVE MUSIC / PUB / TERRACE

A firm favourite with East End indie kids, The Macbeth has welcomed gigs by the likes of Franz Ferdinand and Florence & the Machine. The cute roof garden and smoking terrace often hosts a pop-up cinema in summer months.

Shoreditch: 70 Hoxton St, N1 · 5pm–1am (2am Thu–Sat) · themacbeth.co.uk

The Mayor of Scaredy Cat Town
BAR / COCKTAILS / SSHHH

Enter via the Smeg fridge at the back of the Breakfast Club on street level to reach this industrial-chic basement cocktail bar.

Spitalfields: 12-16 Artillery Lane, E1 · 5pm (3pm Fri; noon Sat, Sun)–midnight (10.30pm Sun) · www.themayorofscaredycattown.com

Nightjar
BAR / COCKTAILS / LIVE MUSIC

An award-winning cocktail destination and a basement speakeasy with a vintage vibe and live music most nights, typically jazz or gypsy swing.

Shoreditch: 129 City Road, EC1 · 6pm–1am (2am Thu; 3am Fri, Sat) · www.barnightjar.com

Number 90 Main Yard
BREAKFAST / BRUNCH / BAR / SUNDAY ROAST

In a former dye-cutting factory on the canal in Hackney Wick, this spacious multi-arts venue, bar and restaurant combo hosts a rich programme of events with a community focus running from a Burger & Movies program every Tuesday night to brunch on Sundays.

Hackney Wick: 90 Main Yard, Wallis Rd, LE9 · Noon–11.30pm. Closed Mon, Tue · www.number90bar.co.uk

The Old Blue Last
PUB / LIVE MUSIC

Hipster pub/club run by *Vice* magazine that's less down at heel since a recent refurbishment. Upstairs hosts packed gigs and magazine nights featuring all the bands of the moment.

Shoreditch: 38 Great Eastern St, EC2 · Noon–midnight (1.30am Fri, Sat) · www.theoldbluelast.com

Oslo NEW
BAR / LIVE MUSIC / SCANDINAVIAN

The latest addition to East London's hectic social scene is a Scandinavian-inspired club and restaurant in a former railway station in Hackney. Grab a craft ale and a salmon BLT then climb upstairs and wait for the gigs to start.

Hackney: 1a Amhurst Road, E8 · Noon–2am (3am Fri, Sat) · www.oslohackney.com

Peg & Patriot NEW
BAR / COCKTAILS

The new cocktail bar inside the Town Hall Hotel pushes 'molecular mixology;' the quirky cocktail menu features for example Salt Beef Sazerac – salt beef beigal cognac, absinthe, sugar and bitters! Bartender Matt Whiley is also distilling three different styles of gin on site, including Moonshine Kid Dog's Nose, a hop gin.

Bethnal Green: Town Hall Hotel, Patriot Square, E2 · 5pm–midnight (1am Fri, Sat); Sun noon–10pm. Closed Mon · www.pegandpatriot.com

Power Lunches Arts Café
BAR / CLUB / GRUNGY / LIVE MUSIC

A casual Dalston hangout that hosts hip live music nights (think cold wave and sound poets) in the minimal basement. Upstairs is an agreeable café serving simple dishes and a small range of wines and spirits.

Haggerston: 446 Kingsland Rd, E8 · 11am–midnight (2am weekends) · powerlunchesltd.co.uk

The Princess of Shoreditch
PUB

This tucked-away hotspot has a country pub feel with a hearty menu for both feeding and watering. It's a warm place to come on a chilly evening and provides a little respite from the madding Shoreditch crowds.

Shoreditch: 76 Paul St, EC2A · Noon–11pm (10.30pm Sun) · theprincessofshoreditch.com

Red Lion
PUB / TERRACE

An agreeable Hoxton boozer with a slightly more mature crowd. In summer, the panoramic roof terrace is a pleasant spot for lunch and beers.

Hoxton: 41 Hoxton St, N1 · Noon (10.30am Sun)–11pm · www.redlionhoxtonst.com

Ridley Road Market Bar
BAR

In the heart of humming Ridley Road Market – come during the day to buy produce from around the world, especially Africa and the Caribbean – this tropical, lo-fi bar keeps the neighbourhood's energy going long after dark.

Dalston: 49 Ridley Rd, E8 · 6pm–2am (11pm Tue, 12.30am Wed); Sun 5–11pm. Closed Mon · www.facebook.com/ridleyroad

Royal Oak
CHIPS / COCKTAILS / PUB / SUNDAY ROAST

The highlight of hip Columbia Rd is a proper East End pub that is the default meeting point for local creatives. The Sunday lunch is renowned.

Bethnal Green: 73 Columbia Rd, E2 · 4pm (noon Sat, Sun)–11pm · www.royaloaklondon.com

Sebright Arms
CHIPS / LIVE MUSIC / PUB

Tucked away up an alley off Hackney Road, this perennially trendy East End haunt hosts regular foodie pop-ups, and has a great selection of beers brewed within the M25.

Haggerston: 31–35 Coate St, E2 · 5pm–11pm (midnight Thu, Fri); Sat noon–midnight; Sun noon–10.30pm · sebrightarms.co.uk

Shacklewell Arms DON'T MISS
BAR / GRUNGY / LATE / LIVE MUSIC

Since launching a few years ago, this bijou gem has become a reliable favourite of the Dalston set, eager to catch residencies and gigs by up-and-coming acts.

Dalston: 71 Shacklewell Lane, E8 · 5pm (noon Sat, Sun)–midnight (3am Fri, Sat) · www.shacklewellarms.com

Shoreditch House
BAR / LITERARY EVENTS / MEMBERS CLUB

Find a member to sign you in, and head for the rooftop pool to scope the incredible views and the parade of up-and-coming locals. The restaurant is worth a stop too.

Shoreditch: Ebor St, E1 · 7am–3am; Sun 8am–midnight · www.shoreditchhouse.com

Spurstowe Arms
PUB

Very good and cool Dalston gastro pub.

Dalston: 68 Greenwood Rd, E8 · 5pm (noon Sat)–midnight (11pm Mon); Noon–11pm Sun · www.thespurstowearms.com

Vogue Fabrics
CLUB

You don't have to be gay, but it helps to be fabulous to enjoy this hilarious hub for East London creatives. It features a disco floor and transvestite staff and is just down the road from Dalston Superstore.

Dalston: 66 Stoke Newington Rd, N16 · Thu 8pm–2am; Fri, Sat 10pm–3am (4am Sat) · voguefabricsdalston.com

Vortex Jazz Club
JAZZ / LIVE MUSIC

Reinvigorated by its move to Dalston, the dynamic club is the epicentre of the UK's vibrant new jazz scene: house label Vortex Babel got off to an amazing start with youthful regulars the Portico Quartet.

Dalston: 11 Gillett St, N16 · 8pm–midnight daily · www.vortexjazz.co.uk

White Lyan
BAR / COCKTAILS

No sugar, no citrus or anything perishable, no ice, almost no branded products... The first solo venture from Ryan Chetiyawardana (69 Colebrooke Row), offers up premixed cocktails. Try for instance the Painted Presidente, with Mr Lyan Rum, vermouth, pomegranate paint and grass. There are also shots to get you prepped for the dance floor downstairs.

Hoxton: 153-155 Hoxton St, N1 · 6pm–late daily · whitelyan.com

Worship St Whistling Shop
BAR / COCKTAILS / SSHHH

A spot-on addition to the capital's trend for speakeasies that boasts a Dickensian interior and windowed laboratory. Drinks are appealing named – with creepy ingredients like 'chlorophyll bitters' that add to the fun.

Shoreditch: 63 Worship St, EC2 · 5pm–midnight (1am Wed, Thu; 2am Fri, Sat). Closed Sun, Mon · whistlingshop.com

Xoyo
CLUB / LIVE MUSIC

A unique events space and club with a great booking policy where you can experience the best in live music and other cultural happenings. Check the programme online.

Shoreditch: 32-37 Cowper St, EC2 · www.xoyo.co.uk

SHOPPING

A Child of the Jago DON'T MISS
FASHION / MENS / VINTAGE

Owned by designer Barnzley and Agent Provocateur's Joe Corre (scion of Vivienne Westwood and Malcolm McLaren) this is a mecca for, as they put it, 'Victorian pimps'.

Shoreditch: 10 Great Eastern St, EC2 (+ branches) · 11am–7pm; Sun noon–5pm · www.achildofthejago.com

A Gold
BRITISH / CAKES / CHOCOLATE / DELI / TAKE AWAY

Old-fashioned village-style shop that's a haven of sweets, organic groceries and specialised deli items. The sandwiches are a great take-away option.

Shoreditch: 42 Brushfield St, E1 · 10am–4pm (5pm Sat, Sun) · www.agoldshop.com

Absolute Vintage
VINTAGE

Bags, accessories and the most incredible selection of vintage shoes in town.

Spitalfields: 15 Hanbury St, E1 · 11am–7pm · www.absolutevintage.co.uk

Ally Capellino DON'T MISS
BAGS / FASHION / MENS

Her simple leather and waxed cotton bags have made Ally Capellino the toast of London fashionistas. Don't miss her equally stylish range of Bags for Bikes.

Shoreditch: 9 Calvert Ave, E2 (+ branches) · 11am–6pm (5pm Sun). Closed Mon · www.allycapellino.co.uk

Artwords
BOOKS

Tiny but incredibly well stocked specialist in books, magazines and videos on the contemporary visual arts. There's another branch on Broadway Market.

Shoreditch: 69 Rivington St, EC2 (+ branches) · 10.30am (11am Sat)–7pm; Sun noon–6pm · www.artwords.co.uk

Bernstock Speirs
HATS

Established in 1982 by Paul Bernstock and Thelma Speirs, this quirky millinery is inspired by the underground club scene, and champions a cheeky and youthful style.

Spitalfields: 234 Brick Lane, E2 · 10am–6pm; Sat, Sun 11am–5pm · www.bernstockspeirs.com

Beyond Retro Dalston DON'T MISS
COFFEE / VINTAGE

Much beloved by stylists, Beyond Retro's Dalston branch is another amazing and massive temple to vintage and features beautiful Art Deco mosaic interiors plus its own fab café.

Dalston: 92-100 Stoke Newington Rd, N16 (+ branches) · 10am–7pm (8pm Thu); Sun 11.30am–6pm · www.beyondretro.com

Bleach
BEAUTY / HAIR

This trailblazing Dalston salon is famed for initiating the dip-dye trend à la Lady Gaga.

Dalston: 420 Kingsland Rd, E8 (+ branches) · 9am–9pm; Sun 11.30am–6pm · bleachlondon.co.uk

Blitz DON'T MISS
BOOKS / INTERIORS / VINTAGE

This two-floor 'vintage department store', founded by a group of second-hand dealers, is a great place to pick up some pristine '50s leather shoes or a stylish leather armchair. There are books and a cute café too.

Shoreditch: 55-59 Hanbury St, E1 · 11am–7pm (8pm Thu–Sat) · www.blitzlondon.co.uk

Boxpark
MALL / POP UP

The 'world's first pop-up mall' is a unique, experimental space made of stripped and refitted shipping containers and filled with a mix of local and global brands – from Swedish Hasbeens to Hype – plus galleries, cafés and restaurants.

Shoreditch: 2-10 Bethnal Green Rd, E1 · 11am–7pm (8pm Thu); noon–6pm Sun · www.boxpark.co.uk

Brick Lane Bikes
BIKES

At the heart of East London's cycling scene, Brick Lane Bikes was the UK's first fixed-gear bike store, specialising in custom-made bikes built in their on-site workshop.

Brick Lane: 118 Bethnal Green Rd, E2 · 9am–7pm; Sat 11am–6pm (5pm Sun) · bricklanebikes.co.uk

Brick Lane Market
MARKET / VINTAGE

On Sundays, at the northern end of Brick Lane and along Cheshire Street, young Londoners flock in search of second-hand furniture, cool vintage bargains and bric-à-brac. The adjacent Old Truman Brewery is also home to 5 separate markets showcasing local artists, designers, collectors, chefs & bakers. Check the site for details.

Shoreditch: The Old Truman Brewery, 91 Brick Lane, E1 · Sun 10am–5pm · www.bricklanemarket.com

Broadway Market
MARKET

Crammed into a little East End street between the Regent's Canal and London Fields is this food and clothes market that's been plying its trade since the 1890s. Organic meat, fruit and vegetables, fresh fish and smoked salmon and oysters, delicious bread, cakes and cheese, plus vintage fashion bargains.

Hackney: Broadway Market, E8 · Sat 9am–5pm · broadwaymarket.co.uk

Columbia Road Market
FLOWERS / MARKET

On Sundays, the charming East End street is transformed into a jungle of plants. There's also window shopping, cupcakes and coffee galore.

Bethnal Green: Columbia Rd, E2 · Sun 8am–3pm · www.columbiaroad.info

E5 Bakehouse
BREAD / CAKES / COFFEE

Ben Mackinnon is bringing the art of sourdough baking to Hackney. Everything he bakes, makes or sells embodies his passion for artisan methods, organic local products and delicious food.

London Fields: Arch 395, Mentmore Terrace, E8 · 7am–7pm · e5bakehouse.com

Fabrique Bakery
BREAD / CAKES / COFFEE

Scandinavian chic at this Shoreditch outpost of the Stockholm bakery. Sample their cinnamon buns, cardamom buns, biscuits and fantastic breads. The coffee is specially blended in Sweden by Johan & Nyström.

Shoredicth: Arch 385, Geffrye St, E2 ·
8am (10am Sat, Sun)–6pm ·
fabrique.co.uk

FARM:shop
ORGANIC

This unique urban farming project
attempts to grow as much food on and
in every inch of the building as it can,
with a mini 'aquaponic' fish farm, rooftop
chicken coops, indoor allotments and a
polytunnel. The produce (along with that
of other local farmers) is available here,
in the shop/ café.

Dalston: 20 Dalston Lane, E8 ·
11am–4pm (5pm Sat, Sun) ·
farmlondon.weebly.com

Fred Perry
FASHION / MENS

The first concept store of the iconic
London brand showcases premium
lines such as collabs, Blank Canvas
projects & the Laurel Wreath Collection.

Spitalfields: 105a Commercial St,
Old Spitalfields Market, E1 ·
11am–7pm (6pm Sun) ·
www.fredperry.com

Goodhood Store
FASHION / INTERIORS / MENS / MULTIBRAND

A huge new flagship for the luxe East End
multibrand, pimping brands like Maiden
Noir, Norse Projects or Perks & Mini, and
now with room for cosmetics, homeware,
kids collections and even a café.

Shoredicth: 151 Curtain Rd, EC2 ·
10am–6pm; Sun 11am–5pm ·
goodhoodstore.com

Hostem
MENS / MULTIBRAND

An elegant but rustic space with a
19th-century vibe provides a unique
environment to browse the international
menswear selection featuring Casely-
Hayford, Rick Owens or The Elder
Statesman. Their 'Chalk Room' offers a
bespoke service where you can tweak
and customise suits, accessories and
footwear by appointment.

Shoredicth: 41-43 Redchurch St, E2 ·
11am–7pm; Sun noon–5pm ·
www.hostem.co.uk

House of Hackney DON'T MISS
DESIGN / FLOWERS / INTERIORS

Hackney's maximalist homewares
brand – making wallpaper, bedlinen,
furniture and fashion – now has its own
shop. Their prints, including Dalston Rose
and Queen Bee, are inspired by Victorian
Hackney in modern times, and blur the

line between fashion and interiors. The
shop also features a satellite of Liberty's
famous Wild at Heart florist.

Shoredicth: 131 Shoreditch High St, E1 ·
10am–7pm; Sun 11am–5pm ·
www.houseofhackney.com

Hub
FASHION / MENS / MULTIBRAND

The Broadway Market outpost of this
excellent Stoke Newington boutique
stocks covetable mid-range designer
labels like Acne, Peter Jensen and See
by Chloé.

Spitalfields: 2a Ada St, E8 · 10.30am–6pm;
Sun 11am–5pm · hubshop.co.uk

Jasper Morrison Shop
DESIGN / INTERIORS

The Brit designer's retail outlet is a
simple little space inside his studio
showcasing beautifully designed,
practical objects – from cutlery to
clocks – designed by his studio as well
as other contemporary talents.

Shoredicth: 24b Kingsland Rd, E2 ·
11am–5pm. Closed Sat, Sun ·
www.jaspermorrisonshop.com

Labour & Wait DON'T MISS
DESIGN / INTERIORS / KNICK KNACKS

Function meets style in this retro-
styled shop stocking covetable wares
for the kitchen, home and garden.
There's a small range of vintage
workwear and adorable gifts for kids
including basic leather satchels.

Hackney: 85 Redchurch St, E2 · 11am–
6pm. Closed Mon ·
www.labourandwait.co.uk

Luna & Curious
DESIGN / INTERIORS / KNICK KNACKS

This dreamy Shoreditch shop showcases
unique pieces by up-and-coming
designers and artists, many of whom are
local to the East End.

Shoredicth: 24-26 Calvert Ave, E2 ·
11am–6pm (5pm Sun) ·
lunaandcurious.com

MHL Shop
FASHION / MENS

The first dedicated boutique in the UK
for the Margaret Howell diffusion line
– a reinterpretation of workwear –
is located in a converted warehouse
in Shoreditch.

Shoredicth: 19 Old Nichol St, E2 ·
11am (10am Sat)–7pm; Sun noon–5pm ·
www.margarethowell.co.uk

Old Spitalfields Market
DON'T MISS / MARKET

The 1887 covered market now stretches
into a restaurant and shopping
precinct. Get in early on Sun before
catching new fashion at (Up)Market in
the nearby Old Truman Brewery.

Spitalfields: Old Spitalfields Market,
16 Horner Square, E1 ·
10am (11am Sat)–5pm ·
www.oldspitalfieldsmarket.com

Pelicans & Parrots
FASHION / INTERIORS / MENS / VINTAGE

The 'first proper shop' in Dalston
is a mixture of classic tailored and
trend-aware vintage fashion, furniture
and interiors.

Dalston: 40 Stoke Newington Rd, N16
(+ branches) · Noon–7pm daily ·
pelicansandparrots.com

Present
COFFEE / MENS / SCANDINAVIAN

Uber cool menswear store thronged
by creative locals that also boasts
the Prufrock Coffee concession from
award-winning barista Gwilym Davies.

Shoredicth: 140 Shoreditch High St, E1 ·
10.30am–7pm; Sat 11am–6.30pm (5pm
Sun) · www.present-london.com

SCP
DESIGN / INTERIORS

Flagship store of the well-established
furniture, lighting and kitchenware
manufacturer that stocks the leading
names in British design.

Shoredicth: 135 Curtain Rd, EC2
(+ branches) · 9.30am–6pm;
Sun 11am–5pm · www.scp.co.uk

Start
FASHION / MENS / MULTIBRAND

His 'n' hers boutiques (her being Fall
guitarist Brix Smith) on opposite sides
of the street that specialise in high-end
labels (Miu Miu, Rykiel) and jeans
(Earnest Sewn, Acne.)

Shoredicth:
40, 42–44 & 59 Rivington St, EC2 ·
10.30am–6.30pm (7pm Thu); Sat
11am–6pm; Sun noon–5pm ·
www.start-london.com

Strut Broadway DON'T MISS
VINTAGE

Fancy a vintage trench? You're sure
to find it at this very cool second-hand
designer clothes shop.

Hackney: 2b Ada Street, Broadway Market,
E8 · 10.30am (noon Sun, Mon)–6pm ·
www.strutlondon.com

Sunspel
FASHION / LINGERIE / MENS

One of England's oldest labels for luxury underwear and basics like perfectly cut tees and polo shirts. The use of meticulously engineered fabrics means you can wear Sunspel pieces over and over and they won't warp with use.

Shoreditch: **7 Redchurch St, E2 (+ branches) · 11am–7pm; Sun noon–5pm · www.sunspel.com**

Topman General Store
MENS

A modish, upmarket boutique with a retro feel, it sells a mix of carefully selected designer pieces alongside its own discreetly branded threads.

Spitalfields: **98 Commercial St, E1 · 10.30am–7pm daily · www.topman.com**

Violet Cakes DON'T MISS
CAKES / ORGANIC

A bespoke cake company created by Claire Ptak, former pastry chef at Chez Panisse in California. The delicate cakes are made with buttercream icings that change with the seasons. (Find them at Broadway Market on Saturdays.)

Hackney: **47 Wilton Way, E8 · 8am–6pm; Sat, Sun 9.30am–5pm. Closed Mon · www.violetcakes.com**

Hackney City Farm
FREE ENTRY / KIDS

This charming city farm is home to a range of farmyard animals including goats, sheep, chickens and a donkey, as well as rabbits and guinea pigs. The chickens and ducks lay eggs daily, which can be purchased in the shop, alongside honey from the bees. The onsite café Frizzante is delicious and healthy.

Hackney: **1a Goldsmiths Row, E2 · 10am–4.30pm. Closed Mon · hackneycityfarm.co.uk**

London Fields
PARKS & GARDENS

The imaginary idyll of the Martin Amis novel is enjoying a real renaissance as the default posing and picnic spot for Hackney scenesters.

NOTES

HANGOUTS
Tatsuo Hino

✕ ✕ ✕

Originally from Kyushu in Japan, Tatsuo has lived in and out of London for the last 15 years. He specialises in media and fashion consultancy, working for **Dazed & Confused** *as well as running the London office for the Japanese lifestyle company* **Beams**. *He also writes regular for the English/Japanese bilingual magazine* **+81**, *and works on exhibition initiatives for* **Rockarchive**, *amongst other ongoing projects.*

instagram - @tatsuo_london

Esters
This artisan coffee and tea hangout in Stoke Newington is arguably the best coffee shop in the neighbourhood. The Has Bean roast changes every 4 weeks.
www.estersn16.com

Life
A Japanese restaurant and bar with a great interior by Graf Design. The hidden basement bar is a good late-night spot for drinking Japanese shochu and whisky.
www.life-oldst.com

Clutch Chicken
Fried, guilt-free, free-range chicken and a variety of sides, plus tasty cocktails, makes for one of East London creatives' favourite hang-outs!
www.clutchchicken.com

Maddy's Fish Bar
A step ahead of your average fish'n'chip shop with locally sourced produce and a bit of a Japanese twist. I highly recommend the super-fresh fish burger!
maddysfishbar.com

Kanada-ya Ramen
London's best Japanese ramen noodle bar is imported from Fukuoka, the hometown of Tonkotsu (pork broth) ramen.
www.kanada-ya.com

Momosan Shop
Momo-san curates a selection of crafted homewares; beautiful, yet simple objects that are practical and functional, and that you won't find anywhere else in London!
momosanshop.com

Skylarking Cafe
A tiny Himalayan cafe in Dalston. You have to try the organic Himalayan coffee and Nepalese dumplings, or Momos - cheap and filling!
skylarkingcafe.weebly.com

Sunday Barnsbury
Islington's best restaurant is perfect for breakfast, brunch, lunch, dinner, cakes and cocktails.
www.facebook.com/sundaybarnsbury

House of Twenty
A mid-century vintage furniture and props specialist in East London with a great selection, good prices and customer service. Scandinavian furniture is constantly arriving from Europe, and they have a restoration workshop out the back.
www.houseoftwenty.com

Backyard Cinema
The best pop-up cinema wher e classic films are screened in unusual locations, like Baz Luhrmann's *Romeo & Juliet* inside St Mary's Church with its vibrant gothic decor alongside a full choir.
www.backyardcinema.co.uk

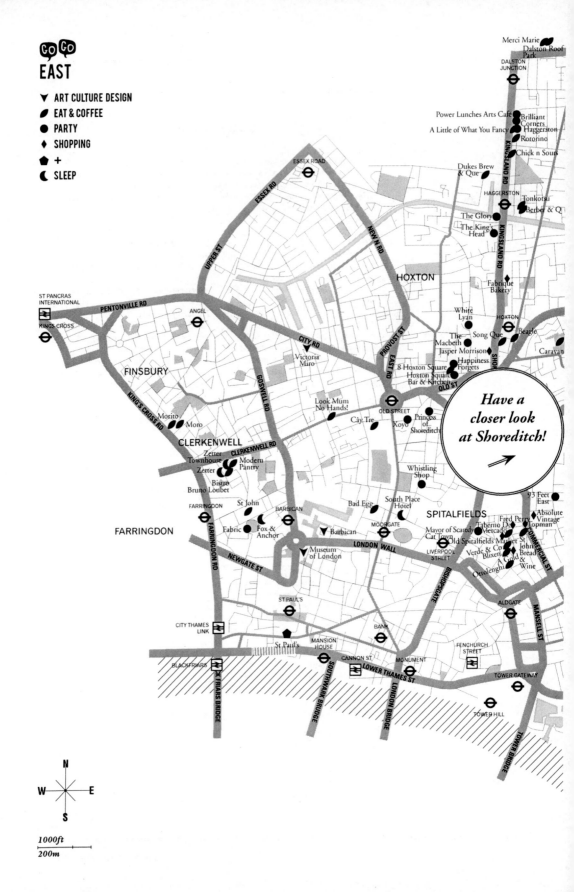

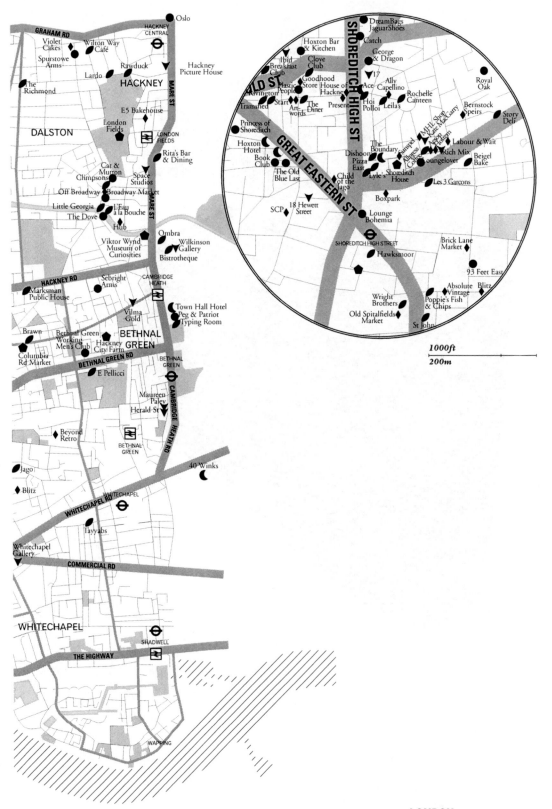

Oslo

GRAHAM RD
HACKNEY CENTRAL

Violet Cakes
Wilton Way Café
Spurstowe Arms
Rawduck
Lardo
HACKNEY
Hackney Picture House

The Richmond
MARE ST

E5 Bakehouse

DALSTON
LONDON FIELDS
London Fields

Rita's Bar & Dining

Car & Mutton
Chimpsons
Space Studios
Off Broadway
Broadway Market
Little Georgia
L'Eau a la Bouche
The Dove
Hub
MARE ST

Viktor Wynd Museum of Curiosities
Ombra
Wilkinson Gallery
Bistrotheque

HACKNEY RD
Sebright Arms
CAMBRIDGE HEATH
Marksman Public House
Vilma Gold
Town Hall Hotel
Peg & Patriot
Typing Room

Brawn
Bethnal Green Working Men's Club
Hackney City Farm
BETHNAL GREEN
Columbia Rd Market
BETHNAL GREEN RD
BETHNAL GREEN
E Pellicci

CAMBRIDGE HEATH RD

Maureen Paley
Herald St

Beyond Retro
BETHNAL GREEN

Jago
Blitz
40 Winks
WHITECHAPEL
WHITECHAPEL RD

Tayyabs

Whitechapel Gallery
COMMERCIAL RD

WHITECHAPEL
SHADWELL
THE HIGHWAY

WAPPING

Shoreditch detail (circle)

DreamBags JaguarShoes
Catch
SHOREDITCH HIGH ST
Hoxton Bar & Kitchen
George & Dragon
Ibid
Breakfast Club
Clove Club
17
Ally Capellino
Royal Oak
OLD ST
Rivington
Plastic People
Goodhood Store
House of Hackney
Ace
Hoi Polloi
Leila's
Rochelle Canteen
Tramshed
Start
Art-words
The Diner
Present
Bernstock Speirs
Story Deli
Princess of Shoreditch
MHL Shop
Kate MacGarry
Sunspel
Labour & Wait
Hoxton Hotel
GREAT EASTERN ST
The Boundary
Aesop
Beigel Bake
Book Club
Dishoom
Pizza East
Rich Mix
Youngelover
Lyle's
Shoreditch House
The Old Blue Last
Child of the Jago
Les 3 Garcons
SCP
18 Hewett Street
Boxpark
Lounge Bohemia
SHOREDITCH HIGH STREET
Brick Lane Market
Hawksmoor
93 Feet East
Wright Brothers
Absolute Vintage
Blitz
Poppie's Fish & Chips
Old Spitalfields Market
St John
1000ft
200m

GoGo
SOUTH

BANKSIDE × BATTERSEA × BERMONDSEY × BRIXTON × ELEPHANT & CASTLE × NEW CROSS
PECKHAM × SOUTHBANK × SOUTHWARK

More than a decade on, the Tate Modern and London Eye symbolise
the CULTURAL/TOURIST remit of the South Bank.
Spanning BRUTALIST temples (The Hayward, National Theatre)
and ROMANTIC prospects of the Thames, it stretches east
to the FOODIE paradise of Borough Market. The historically rich
vaults of nearby London Bridge are a CLUBBING mecca again,
while due south gritty Elephant & Castle, Chaplin's birthplace,
boasts the cutting-edge Corsica Studios. Back in 2007, Peckham
was big news for its artists' SQUATS and the pioneering SOUTH
LONDON GALLERY, but much momentum has shifted west
to foodie and clubbing hub BRIXTON, while live music fans head
east to join Goldsmiths' students in thriving NEW CROSS.

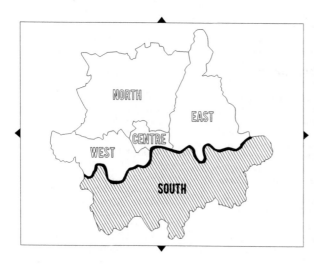

GETTING AROUND

The **Thames Path** makes for a great
cultural stroll: head down from **London
Bridge** and you'll pass **Borough Market**,
before reaching the **Tate** (the best
views of this, though, via the **Millennium
Bridge** from **St Paul's**). From here
there's the Tate to Tate boat, or continue
on past the restaurants of **Gabriel's
Wharf** to the **South Bank Centre** and
transport hub **Waterloo**. For **Elephant
& Castle** and **Brixton**, take the Northern
Line, while the East London Line links
to **New Cross**. **Peckham** is edgy
for a reason, so take the bus (12 from
Oxford Circus, 78 from Liverpool St).

ART CULTURE DESIGN

British Film Institute
BAR / BOOKS / FILM / MYTHIC / TERRACE

The ex-NFT offers constantly rotating retrospectives of the masters alongside acclaimed world film. Each October you can get one up on the best of independent cinema by catching the London Film Festival here.
South Bank: Belvedere Rd, SE1 · www.bfi.org.uk

Design Museum
DESIGN / MUSEUM

The striking Thameside warehouse is a temple to contemporary design from furniture to graphics, architecture and fashion, and includes a stylish shop.
South Bank: Shad Thames, SE1 · 10am–5.45pm · designmuseum.org

Dulwich Picture Gallery
ART

England's first public art gallery features a much-imitated design by architect Sir John Soane. Intended as the Royal Collection of Poland, the worthy spread of Old Masters encompasses Rembrandt, Van Dyck and Rubens.
Dulwich: Gallery Rd, SE21 · 10am (11am Sat, Sun)–5pm. Closed Mon · www.dulwichpicturegallery.org.uk

Fashion & Textile Museum
FASHION / MUSEUM

A home for contemporary fashion, textiles and jewellery founded by fuschia-haired Brit designer Zandra Rhodes. Alongside an archive and temporary exhibitions, the shop stocks rare accessories by up-and-coming designers.
Lambeth: 83 Bermondsey St, SE1 · 11am–6pm (8pm Thu). Closed Sun, Mon · ftmlondon.org

Hannah Barry Gallery
DON'T MISS / ART

A pioneer of the Peckham scene, Hannah Barry's eponymous gallery is a critical platform for young artists. Since 2008, it has held the very cool summer sculpture show 'Bold Tendencies' in a multistory car park nearby.
Peckham: 44 Holly Grove, SE15 · 3–6pm; Sat 10am (noon Sun)–6pm. Closed Mon–Wed · www.hannahbarry.com

Horniman Museum & Gardens
FREE ENTRY / KIDS / MUSEUM / PARKS & GARDENS

This museum has been around since the Victorian age. It showcases anthropology, musical instruments and natural history collections across six free galleries, plus an acclaimed aquarium and award-winning gardens.
Forest Hill: 100 London Rd, SE23 · 10.30am–5.30pm · www.horniman.ac.uk

National Maritime Museum
ART / MUSEUM

A triple curiosity: maps, models and regalia chart seafaring history in the museum, a walkway leads to the Hogarths and Gainsboroughs in the Inigo Jones-designed Queen's House and, up on the hill, the Royal Observatory and Planetarium help you zone in on Greenwich Mean Time.
Greenwich: Romney Rd, SE10 · 10am–5pm (8pm Thu) · www.rmg.co.uk

Old Operating Theatre, Museum & Herb Garrett
MUSEUM

Britain's sole surviving 19th-century operating theatre conjures the horrors of pre-anaesthetic surgery and shares roof space in the Baroque St Thomas's Church with a fascinating herbal apothecary.
Southwark: 9a St Thomas St, SE1 · 10.30am–5pm · www.thegarret.org.uk

Ritzy Cinema DON'T MISS
BAR / FILM / LIVE MUSIC

An exceptional listed Edwardian building houses one of London's favourite arthouse cinemas. Upstairs is a bar and live music venue with an eclectic weekly line-up featuring anything from jazz to Balkan.
Brixton: Brixton Oval, Coldharbour Lane, SW2 · www.picturehouses.co.uk

Shakespeare's Globe
THEATRE / MUSEUM / MYTHIC

The new attraction is the £7.5-million Sam Wanamaker Playhouse, a 350-seat indoor candlelit theatre. The open-air main theatre is a faithful recreation of the Bard's famous Bankside playhouse offering an original 'Shakespeare in performance' experience.
Bankside: 21 New Globe Walk, SE1 · www.shakespearesglobe.com

Southbank Centre
DANCE / JAZZ / LIVE MUSIC / TERRACE

Home to the refurbished Royal Festival Hall and the under renovation Queen Elizabeth Hall, this giant arts' complex covers everything from classical to electronic and world music. Grab a drink and sit on the café terrace overlooking the Thames.
South Bank: Belvedere Rd, SE1 · www.southbankcentre.co.uk

South London Gallery
DON'T MISS / ART / LATES

The jewel in Peckham's crown helped launch the YBAs and remains at the cutting edge of London's contemporary art scene. It is buoyed by new small-scale galleries, an artist's flat and café.
Camberwell: 65–67 Peckham Rd, SE5 · 11am–6pm (9pm Wed). Closed Mon · www.southlondongallery.org

Tate Modern DON'T MISS
ART / BOOKS / FREE ENTRY / LATES / MUSEUM / WOW

A decade on, the Tate Modern holds masterpieces from all the major 20th-century movements and includes the famous Rothko Room.
Southwark: 53 Bankside, SE1 · 10am–6pm (10pm Fri, Sat) · www.tate.org.uk

White Cube Bermondsey
DON'T MISS / ART / BOOKS

The third London outpost of Jay Jopling's empire is the biggest of the three, and may even be the largest commercial art gallery in Europe. Three exhibition spaces provide an ample canvas for the gallery's starry stable of artists.
Bermondsey: 144-152 Bermondsey St, SE1 · 10am (noon Sun)–6pm. Closed Mon · whitecube.com

Young Vic
BAR / TERRACE / THEATRE

More vivacious and edgy than the Old Vic just down the road, this theatrical big-hitter pleases the critics with a programme of European classics. The split-level bar and restaurant is always rammed with an eclectic crowd.
South Bank: 66 The Cut, SE1 · www.youngvic.org.

EAT & COFFEE

40 Maltby Street £
BAR / MODERN EURO

Natural wine seller Gergovie Wines has set up a small kitchen in its warehouse where they serve excellent rustic Italian fare to go with the bottles (£10 corkage).
Bermondsey: 40 Maltby Street, SE1 · No reservations · 5.30 (12.30pm Fri)–10pm; Sat 11am–5pm. Closed Sun, Mon, Tue · www.40maltbystreet.com

Agile Rabbit £
BUDGET / LIVE MUSIC / MARKET / PIZZA / TAKE AWAY

A bohemian pizzeria and hangout inside Brixton Market, with live bands on Fri and Sat, 7–10pm.
Brixton: 24 Coldharbour Lane, SW9 · 020 7998 3448 · 11am (10am Sat, Sun)–11pm (midnight Sat)

Anchor & Hope ££
BRITISH / PUB / SUNDAY ROAST

Waterloo's most famous gastropub offers carefully sourced British ingredients, big flavours and consistently great cooking. The no bookings policy means you should avoid peak times – and, in any case, it's so near the Young Vic it makes perfect sense as a pre- or post-theatre jaunt.
Waterloo: 36 The Cut, SE1 (+ branches) · No reservations · 11am (5pm Mon)–midnight; Sun 12.30–6pm

Artusi ££ DON'T MISS
ITALIAN

Elegant and precise contemporary Italian fare from the chef with an almost comically English name, Jack Beer (ex Clove Club). His chalkboard menu might feature tagliatelle with ox cheek ragu, or cod with sprouting broccoli, Tokyo turnips and pickled puntarelle. Wines are Italian too. The set lunch menu on Sundays is a joy.
Peckham: 161 Bellenden Rd, SE15 · 020 3302 8200 · Noon–2.30pm, 6–10pm. Sun noon–3pm. Closed Mon lunch · artusi.co.uk

Ben's Canteen ££
BREAKFAST / BRUNCH

'The place on the hill' is a relaxed all-day cafe with tables outside on the street and a tasty weekend brunch.
Battersea: 140 St John's Hill, SW11 · 020 7228 3260 · 9am–midnight · www.benscanteen.com

Birdhouse £
BREAKFAST / COFFEE

This smart little cafe serves great coffee made from beans from London's own Climpson & Sons, plus tasty snacks.
Battersea: 123 St John's Hill, SW11 · No reservations · 7am–4pm; Sat, Sun 9am–5pm · www.birdhou.se

Brindisa Food Rooms ££
DELI / MARKET / SPANISH / TAKE AWAY

The new Brixton Market outpost of the popular Borough Market address is a hybrid shop and bar selling their delicious selection of cured, salted and seasoned foods from Spain, to eat in or take away.
Brixton: 41–43 Atlantic Rd, SW9 · 020 7733 0634 · Shop: 10am–7pm (4pm Sun). Café: 5pm (10am Fri–Sun)–10pm · www.brindisa.com

Brixton Cornercopia ££
DON'T MISS / BRITISH / GROCERY / MARKET / TAKE AWAY

This neighbourhood restaurant and new-gen cornershop is all about ultra-local food and sustainability, celebrating the abundance and diversity of ingredients available from Brixton Market and from other local growers and artisan makers.
Brixton: 65 Brixton Village Market, SW9 · No reservations · 11am–6pm. Closed Mon, Tue · brixtoncornercopia.co.uk

Brunswick House Café £
DON'T MISS / BRUNCH / COCKTAILS

Ornate chandeliers and other vintage pieces adorn the interior of this cafe, located in the industrial salvage shop Lassco (see below). The fresh and contemporary menu complements the place's bohemian charm. The weekend brunch and cocktails are excellent too.
Vauxhall: 30 Wandsworth Rd, SW8 · 020 7720 2926 · 9.30am (10am Sat)–midnight; Sun 10am–5pm · www.brunswickhouse.co

The Canton Arms ££
BRITISH / PUB

Thriving after takeover by the people behind Waterloo's Anchor & Hope, this rustic local features fine real ales and classic British fare like the renowned foie gras toastie.
Stockwell: 177 South Lambeth Rd, SW8 · No reservations · 11am (5pm Mon)–11.30pm · cantonarms.com

Coma y Punto £ DON'T MISS
COLOMBIAN / MARKET

Calorie-rich Colombian fare at this unpretentious and friendly cafe inside Brixton Market. The Colombian pop music on the TV provides an extra guilty pleasure.
Brixton: 94-95 Granville Arcade, SW9 · 020 7326 0276 · 8.30am–5.30pm (3.30pm Wed). Closed Sun.

Craft London ££ NEW / DON'T MISS
BAR / BRITISH / COCKTAILS

Chef Stevie Parle and his team roast their own coffee, cure meat, ferment vegetables and have their own kitchen garden just outside with an orchard, smoke house, herb and veg boxes and bee hives. Tom Dixon took care of the striking interiors.
Greenwich Peninsula: 1 Green Place, SE10 · 020 8465 5910 · Lunch: Wed–Sun, Dinner: Mon–Sat; Bar, 5pm–1am. Closed Sun; Café 8am–6pm daily · craft-london.co.uk

The Dairy ££
DELI / MODERN EURO / TAKE AWAY

Chef Robin Gill and his wife Sarah turn out dishes of great creativity and finesse, prepared with ingredients grown in their rooftop garden. There's also a bakery and smokehouse. And now take treats home from the artisanal delicatessen, next door.
Clapham: 15 The Pavement, Clapham Oldtown, SW4 · 020 7622 4165 · Noon–3pm (4pm Sun); 6–10pm. Closed Mon, Sun dinner and Tue lunch · the-dairy.co.uk

Elliot's ££ DON'T MISS
BREAKFAST / BRITISH / COFFEE

Inside Borough Market, enjoy a daily changing, ingredient driven menu that makes the most of fine produce cooked over wood and charcoal, and paired with London's "most natural wine list." They take their coffee seriously too, offering 2 single-origin coffees brewed through paper percolation in a Marco shuttle.
Southwark: 12 Stoney St, SE1 · 020 7403 7436 · 7am–10pm. Closed Sun · www.elliotscafe.com

Federation Coffee £ DON'T MISS
COFFEE / MARKET / TAKE AWAY

These South London-based coffee roasters sell their fine brews, plus tasty sweet and savoury baked fare, from their popular Brixton Market café.

Brixton: Unit 77-78, Brixton Village Market, SW9 · No reservations · 8am–5pm; Sat, Sun 9am–6pm (5pm Sun) · federationcoffee.com

Four O Nine ££
AFTERNOON TEA / MODERN EURO / TERRACE

This secret Clapham restaurant – access is via a private entrance – serves an inventive menu of mod-Euro and French cuisine, matched with great wine.
Clapham: 409 Clapham Rd, SW9 · 020 7737 0722 · Mon–Sat, 6–10.30pm; Sat, Sun noon–4pm · www.fouronine.co.uk

Franco Manca £ DON'T MISS
MARKET / PIZZA

Tucked into one of the arches of Brixton Market, this remarkably cheap pizzeria has been justly showered with acclaim for its simple menu and slow-rising sourdough bases.
Brixton: 4 Market Row, Electric Lane, SW9 (+ branches) · No reservations · Noon–11pm (5pm Mon, 10.30pm Sun) · www.francoma nca.co.uk

Hixter Bankside ££
BAR / BRITISH / COCKTAILS / STEAK

The recipe at Hixter is simple: chicken or steak to share. And that's Himalayan salt dry-aged steak from hand-selected cows, and barn-reared chicken from Swainson House Farm in Lancashire. Mark's Bar in the basement serves cocktails that champion British drinks' producers.
Bankside: 16 Great Guildford St, SE1 (+ branches) · 020 7921 9508 · 11.30am–midnight (11pm Sun). Bar: noon–1.30am (12.30am Sun) · www.hixterbankside.co.uk

Honest Burgers £
BURGERS / MARKET

From their Brixton Market outpost, Honest Burgers demonstrates a serious commitment to burgers, using aged beef sourced from top London butcher Ginger Pig, served with triple-cooked chips sprinkled with rosemary salt and a fine selection of craft beer.
Brixton: Unit 12, Brixton Village, SW9 (+ branches) · No reservations · Noon–10.30pm (4pm Mon, 10pm Sun) · www.honestburgers.co.uk

Lab G £
ICE CREAM / MARKET / TAKE AWAY

Artisanal gelato, made daily in their lab inside Brixton Market with the freshest ingredients and a passion for flavour.

Brixton: 6 Granville Arcade, Coldharbour Lane, SW9 · No reservations · 11am–5pm (11pm Thu–Sat). Closed Mon · lab-g.co.uk

The London Particular £
DON'T MISS / BREAKFAST / BRITISH / BRUNCH / ORGANIC

Specialising in classic Brit cuisine, this New Cross cafe uses only the finest artisanal and organic ingredients to deliver some of London's tastiest grub. A home away from home for art students from nearby Goldsmiths' College.
New Cross: 399 New Cross Rd, SE14 · 020 8692 6149 · 10am–10pm (4.30pm Sun–Wed) · www.thelondonparticular.co.uk

Mama Lan £
BUDGET / CHINESE / MARKET

Inside Brixton Market, enjoy handmade dumplings, noodle soups and street snacks, Beijing style. (Cash only.)
Brixton: Unit 18, Brixton Village, SW9 · No reservations · Noon–10pm (4pm Mon) · mamalan.co.uk

The Manor ££ NEW / DON'T MISS
BAR / MODERN EURO

A new bistro from The Dairy crew. As you'd expect the food is brilliant, a kind of Nordic contemporary, enamoured with smoking, fermenting and scorching. You can also just drop in for a drink – a kombucha sour anyone? – and a snack.
Clapham: 148 Clapham Manor St, SW4 · 020 7720 4662 · Noon–3pm (4pm Sun), 6–10pm. Closed Mon, Tue and Sun dinner · www.themanorclapham.co.uk

Monmouth Coffee £
COFFEE / TAKE AWAY / MARKET

The Borough Market outpost of Covent Garden's superlative roasters and grinders of single origin coffee, available to drink in or take home in a cup, or as whole or ground beans.
Southwark: 2 Park St, SE1 · No reservations · 7.30am–6pm. Closed Sun · www.monmouthcoffee.co.uk

Naughty Piglets ££ NEW
MODERN EURO / WINE BAR

A "happy and casual" wine bar and bistro with a creative chalkboard menu listing dishes such as quail, pork belly or lamb cooked over the charcoal grill.
Brixton: 28 Brixton Water Lane, SW2 · 020 7274 7796 · Lunch Thu–Sat noon–3pm (2.30pm Thu), Sun noon–4pm; Dinner Tue–Sat 6–10pm. Closed Mon · naughtypiglets.co.uk

Roast £££
BREAKFAST / BRITISH / BRUNCH / SUNDAY ROAST

Perched above Borough Market and perfect for people watching, this buzzing spot specialises in the best of British cooking and also does wonderful breakfasts.
Southwark: The Floral Hall, Stoney St, SE1 · 084 5034 7300 · 7am (8.30am Sat)–11pm; Sun 11.30am–6.30pm · www.roast-restaurant.com

Rooftop Café ££
BREAKFAST / BRITISH / BRUNCH / VIEW

A seasonal, straightforward approach to food from chef Peter Le Faucheur and one of the best views in London. The furniture and interiors are by young Spanish designer Dr Cato and help create a warm but striking atmosphere.
London Bridge: 28 London Bridge St, SE1 · 0203 102 3770 · 8am–3pm daily; 6–10.30pm Wed–Sat · www.theexchange.so/rooftop

The Rookery ££ DON'T MISS
BAR / TERRACE / VIEW

Excellent food and a quality bar with a smart 'Lower East Side' vibe, overlooking Clapham Common.
Clapham: 69 Clapham Common, SW4 · 020 8673 9162 · 5.30–11pm (midnight Fri); Sat, Sun 12.30pm–midnight (10.30pm Sun) · www.therookeryclapham.co.uk

Rosie's Deli Café £
BREAKFAST / BRITISH / BRUNCH / COFFEE / DELI

Boudoir meets 1950s corner shop in this adorable daytime deli and cafe. The menu includes excellent breakfasts (cinnamon toast) and inventive sandwiches. It's worth checking out the owner's Spooning with Rosie cookbook.
Brixton: 14e Market Row, SW9 · No reservations · 9.30am–5.30pm. Closed Sun · www.rosiesdelicafe.com

Salon ££ DON'T MISS
BRITISH / BRUNCH / GROCERY / TAKE AWAY

Go for the inventive 4-course set-menu of seasonal British fare, prepared with plenty of produce grown, produced or foraged in Brixton. The downstairs shop sells deli items and grilled cheese sandwiches to go.
Brixton: 18 Market Row, Coldharbour Ln, SW9 · 020 7501 9152 · Tue–Sat 6.30–10.30pm; Sat, Sun 10.30am–3.30pm. Closed Mon · salonbrixton.co.uk

ScooterCaffè £
COFFEE / ITALIAN

The Vespa repair shop here has moved on, but the staff's vintage Faema espresso machine served such good coffee that the owner kept the little space open as a cafe. You can even bring your own food.

South Bank: 132 Lower Marsh, SE1 · No reservations · 8.30am (10am Fri, Sat)–11pm (midnight Fri, Sat) ·

Sea Cow £
FISH & CHIPS / TAKE AWAY

This new generation fish and chip shop is all about the fish, with nice big tables to spread out on.

East Dulwich: 37 Lordship Lane, SE22 · 020 8693 3111 · Noon (5pm Mon–Wed)– 11pm (10pm Sun) · www.theseacow.co.uk

Seven at Brixton £
BAR / BREAKFAST / BRUNCH / COCKTAILS / MARKET / SPANISH / TAPAS

This chic and roomy all-day bar and cafe in the Brixton Market has a Spanish flavour, serving up tapas, *pintxos* and cocktails, as well as presenting some local art upstairs.

Brixton: Unit 7 Market Row, SW9 · 020 7998 3309 · 9am–11.30pm (6pm Mon) · sevenatbrixton.wordpress.com

St John Bakery Room £
DON'T MISS / BREAKFAST / BREAD / CAKES / MARKET / TAKE AWAY

Added to St John's hugely popular take-away bakery stand at Maltby Street Market comes the new Bakery Room – a sit-in spot open on weekends only to enjoy breakfast, lunch, fresh baked madeleines and their addictive doughnuts!

Bermondsey: Arch 42, Ropewalk, Maltby St Market, SE1 · No reservations · Sat, Sun 10am–6pm · www.stjohngroup.uk.com

Table £
BREAKFAST / BRUNCH / BUDGET / ORGANIC / TAKE AWAY

Housed in an architects' head office, this stylish self-service canteen does great salads and quiche to take away or enjoy at communal table. By night, candles are lit and diners are spoilt with an appealing à la carte menu.

South Bank: 83 Southwark St, SE1 · 020 7401 2760 · 7.30am–10.30pm (4.30pm Mon); Sat, Sun 8.30am–4pm · thetablecafe.com

Union Street Café ££
BAR / ITALIAN

Not far from Borough Market, Gordon Ramsay's latest is a reliable modern Italian with a daily changing menu prepared from an open kitchen. The décor is Manhattan loft style, and there's a lovely bar in the basement.

Southwark: 47-51 Great Suffolk St, SE1 · 020 7592 7977 · Noon–3pm (4pm Sat, Sun), 6–11pm (10.30pm Sat, Sun) · www.gordonramsay.com

Queenswood ££ NEW
BREAKFAST / MODERN EURO / VEGETARIAN

Serving coffee, juice and breakfast to dinner, wine and cocktails, this all-day neighbourhood brasserie has an eclectic menu with lots of veggie options.

Battersea: 15 Battersea Square, SW11 · 020 7228 8877 · 8am–late, daily · www.queenswoodldn.com

Wild Caper £
BREAD / COFFEE / DELI / ORGANIC / TAKE AWAY

As if Franco Manca's owners hadn't done enough for South Londoners, their nearby organic café/deli delights with the finest Italian olive oils, mozzarella, sausages, interesting organic wines and great Monmouth coffee.

Brixton: 11a-13 Market Row, SW9 · 0207 737 4410 · 9am–10pm daily · www.wildcaper.co.uk

Wright Brothers Oyster & Porter House ££
BRUNCH / OYSTERS

Wright Brothers supply many top London restaurants, and their Japanese-style rock oysters are hard to beat. There's another branch in Soho, but this small but perfectly-formed branch, overlooking the bustle of Borough Market, is brilliantly atmospheric.

Southwark: 11 Stoney St, SE1 (+ branches) · 020 7403 9554 · Noon (11am Sat)–11pm (10pm Sun) · www.thewrightbrothers.co.uk

You Don't Bring Me Flowers £
COFFEE / FLOWERS

Sip your fair trade coffee among a selection of beautiful and unusual plants and flowers at this unique and charming florist/cafe selling home-made cakes, tarts, pastries, sandwiches, soups and more.

Hither Green: 15 Staplehurst Rd, SE13 · No reservations · 8am (9am Sat)–6pm; Sun 10am–5pm. Closed Mon · www.youdontbringmeflowers.co.uk

Zucca ££
ITALIAN

A classic modern Italian restaurant with a charming Bermondsey location. The antipasti (sea bream carpaccio, or *zucca* – Italian for pumpkin) are pleasingly cheap, and there are excellent breads and dipping oil.

Southwark: 184 Bermondsey St, SE1 · 020 7378 6809 · Noon–3pm (3.30pm Sat), 6–10pm; Sun noon–4pm. Closed Mon · www.zuccalondon.com

PARTY

The Amersham Arms
BUDGET / LIVE MUSIC / PUB / SUNDAY ROAST

Traditional boozer that's frequented by local Goldsmiths students. Expect gigs aplenty as it's also the default HQ of SE London's live music scene.

New Cross: 388 New Cross Rd, SE14 · Noon–midnight (late on weekends) · www.theamershamarms.com

Bar Story
BAR / BUDGET

A quirky dive bar with a tasty bar menu attracts the hipster students from nearby art colleges.

Peckham: 213 Blenheim Grove, SE15 · 3pm–10pm (11pm Fri); Sat 2pm–11pm (9pm Sun) · www.barstory.co.uk

Bermondsey Arts Club
BAR

Public conveniences from the Victorian era transformed into an arty-chic cocktail bar. The marble bar and table tops are made from upcycled toilet cubicle separators!

Bermondsey: 102A Tower Bridge Rd, SE1 · 6pm–2am. Closed Sun, Mon · bermondseyartsclub.co.uk

Bump Caves
BAR / COCKTAILS

A freaky laboratory, a dive bar and distillery, that takes you 'furthur' (a nod to Tom Wolfe's The *Electric Kool-Aid Acid Test*) with its selection of experimental house-made concoctions. Try barman Max Chater's house cocktail, the #EKAAT: 'bump' malt, Campari, C&PP, and sparkling Piquepoul served with a 9V battery and citric acid.

Bermondsey: 206-208 Tower Bridge Rd, SE1 · 5pm–1am (2am Fri, Sat). Closed Mon, Tue · www.bumpcaves.co.uk

 TO LISTEN TO
THE CHEMICAL BROTHERS
BORN IN THE ECHOES
(VIRGIN EMI)

Bunga Bunga
BAR / BRUNCH / ITALIAN / LIVE MUSIC / PIZZA

A kitsch pizzeria from the duo behind Sloane clubs Bart's and Kitts that takes party animal Silvio Berlusconi as its poster boy. Grab a prosecco-based Berlusconi Bellini, several slices of pizza, and enjoy live music like Tyrolean yodelling. Not for the shy.
Wandsworth: 37 Battersea Bridge Rd, SW11 · 6pm–1am (2.30am Fri); Sat 11.30am–5.30pm, 7pm–2.30am. Closed Sun & Mon · bungabunga-london.com

Call Me Mr Lucky
BAR / COCKTAILS / SSHHH

A joyful dive bar hidden out the back of the The Breakfast Club's basement kitchen. (Just tell one of the staff you're there 'to get lucky.') The house shot £5 is in fact a trio starting with Ocho blanco tequila, followed by Jalapeño pickle, pomegranate molasses, coriander and habanero, and finishing up with mint infused coconut water. Manda huevos!
Southwark: 11 Southwark Street, SE1 · 5pm–1am (midnight Mon–Wed; 11pm Sun) · callmemrlucky.com

The Camberwell Arms
MODERN EURO / PUB

A relaunched local boozer, now a brilliant gastropub from the crew behind Waterloo's ever-popular Anchor & Hope. The nose-to-tail menu is for the adventurous foodie.
Camberwell: 65 Camberwell Church St, SE5 · No reservations · Noon–2.30pm, 6–10pm; Sun noon–4pm. Closed Mon lunch · thecamberwellarms.co.uk

Coronet Theatre
CLUB / LIVE MUSIC

Unique 3-floor venue in a 1920s Art Deco building that hosts major parties from the likes of Warp, Bugged Out!, Ed Banger and Eat Your Own Ears.
Elephant & Castle: 28 New Kent Rd, SE1 · www.coronettheatre.co.uk

Corsica Studios
CLUB / GRUNGY / LIVE MUSIC / TERRACE

Brave the Elephant & Castle roundabout for London's most progressive club and arts' space. Now with a new open-air venue The Paperworks, located just 5 minutes away at 48-50 Newington Causeway. There they extend the cutting-edge musical programme by adding creative arts experiences, street food and cocktails.

Elephant & Castle: 5 Elephant Rd, SE17 · 10pm–6am; Sun 6pm–3am · www.corsicastudios.com

Dandelyan NEW / DON'T MISS
BAR / COCKTAILS / VIEW

This glam bar, designed by Tom Dixon, is the sister establishment to Hoxton hotspot White Lyan. Inspired by the botanical wilds of the British countryside and around the world, award-winning bar impresario Ryan Chetiyawardana oversees operations, serving both experimental cocktails and refined interpretations of the classics.
South Bank: Mondrian London, 20 Upper Ground, SE1 · Noon–1.30am (12.30am Sun); 4pm–1am, Mon–Wed · www.mondrianlondon.com

The Miller
BEER / LIVE MUSIC / PUB / TERRACE

The with-it team behind the Sebright Arms in Haggerston has turned this London local into a go-to gastropub pushing craft beer and hot dogs.
London Bridge: 96 Snowfields Rd, SE1 · Noon–11pm (midnight Thu; 1am Fri); 6pm–1am Sat. Closed Sun · www.themiller.co.uk

Plan B
CLUB

Pared-down warehouse that reopened with a Hot Chip party in 2009 and attracts a Hoxton crowd with its Funktion 1 sound system and hep music policy (nights by Snack Crackle & Pop and Deadly Rhythm).
Brixton: 418 Brixton Rd, SW9 · Fri 9pm–6am; Sat 10pm–5am · www.planb-london.com

The Prince of Wales NEW
COMEDY / LATE / LIVE MUSIC / PIZZA / PUB

Opposite the Ritzy Cinema, this one-stop party powerhouse combines a (gastro)pub, club and rooftop terrace and is home to a non-stop events programme covering live gigs, DJs, comedy, or the monthly pizza and ping-pong 'pongathon.'
Brixton: 467-469 Brixton Rd, SW9 · Noon–11pm (5am Fri, Sat) · www.pow-london.com

Tooting Tram & Social
DON'T MISS / BAR / LIVE MUSIC

Chill out in this massive bar inside a converted tram shed. With ridiculously high ceilings, giant Italianate chandeliers, leather sofas and a modular layout, there's wow factor galore.

Tooting: 46-48 Mitcham Rd, SW17 · 5pm–midnight (1am Thu, 2am Fri); Sat, Sun noon–2am (midnight Sun) · tootingtramandsocial.co.uk

SHOPPING

Battersea Car Boot Sale
MARKET / VINTAGE

Open every Sunday afternoon, this long-standing option is the best of the car boot markets. Bargain hunters comb through vintage fashion, house clearance, furniture and antiques, and some new stuff too.
Battersea: Battersea Park School, Battersea Park Rd, SW11 · Sun 1.30–5pm · www.batterseaboot.com

Bermondsey 167
FASHION / INTERIORS / MENS

South London gets its own slick concept store courtesy of Michael McGrath, ex-head of menswear for Burberry. Alongside his own line M2CG, you'll find pristine homewares, books and a small range of highbrow fashion for women.
Southwark: 167 Bermondsey St, SE1 · 11am–7pm; Sun noon–6pm. Closed Mon · bermondsey167.com

Borough Market DON'T MISS
MARKET

The capital's most renowned food market attracts incognito celebrities and off-duty chefs alike, offering every conceivable kind of artisanal product, free samples and myriad on-site restaurants. Thursdays are far less frantic.
Southwark: Thu 10am–5pm; Fri 10am–6pm; Sat 8am–5pm · www.boroughmarket.org.uk

Brixton Market DON'T MISS
MARKET

The vibrant neighbourhood's culinary and cultural heart, with hundreds of great shops and stalls down Electric Avenue and nearby, selling food, homewear, vintage fashion and much more, including world goods like fabrics and tropical foods. But it's especially a destination from some of London's most exciting restaurants and bars. There's late night opening on Thu and Fri nights, and don't miss the Farmer's Market on Sun (10am–2pm).
Brixton: Electric Ave, SW9 · 9.30am–6pm (shops); 9.30am–5.30pm (arcades) · brixtonmarket.net

I Knit London
BAR / KNITTING

Combining endless exotic yarns and knitting literature with alcohol-fuelled communal soirées (Wed/Thu at 6pm) makes for one crafty set-up indeed.

Waterloo: 106 Lower Marsh, SE1 · 10.30am–6pm (8.30pm Tue–Thu). Closed Sun · www.iknit.org.uk

Lassco
ANTIQUES / VINTAGE

Browse incredible architectural salvage, from industrial lampshades to Edwardian mirrors or old pots, jars, boxes and bottles, then head to the site's excellent Brunswick House Cafe (see above).

Vauxhall: 30 Wandsworth Rd, SW8 · 9am (Sat 10am, Sun 11am)–5pm · www.lassco.co.uk

Leftovers
MARKET / VINTAGE

This vintage and antique fashion shop inside Brixton Village stocks pre-industrially made clothes, bags, hats, gloves, buttons and other accessories from the Victorian era to the 1960s, hand-picked by the owner Margot, who has a background in fashion design.

Brixton: Unit 71, Brixton Village, SW9 · 11am–5.30pm (4pm Sun). Closed Mon, Tue · leftoverslondon.com

Maltby Street Market DON'T MISS
MARKET

This smaller, cooler version of neighbouring Borough Market has expanded from the railway arches (Ropewalk) on Maltby Street to include the adjacent Spa Terminus site. You'll find some of London's best indie producers there, like The London Honey Company, Monmouth Coffee, Neal's Yard Dairy or St John Bakery.

Bermondsey: Druid St and Dockley Rd, SE1 · Sat 9am–5pm; Sun 11am–5pm · www.spa-terminus.co.uk · www.maltby.st

Radio Days
MENS / INTERIORS / VINTAGE

Step back in time at this heady vintage emporium, where magazines, memorabilia and authentic home accessories vie for attention with a well-selected sample of threads from the '20s to the '70s.

Waterloo: 87 Lower Marsh, SE1 · 10am–6pm. Closed Sun · www.radiodaysvintage.co.uk

What the Butler Wore
FASHION / MENS / VINTAGE

Reasonably priced vintage threads from the 60s and 70s for men and women, with a particularly good selection of shoes and Mod clothing.

South Bank: 131 Lower Marsh, SE1 · 11am–6pm; Sun noon–5pm · whatthebutlerwore.co.uk

Kew Gardens
PARKS & GARDENS / VIEW

A 300-acre haven of landscaped lawns and botanical greenhouses that maintains the largest plant collection in the world. Particular delights are the steamy wrought-iron Palm House and the Fibonacci-sequenced Xstrata Treetop Walkway.

Richmond: 9.30am–nightfall · www.kew.org

The London Eye
MONUMENT / VIEW

A decade on, the world's largest observation wheel is imprinted on the London skyline. Go on a clear day to spot Windsor Castle or reserve an atmospheric night flight. (Booking is advisable.)

South Bank: Riverside Building, County Hall, Westminster Bridge Rd, SE1 · 10am–8pm · www.londoneye.com

Tooting Bec Lido
KIDS / SWIMMING / WOW

South London families flock to this iconic lido – the country's largest freshwater pool – with stylish Pantone changing cubicles. There's a paddling pool for kids, a nice cafe and lockers for valuables.

Tooting: Tooting Bec Rd, SW16 · May–Aug 6am–8pm. Sep 6am–5pm · www.placesforpeopleleisure.org

NOTES

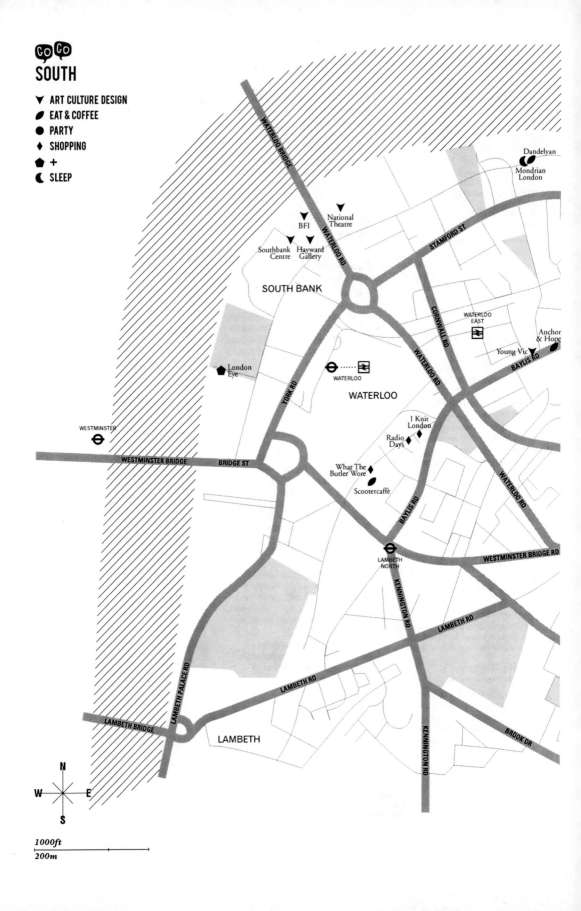

GO GO SOUTH

- ▼ ART CULTURE DESIGN
- 🍃 EAT & COFFEE
- ● PARTY
- ♦ SHOPPING
- ⬠ +
- ☾ SLEEP

Dandelyan
Mondrian London

National Theatre
BFI

Southbank Centre
Hayward Gallery

STAMFORD ST

SOUTH BANK

WATERLOO BRIDGE

WATERLOO RD

CORNWALL RD

WATERLOO EAST

Anchor & Hope

Young Vic

BAYLIS RD

London Eye

WATERLOO

WATERLOO RD

YORK RD

I Knit London

Radio Days

What The Butler Wore

Scootercaffe

WESTMINSTER

WESTMINSTER BRIDGE

BRIDGE ST

BAYLIS RD

WESTMINSTER BRIDGE RD

LAMBETH NORTH

KENNINGTON RD

LAMBETH RD

LAMBETH PALACE RD

LAMBETH BRIDGE

LAMBETH RD

LAMBETH RD

KENNINGTON RD

BROOK DR

LAMBETH

N
W E
S

1000ft
200m

BLACKFRIARS BRIDGE

SOUTHWARK BRIDGE

LONDON BRIDGE

Shakespeare's Globe Theatre

Tate Modern

BLACKFRIARS RD

BANKSIDE

MARSHALSEA RD

SOUTHWARK ST

Table

TOOLEY ST

Design Museum

LONDON BRIDGE

Elliot's
Wright Bros
Oyster Bar

Old Operating Theatre

Roast
Monmouth
Borough Market

Brindisa

The Shard

Hixter Bankside

SOUTHWARK ST

ST THOMAS ST

Call Me Mr Lucky

BOROUGH HIGH ST

SOUTHWARK

GREAT SUFFOLK ST

UNION ST

Fashion & Textile Museum

White Cube Bermondsey

Union Street Café

167 Bermondsey

NEWCOMEN ST

Zucca

MARSHALSEA RD

The Miller

SOUTHWARK

BLACKFRIARS RD

WEBBER ST

BOROUGH

LONG LANE

GREAT SUFFOLK ST

GREAT DOVER ST

BOROUGH RD

BOROUGH HIGH ST

TRINITY ST

LONDON RD

ST GEORGE'S RD

OSWIN ST

NEW KENT RD

Coronet Theatre

ELEPHANT & CASTLE

Corsica Studios

ELEPHANT & CASTLE

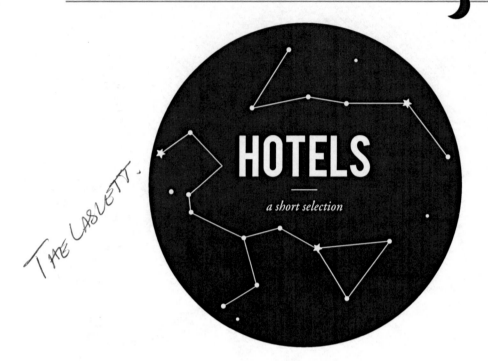

THE LASLETT.

HOTELS

a short selection

20 Nevern Square £
25 rooms.
Earl's Court: 20 Nevern Square, SW5 ·
020 7565 9555 ·
www.20nevernsquare.com

A

Ace Hotel London £££
258 rooms.
Shoreditch: 100 Shoreditch High St, E1 ·
020 7613 9800 · www.acehotel.com/london

Artist Residence £££
10 rooms.
Pimlico: 52 Cambridge St, SW1 ·
0207 931 8946 ·
artistresidencelondon.co.uk

B

The Beaumont ££££
73 rooms.
Mayfair: 8 Balderton St, W1K ·
020 7499 1001 · www.thebeaumont.com

The Boundary £££
17 rooms.
Shoreditch: 2-4 Boundary St, E2 ·
020 7729 1051 ·
www.theboundary.co.uk

C

Café Royal ££££
159 rooms.
West End: 68 Regent St, W1 ·
020 7406 3333 ·
www.hotelcaferoyal.com

Charlotte Street Hotel ££££
52 rooms.
Fitzrovia: 15 Charlotte St, W1 ·
020 7806 2000 ·
www.charlottestreethotel.com

Chiltern Firehouse ££££
26 rooms.
Marylebone: 1 Chiltern St, W1U ·
020 7073 7690 ·
www.chilternfirehouse.com

Church Street Hotel ££
30 rooms.
Camberwell Green:
29-33 Camberwell Church St, SE5 ·
020 7703 5984 ·
churchstreethotel.com

Corinthia Hotel ££££
294 rooms.
Embankment: 10 Whitehall Place, SW1 ·
020 7930 8181 · www.corinthia.com

D

Dean Street Townhouse £££
39 rooms.
Soho: 69-71 Dean St, W1 ·
020 7434 1775 ·
www.deanstreettownhouse.com

F

Fox & Anchor ££
6 rooms.
Clerkenwell: 115 Charterhouse Square, EC1 ·
020 7250 1300 · foxandanchor.com

G

Great Northern Hotel £££
91 rooms.
King's Cross: King's Cross, N1 ·
020 3388 0800 ·
www.gnhlondon.com

H

Haymarket Hotel ££££
50 rooms.
Piccadilly: 1 Suffolk Place, SW1 ·
020 7470 4000 · www.firmdalehotels.com

High Road House £££
14 rooms.
Chiswick: 162 Chiswick High Rd, W4 ·
020 8742 1717 ·
www.highroadhouse.co.uk

Hoxton Holborn ££
174 rooms.
Holborn: 199-206 High Holborn, WC1 ·
020 7661 3000 ·
thehoxton.com/london/holborn/

Hoxton Hotel £
208 rooms.
Shoreditch: 81 Great Eastern St, EC2 ·
020 7550 1000 · www.hoxtonhotels.com

L

The London Edition
177 rooms.
Fitzrovia: 10 Berners St, W1 ·
020 7781 0000 ·
www.editionhotels.com/london

M

The Mayflower ££
47 rooms.
Earl's Court: 26-28 Trebovir Rd, SW5 ·
020 7370 0991 ·
www.themayflowerhotel.co.uk

Mondrian London ££££
359 rooms
South Bank: 20 Upper Ground, SE1 ·
020 3747 1000 · www.mondrianlondon.com

N

New Linden Hotel ££
50 rooms.
Bayswater: 59 Leinster Square, W2 ·
020 7221 4321 · www.newlinden.com

Number Sixteen £££
42 rooms.
South Kensington: 16 Sumner Place, SW7 ·
020 7589 5232 · www.firmdalehotels.com

O

One Leicester Street £££
15 rooms.
Soho: 1 Leicester St, WC2 · 020 3301 8020 ·
www.oneleicesterstreet.com

P

Pavilion Hotel £
29 rooms.
Bayswater: 34-36 Sussex Gardens, W2 ·
020 7262 0905 · www.pavilionhoteluk.com

Q

Qbic London City Hotel £
171 rooms.
The City: 42 Adler St, E1 ·
020 3021 3300 · london.qbichotels.com

R

The Rockwell ££££
40 rooms.
Kensington: 181 Cromwell Rd, SW5 ·
020 7244 2000 · www.therockwell.com

Rose & Crown ££
6 rooms.
Stoke Newington:
199 Stoke Newington Church St, N1 ·
020 7923 3337 ·
www.roseandcrownn16.co.uk

Rough Luxe £££
9 rooms.
King's Cross: 1 Birkenhead St, WC1 ·
020 7837 5338 · www.roughluxe.co.uk

S

Shoreditch Rooms ££
26 rooms.
Shoreditch: Ebor St, E1 ·
020 7739 5040 ·
www.shoreditchrooms.com

South Place Hotel ££££
80 rooms.
Spitalfields: 3 South Place, EC2 ·
020 3503 0000 · www.southplacehotel.com

St Pancras Renaissance ££££
245 rooms.
King's Cross: Euston Rd, NW1 ·
020 7841 3540 ·
stpancrasrenaissance.co.uk

The Sumner £££
20 rooms.
Marylebone: 54 Upper Berkeley St, W1 ·
020 7723 2244 · www.thesumner.com

T

Town Hall Hotel ££
98 rooms.
Bethnal Green: Patriot Square, E2 ·
020 7871 0460 · townhallhotel.com

V

Vancouver Studios ££
47 rooms.
Bayswater: 30 Prince's Square, W2 ·
020 7243 1270 ·
vancouverstudios.co.uk

W

W Hotel ££££
192 rooms.
Soho: 10 Wardour St, W1 ·
020 7758 1000 ·
www.starwoodhotels.com/whotels

Y

York & Albany £££
10 rooms.
Camden: 127-129 Parkway, NW1 ·
020 7387 5700 · www.gordonramsay.com

Z

Z Hotel Soho ££
85 rooms.
Soho: 17 Moor St, W1 · 020 3551 3700 ·
www.thezhotels.com

Zetter Hotel £££
59 rooms.
Clerkenwell: St John's Square,
86-88 Clerkenwell Rd, EC1 ·
020 7324 4444 · www.thezetter.com

Zetter Townhouse £££
13 rooms.
Clerkenwell: 49-50 St John's Square, EC1 ·
020 7324 4567 ·
thezettertownhouse.com

DIRECTORY
A·Z

BANKING see Money

BOOKING TICKETS
A couple of the major ticket agencies that venues rely on are www.ticketweb.co.uk and www.ticketmaster.co.uk. Increasingly concerts and clubs are using e-ticketed barcodes which are then printed and scanned at the door, although there is usually a way to circumvent this. If events are sold out, great resources are www.gumtree.com and www.seatwave.com, offering fan-to-fan ticket exchange.

CELL PHONES see mobile phones

CLUBBING
Most venues are open until 3am on Fri/Sat and larger ones from Thu through to Sun. Since drinks can be expensive (pub averages are around £4–£5 for a pint, and £4–£6 for spirits and mixers, but can rise steeply particularly in central clubs), most Londoners drink at home or in a local bar before heading out around midnight. Superclubs like Fabric don't get started until 2 or 3am, so pace yourself and expect to dance until noon the next day (some rise at 6am and then go out!). Bags are often searched on entrance to live music clubbing events, with no drinks, drugs (and even water) allowed into venues. Entrance ranges from a couple of pounds (mid-week in smaller venues) up to £25 for star DJs. Many neighbourhood venues, though, are free or reduced before 11pm–midnight.

CONDOMS
Condoms are sold in chemists and supermarkets, and there are vending machines in the toilets of train stations, clubs and bars.

COST OF LIVING
Newspaper 40p (tabloids, *The Sun* etc.) to £1.80 for reputable broadsheets (*Guardian*, *Independent*, *Times*). Cigarettes: a packet of 20 typically costs around £9, with a similar figure for a 25g packet of rolling tobacco. Big Mac £2.89, an espresso (Starbucks) £1.60, cinema ticket £10 to £17 in the West End and multiplexes.

CREDIT CARDS
Visa and Mastercard are widely accepted; American Express and Diners Club cards are less so. If your card is lost or stolen, call: **American Express** (012 7369 6933),

Diners Club (0845 862 2935), **Visa** (0800 891 725). **Mastercard** (0800 964 767).

DENTISTS
For urgent care, you can visit the **Dental Emergency Care Service**, Guy's Hospital, St Thomas St, Southwark, SE1. Open Mon–Fri 9am–5pm. Queues start forming at 8am, so get there by 10am to be sure of being seen. For less urgent care, you can also find a dentist on www.nhs.uk/Service-Search/Dentists/LocationSearch/3

DINING
If Londoners are not eating 'al desko' – the popular phrase satirising office worker's sandwich lunches in front of their computer – most tend to grab up to an hour between noon and 3pm. Dinner is usually from around 7.30–10.30pm (last orders in restaurants), but it's common to snack while drinking and then grab a takeaway on the way home from the pub or go for a late-night curry.

DOCTORS
As well as British citizens, residents (e.g. overseas students) and people with a UK work permit can all visit a General Practitioner free of charge. Anybody else can still visit a GP but will have to pay. You can find your nearest surgery at www.nhs.uk or simply walk in to one of the new GP-led health centres. Open from 8am to 8pm, every day of the year, they don't require an appointment. Also useful is **NHS Direct** – a confidential 24-hour telephone helpline offering medical advice from nurses on 111. The national emergency number – for police, fire or ambulance services – is 999.

DRINKING AND DRUGS
You must be 18 to buy cigarettes or to buy or be served alcohol, and it's very common to be asked for photo ID (passport, driver's licence) if you don't look clearly over 25. As in most major capitals, illicit drugs are fairly common, and legal highs like poppers are omnipresent in edgier areas like Camden and sex shops in Soho.

DRY CLEANERS
Posh – by appointment to the Queen! – but reliable **Jeeves of Belgravia** has 9 branches throughout London and offers a complimentary collection and delivery service www.jeevesofbelgravia.co.uk but

you'll find a no-nonsense cheap dry cleaner on practically every street corner.

ELECTRICITY
The UK uses 230V, 50-cycle AC voltage and three-pin plugs (the US and Canada use 110 volts and European countries use 220 volts). European and US appliances will need adaptors, which are most readily available at branches of **Boots** www.boots.com the chemist and the electrical chain **Currys** www.currys.co.uk and some supermarkets.

EMBASSIES
American Embassy: 24 Grosvenor Square, Mayfair, W1 · 020 7499 9000 · www.london.usembassy.gov
Australian High Commission: Australia House, Strand, Holborn, WC · 020 7379 4334 · www.uk.embassy.gov.au
Canadian High Commission: 7 Trafalgar Square, SW1 · 020 7004 6000 · www.unitedkingdom.gc.ca
French Embassy: 58 Knightsbridge, SW · 020 7073 1000 · passport & visa 084 5730 0118
Irish Embassy: 17 Grosvenor Place, Belgravia, SW · 020 7235 2171 · passport & visa 020 7373 4339 · www.dfa.ie
Embassy of Japan: 101-104 Piccadilly, Mayfair, W1 · 020 7465 6500 · www.uk.emb-japan.go.jp
New Zealand High Commission: New Zealand House, 80 Haymarket, St James's, SW · 020 7930 8422 · www.nzembassy.com
South African High Commission: South Africa House, Trafalgar Square, St James's, WC · 020 7451 7299 · www.southafricahouseuk.com

EMERGENCIES
To contact the police, fire or ambulance services dial 999 free from any public or private telephone. The single European emergency number (112) also works in the UK. In case of accident most major hospitals have 24-hour Accident and Emergency (A&E) departments, with free treatment open to EU nationals and non-EU visitors with a passport.

FLOWERS
Markets are a good bet for flowers in London: **Wild Bunch** in Covent Garden offers not a shop but seven adjoining stalls, while **Columbia Road Flower Market** (pg 60) is the undisputed place for flower and plant-shopping on weekends. **McQueens'**

(www.mcqueens.co.uk) flagship in Clerkenwell is both extremely elegant (they cater for the *Vanity Fair* post-Academy Awards) and affordable.

GAY AND LESBIAN

The gay scene in London is huge and ever-changing. Popular publications are *Gay Times*, *Attitude* and *Diva* (for girls) with the light-hearted *Boyz* free in gay stores, bars and clubs. The main gay-friendly areas are Soho (home to G-A-Y) and 'Vauxhall Village' where RVT and Fire/Lightbox are the key venues, but think shirt-off hardcore clubbing. Patroc (www.patroc.com/london) is a useful site that has maps of gay Soho and Vauxhall. But the scene is moving East, where Shoreditch's George & Dragon (pg 58) and Dalston's Vogue Fabrics (pg 59) and Dalston Superstore (pg 57) are a far more stylish option. For girls, Soho's she-soho.com is a youthful go-to spot.

GYMS

The efficient chain **Soho Gyms** has branches throughout London. You can pick up a 1 day pass for £12, or a one week pass for £34. A weekend pass will cost you £26.95. www.sohogyms.com The upbeat **Gymbox** has 7 locations at Bank, Covent Garden, Farringdon, Holborn, Old Street, Stratford, & Westfield London. www.gymbox.com Luxe club **Thirty Seven Degrees** has two outposts at Tower Bridge & Olympia. www.thirtysevendegrees.co.uk The Central **YMCA** in Bloomsbury is another more affordable option. www.ymcaclub.co.uk.

HAIRDRESSERS

Two well-regarded salons often featuring in edgy magazines are **Tommy Guns** (Soho and Shoreditch branches) www.tommyguns.co.uk and the **Taylor Taylor** flagships in Shoreditch, Notting Hill and the City (www.taylortaylorlondon.com). **Toni & Guy** (www.toniandguy.com) is reliable and has chains throughout town. Also check out addresses under our HAIR tag.

HEALTH INSURANCE

EU residents are entitled to NHS treatment at a reduced cost or free of charge with an EHIC (the new E111) card, and non-EU nationals should take out health insurance before coming to London. It's worth remembering this is not an alternative to travel insurance and will not cover private medical healthcare or costs for e.g. rescue services, travel disruptions etc.

LOST PROPERTY

Property found on London Underground, buses or the overground will be held at the local station before being sent on to TFL's **Lost Property Office** within 2–7 days (200 Baker St, NW1, 0343 222 1234, Mon–Fri 8.30am–4pm, except Bank Holidays). You can also fill out an online form at www.tfl.gov.uk that will be searched for 21 days. If you lose property marked with an address in a black cab, the office will write to you, but can also be found at 15 Penton St N1, Angel, Mon–Fri 9am–4pm, 0207 918 2000. The local police station (via Directory Enquiries) can help out in all other instances.

MINI CABS

See our entry on Taxis (Black Cabs) and Mini Cabs in the Transport section on page 85 .

MEMBERS CLUBS

Times have not really changed since 18th-century gentlemen's clubs gave aristos, politicos and the male English gentry a place to quaff brandy and chomp cigars. Indeed, these days there is a rash of new members' clubs, each attempting to draw a crowd of celebrity creatives – from the notorious **Groucho Club** (www.thegrouchoclub. com) to the international **Soho House** (www.sohohouselondon.com) chain and elegant neo-classical **Home House** (homehouse.co.uk). Offering restaurants, sleek bars and the odd bowling alley, they are home to every celebrity party in town (especially **Shoreditch House,** www.shoreditchhouse.com). The latter's expansion to accommodation (**Shoreditch Rooms**) offers a chance for non-members to gain access. But you can enter for free if you do the neighbourhood circuit and find a member who will sign you in. The popular **Dean St Townhouse** (www.deanstreettownhouse. com) mimes the classic members club vibe but its restaurants and rooms are open to all-comers and they can even help sort out access to the nearby **Soho House** (they're part of the same group). Find our featured Members Club in the INDEX on page 99)

MOBILE PHONES

Most dual and tri-band mobile phones with GSM 900 or 1800 will work in Britain. Check with your mobile provider that the roaming function is activated on your phone before leaving home. The main UK service providers are **EE** ee.co.uk, **Vodafone** www.vodafone.co.uk, **O2** www.o2.co.uk, **Three** www.three.co.uk. Cheap, basic phones with credit on British networks can be bought from most mobile phone shops.

MONEY

Despite being a member of the European Union the UK has not adopted the Euro. The British currency is still Pounds Sterling with 100 pence in each pound. You will usually hear British people say 'p' rather than pence, as in 50p. More colloquially, a pound is known as a 'quid', a five pound note is a 'fiver' and a ten pound note a 'tenner'. To change money and travellers' cheques, head to any bank, bureau de change or post office. There are numerous bureaux de change in Central London – often located inside banks, travel agents or Post Offices, as well as at London's airports and major train stations. **Thomas Cook** is a reliable chain www.thomascook.com. It might be cheaper to use a credit or debit card to get money out of a cash machine, situated inside and outside all High Street banks, in supermarkets, shops, railways and bus stations. (Avoid the machines in bars and newsagents which often charge £1.50-£2 per transaction, on top of the charge your bank will make for using a foreign card.) Supermarkets also offer cash back services (extra cash, added to your card when you pay for items), while banks can give advances on your Visa and Mastercard.

NAILS

Nails Inc www.nailsinc.com (swift, cheap, manicures start at £18) has multiple London outposts and cult nail salon **Wah Nails** (pg 26), inside Topshop Oxford Circus, 'translates fashion trends into fingertip art'. wah-nails.com

OPENING HOURS

Museums and attractions are usually open from Tue to Sun, or from Mon to Sat. The majority open at 10am and close at 6pm but times vary. Many are now staying open late at least once a week – usually on a Fri. Shops are open Mon to Fri from 9am–6pm and on Saturdays from about 10am–7pm. In the centre, they have limited Sunday opening hours (until about 5pm). Late-night shopping is usually on Thu, when the major shops stay open until 8 or 9pm. Most supermarkets are now open until 8pm or later in the week, and until 4 or 5pm on Sun. Government offices all close on Public (Bank) holidays (see list below) however shops tend to stay open (except for Christmas Day).

ORGANIC

There's lots of places besides farmers' markets to buy organic food in London, and most supermarket chains now stock good ranges too. **Whole Foods** (www.wholefoodsmarket.com) is possibly the most high-profile organic food retailer, with a huge flagship branch in Kensington, and chains in Camden, Clapham Junction, Soho and Stoke Newington. **Planet Organic** www.planetorganic.com has 6 branches in London, but the best place to source organic is undoubtedly the famous **Borough Market** (see page 72).

PHARMACIES

Branches of **Boots** (www.boots.com) and larger supermarkets have pharmacies with staff on hand to advise for over-the-counter medicines. There are also independents on most high streets. Opening hours are usually 8.30am–7pm, Mon–Sat but there are a handful of late-night pharmacies: **Boots**, 114 Queensway, Bayswater, W2 (until midnight; 6pm Sun); **Bliss Chemists** (www.blisslife.co.uk), 5-6 Marble Arch, Bayswater (midnight daily) and London's only 24-hour pharmacy, **Zafash** (www.zafashpharmacy.co.uk), 233–235 Old Brompton Rd, Earl's Court.

PHOTO LABS

Snappy Snaps (www.snappysnaps.co.uk) has processing branches throughout London. Self-service digital photo kiosks are available in many chains of High Street chemist **Boots** (they also have an online service www.bootsphoto.com).

POST OFFICES

Post offices are usually open from 9am-6pm Mon-Fri and 9am-noon Sat (Trafalgar Square Post Office at 24-28 William IV St, WC2 until 5.30pm Sat.)

Expect long queues at peak hours. Books of 6 or 12 stamps can be bought from machines outside, and also at newsagents and supermarkets. www.royalmail.com

PRESS

The capital's glut of free papers has largely passed since 2009, and only a couple remain. **Metro**, distributed on the transport networks, is gossip and showbiz focussed, while the daily national tabloid **The Evening Standard** (it scrapped its cover price in 2009) is more in-depth and has a good glossy supplement on Fridays. The comprehensive cultural weekly **Time Out** is now distributed for free on Tuesday mornings at most tube and train stations in zones 1 & 2. The major national dailies are, on the Left of centre, **The Guardian** (sister paper the **Observer** is published on Sundays) and **The Independent**, and on the Right the **Daily Telegraph**, **The Times** and tabloids **The Sun** and **Daily Mail**.

PUBLIC (BANK) HOLIDAYS

The dates for 2016 are: New Year's Day, **1 Jan**; Good Friday, **25 Mar**; Easter Monday, **28 Mar**; May Day, **2 May**; Spring Bank Holiday, **30 May**; Summer Bank Holiday, **29 Aug**; Boxing Day, **26 Dec**; Christmas Day, **27 Dec**.

SALES

There are traditionally two sale periods in London: January and June. The summer sales begin in June but it's the Christmas ones (beginning on Boxing Day, 26 Dec and running throughout Jan, though some now even begin a few days before Christmas) that get shoppers sharpening their elbows.

SMOKING

Cigarettes and tobacco are sold in independent newsagents or at branches of **WH Smith** and in supermarkets. Although smoking is banned in all enclosed public areas, many bars and clubs now have decent terraces for the purpose – most more rammed than the main venue itself.

TATTOOS

Never say never. Camden is the home of tattoo parlours, but most are worth avoiding: **Evil from the Needle** is an exception, evilfromtheneedle.com. A central gem is **Frith Street Tattoos**,

frithstreettattoo.co.uk and **Into You**, arguably London's most famous tattoo studio, www.into-you.co.uk.

TELEPHONES

The dialling code for London is 020, followed by an 8-digit number. If you are dialling from outside the UK, dial the international access code from the country you are calling from, then the UK code, 44, then the full London number omitting the initial '0' from the local code. Dial '00' to dial abroad from the UK.

TIPPING

It is customary to leave 10-15% of the bill when eating out, however restaurants often add on a 'service charge', so check your bill to avoid tipping twice. Sometimes the service charge will be described as 'optional', 'discretionary' or 'suggested', in which case it has not been included in the bill. People generally do not tip in pubs in London, but may offer to buy a drink for the bartender. Tipping in London bars is more commonplace. It's good karma to tip 10-15% of the taxi fare for black cabs and licensed mini cabs in London. Most people simply round up the fare to the nearest £1 and tell the driver to 'keep the change'.

TOURIST INFORMATION

Visit London is the official visitor organisation for the capital (www.visitlondon.com). The main Tourist Information Centre is open daily at 1 Lower Regent St, SW1 (Piccadilly Circus Tube) but there are others around the city.

WAXING

Department stores and the capital's endless spas (Bliss, Elemis) all offer the gamut of facial and body waxing. But it's threading that's becoming increasingly popular, so take advantage of gurus like Shavata (at Harrods Urban Retreat) or pricey but unrivalled superfacialists www.vaishaly.com. The walk-in brow bar Blink at Selfridges (other locations at www.blinkbrowbar.com) is a convenient budget option.

WIFI

Most bars and cafes have free wifi available.

TRANSPORT

GETTING TO AND FROM LONDON

AIRPORTS

Heathrow

Located 32 km to the west of central London and one of the world's busiest airports, with over 73,000,000 passengers in 2014. There are 5 terminals.
www.heathrowairport.com

The fastest way into central London, the **Heathrow Express** will take you from Heathrow to London Paddington in just 15 minutes. The first train departs around 5am from Terminals 1, 2 & 3, with trains running every 15 minutes until 11.48pm. A transfer service operates from terminals 4 & 5. The schedule is practically the same for the return trip. Single tickets cost £21 if purchased online or from the ticket machine or office at Heathrow Airport, and £26 if purchased onboard. An added bonus: Heathrow Express provides free on-board wifi.
www.heathrowexpress.com

Taking the **Underground** is always an option. The trip will take a bit longer (around 50 minutes), but is considerably cheaper. Take Piccadilly Line from Heathrow into London, where you can connect to the rest of the London Tube network. Trains run every few minutes, from around 5am to 11.45pm. A single ticket costs £5.70, but it's worth buying an Oyster card if you plan to use the Tube frequently (see page 84 for more info).
www.tfl.gov.uk

Another option is the **National Express** bus service from Heathrow to Victoria Coach Station. Buses leave every 30 minutes, from 3 different stops (the Central Bus Station, and in front of both Terminal 4 and Terminal 5) and the journey takes between 40 minutes and 1 hour 30 minutes, depending on the route (and traffic). Some services stop en route in Hammersmith or Earl's Court. Services from Heathrow commence around 5.30am and run until 9.30pm. Coaches from Victoria depart from around 7.15am until midnight. Tickets start at £15, one-way. Book at least 30 days in advance.
www.nationalexpress.com

For those arriving or departing after midnight, the **N9 night bus** runs every 20 min to central London (Trafalgar Square) between midnight and 5.30am. Journey time is approximately 65 min. Standard bus fares apply, or an Oyster card will work here as well.
www.tfl.gov.uk

A **taxi** between Heathrow and central London takes about an hour and should cost between £43 and £75, depending, of course, on time of day and exact destination. Be sure to ask your driver how much the fare will be in advance. In Black Cabs, there is an extra charge of £2 for journeys that start from Heathrow Airport ranks and finish within Greater London.

Gatwick

The UK's second biggest airport after Heathrow, Gatwick is a bit farther from the city, sitting about 50 km south of central London. Two terminals (North & South).
www.gatwickairport.com

Gatwick Express provides the quickest route into central London. The trip takes about 30 min, with trains leaving every 15 min from South Terminal to Victoria Station. Service runs from around 5am to midnight, in both directions. Single tickets cost £17.70 online (£19.90 on board).
www.gatwickexpress.com

With five London destinations – to London Bridge, City Thameslink, Blackfriars, Farringdon and St Pancras International stations – the **Thameslink** offers a bit more flexibility at a reduced price. Trains run approx. every 10 min, and you can expect a 30 min (London Bridge) to 48 min (St Pancras) journey into central London. Tickets cost between £10 and £19 and can be bought online. The train station is located in the South Terminal building with a short, free train transit to the North Terminal.
www.thameslinkrailway.com

The **National Express** bus service runs approximately every hour between Gatwick and Victoria Coach Station. Journey time varies according to route and, of course, traffic, but most are about 1 hour 50 min. Some services stop at Hooley, Wallington, Mitcham Junction, Mitcham London Rd, Streatham, Stockwell and Pimlico. Tickets cost £10.
www.nationalexpress.com

A budget option, **Easybus** runs from both North and South Terminals to Earl's Court/ West Brompton, right near Earl's Court Exhibition Centre. The trip takes a little over 1 hour, with buses departing every 15 to 20 mins. Ticket prices start at just £2, but you must book in advance via the website.
www.easybus.co.uk

A **taxi** to central London should cost between £78 and £95, depending, of course, on time of day and exact destination. Be sure to ask your driver how much the fare will be in advance.

Stansted

Britain's 3rd busiest airport and one of the fastest growing airports in Europe. Located 64km to the north-east of London, it is home to many of the UK's low-cost airlines (Ryanair, EasyJet etc), serving mostly European and Mediterranean destinations.
www.stanstedairport.com

The fastest option for central London, the **Stansted Express** meets up with the Tube at Tottenham Hale station after a 30 min trip. The complete trip to Liverpool Street station terminus takes about 45 min. Trains leave every 15 min, from around 5am to midnight. Single tickets cost £21 to Tottenham Hale and £23.40 to Liverpool St.
www.stanstedexpress.com

EasyBus runs between the airport and Baker Street or Old Street almost 24 hours a day. The journey takes about 1 hour 15 min for Baker Street and 1 hour for Old Street, with buses departing every 15-20 min, and tickets start at just £2. You must book in advance via the website.
www.easybus.co.uk

The **National Express** now offers 3 routes: the A6 route runs to Victoria Coach Station, stopping along the way at Golder's Green, Finchley Road Tube, St John's Wood, Gloucester Place, Baker Street, Marble Arch and Hyde Park Corner in 1 hour 45 min ; the A9 route runs direct between to Stratford in 50 minutes; the A8 route runs between Stansted Coach Station to Liverpool Street Street via Bow Road, Mile End and Whitechapel in 65 minutes. Buses depart every 15-30 minutes, 24 hours a day. Prices start at £6. Buy your ticket online or directly from the driver.
www.nationalexpress.com

Terravision runs to both Victoria Coach Station (I hour 15 min) and Liverpool Street Railway Station (55 min). Coaches leave approximately every 30 min. Tickets cost £9. www.terravision.eu

Luton

Located 51km northwest of London, Luton Airport (LTN) is another major base for low-cost air travel. www.london-luton.co.uk

A regular **shuttle** links the airport to Luton Airport Parkway Station. From there you can catch the Tube to central London (St Pancras).

The **Easybus** service runs from Luton Airport to Brent Cross, Finchley Road, Baker Street, Oxford Street/ Marble Arch and London Victoria. Buses leave every 15 min, 24hrs a day (except Christmas Day). The journey takes about 50 minutes, and tickets start at just £2 but you must book in advance via the website. www.easybus.co.uk

Terravision bus service to London Victoria bus station has stops at Buckingham Palace Road, Brent Cross, Baker Street, Marble Arch. At peak times there are departures every 20 min, and the journey takes approximately 1 hour. Tickets cost £10. www.terravision.eu

The **National Express** arrives and departs from bays 4, 5, 6 and 10, situated in the front of the terminal building. The A1 service runs to central London via Finchley Road, St John's Wood, Marylebone, Portman Square, Golders Green, Victoria Rail Station and Victoria Coach Station. Journey time is approx 65 minutes. Ticket prices start at £5. Buy your ticket online or directly from the driver. www.nationalexpress.com

London City

One of London's smaller airports, London City is situated only 9.5km east of Central London and just 4.8km from Canary Wharf. A single runway handles flights, with a strong emphasis on business travel to Europe and New York. www.londoncityairport.com

Docklands Light Railway is an overground system connecting East London to the London Underground. Trains run every 8 to 15 min from the airport to Canning Town, Woolwich Arsenal and Bank. The trip takes between 7 and 22 min. The DLR is part of the Tube network, so costs the same as a trip on the Underground. www.tfl.gov.uk

RAIL

Eurostar

The Very Fast Train connecting London to both Paris and Brussels. A trip between Paris and London will take around 2 hours 15 min. The Eurostar arrives at King's Cross St Pancras International, and from there you can catch a bus or the Tube (Northern, Victoria and Piccadilly lines). www.eurostar.com

COACH

Eurolines offers a coach service that connects London with a number of European cities. Coaches arrive at Victoria coach station, 300m from Victoria train station, where you can continue your journey by bus or Tube (Circle, District, Victoria lines). www.eurolines.com

The SNCF's new **iDBUS** service, also from Victoria coach station, connects London with Amsterdam, Lille, Brussels, Paris (Bercy) and Paris (CDG). uk.idbus.com

GETTING AROUND LONDON

London is a big city, and it has an appropriately expansive transport network, including the London Underground (aka the Tube) and an extensive bus network. The Tube system is organized into 9 zones with 'central' London concentrated in zones 1 & 2. Prices for tickets are organised around these different zones, so travelling within a zone or from zone 1 to 3 is cheaper than travelling from 1 to 4. Single ticket for zones 1–2 costs £4.80. Zones 1–6 cost £6. A daily Travelcard, for zones 1–2 only, costs £12. More cost-efficient is the **Oyster Card**: a single ticket for zones 1–2 costs £2.90 or £2.30 (offpeak), and daily use is capped at £6.40. The Oyster card is

a blue plastic card you use instead of paper tickets. You can charge Travelcards, passes and railcards on it, as well as credit which you use up as you travel. You place it on the yellow card reader as you go through the turnstile or when you get on the bus. You buy your Oyster Card from the ticket offices in the Tube for £5 (refundable deposit) or you can order online. (Oyster Cards are also available for purchase in the Eurostar.) www.tfl.gov.uk

London Underground

The second longest metro system in the world, and buried deeper underground than most other subway systems, the London Underground was also the first underground railway system in the world, opening its first section in 1863. In 1890 it became the first to operate electric trains. Known colloquially as the Tube, the system is comprised of 11 colour-coded lines, each with its own name: the Victoria line, the Bakerloo etc. Northbound, Southbound, Eastbound or Westbound indicates the direction the train is travelling. The first train departs around 5am, and the last between 11pm and midnight.

Night Tube

From the early hours of Sat 12 September 2015, in time for the Rugby World Cup in England, Londoners and visitors to the Capital will be able to travel on the Jubilee, Victoria and most of the Piccadilly, Central and Northern tube lines all night on Fridays and Saturdays.

Buses

Buses are cash-free. You can only use Oyster or a contactless payment card to pay as you go, a Travelcard or a Bus & Tram Pass. A single adult fare is £1.50 with Oyster or a contactless payment card. There is no zone system for the bus network. Ticket machines are located next to the main bus stops on these routes. (You'll need exact money, as the machines do not give change.) Most buses are low-floor vehicles, making them very accessible for pushchairs (strollers) and wheelchairs. People in wheelchairs travel for free.

Night Buses

Night bus services keep the city covered from the time the Tube closes to the start of daytime bus services.

Though now you can take the Night Tube on the weekend too, see above. Additionally, many standard London bus routes run for 24 hours. If you're not familiar with the routes, head to Trafalgar Square (the hub for night buses) or check any bus-stop information board. Bear in mind that services are less frequent at night and night buses stop on request only so you need to indicate your stop clearly to the driver when boarding or disembarking.

Taxis (Black Cabs)

The traditional **Black Cab** (also called a Hackney Carriage) is a quintessential London experience. Drivers are required to pass a rigorous exam of London's geography called 'The Knowledge' and are great for idle banter. With stands outside stations and in central areas, they can be hailed fairly easily, with an illuminated yellow light on the top indicating they're available for hire. Black Cabs are all metered, with a flat rate of £2.40 and drivers will expect a tip of about 10%. They can also be booked by telephone (there is an extra charge of up to £2). Black Cabs are legally obliged to take on any job for journeys up to 20km (30 km for cabs at the Heathrow Airport taxi ranks), or up to one hour duration. They are licensed to carry up to 5 people (6 in the special Metrocabs and Mercedes Vitos) plus luggage. All licensed taxis are accessible to people using wheelchairs and most have a variety of other features to make access easier. The fare payable at the end of the journey will be shown on the taxi meter. There is no extra charge for additional passengers or luggage. Price is calculated according to the time of day, the length of the journey and the distance. You can tip taxi drivers as much as you like, but most people round up to the nearest pound. Text CAB to **60835**, and you'll receive two minicab numbers and one Black Cab number straight to your mobile phone by text. (*Text charged at 35p per enquiry plus standard text message rate. Roaming rates apply to overseas networks.) The free and official **Cabwise** app lets you book your nearest licensed minicab or black cab. A new dedicated black cab booking app **Gett** takes on Uber with a £10 flat fare in central London.

Mini Cabs

Mini cabs are a cheaper and more flexible alternative than the traditional Black Cab, although lower on charm – but beware the capital's famed 'dodgy cabs' which are unlicensed vehicles cruising for fares. With Cabwise, you can text 'HOME' to **60835*** and receive the numbers of two licensed minicabs and a Black Cab firm in the area you are texting from. (*Text charged at 35p per enquiry plus standard text message rate.) **Addison Lee** is a reputable company on **020 7387 8888**, they also have a free App to speed orders up even further. The free and official **Cabwise** app lets you book your nearest licensed minicab or black cab.

Private Driver Apps

An alternative to taxis are the new private car companies that work via apps on your smartphone, notably **Uber**, www.uber.com.

Bikes

Since April 2015, London's public bicycle hire scheme is known as **Santander Cycles**, the new bank sponsor replacing Barclays. According to their website "There are more than 10,000 bikes at over 700 docking stations situated every 300 to 500 metres in London." One can subscribe for one day at £2, one week at £10 or one year at £90. The first 30 minutes are free and then the next 30 minutes of use is £2, and after that the price escalates steeply. The cost of the Cycle Hire member key is £3 but casual users can also purchase 24 hour or 7 day access from docking station terminals with Chip and PIN payment cards. tfl.gov.uk/modes/cycling/santander-cycles

Cars

If you choose to drive, be aware there is a **congestion charge** operating in central London from 7am to 6pm Monday to Friday. If you pay on the day of travel it's £11.50 and if you pay the following day it's £12. You can pay the charge online, by SMS, and in newsagents and petrol (gas) stations that display the Congestion Charging sign. See **www.tfl.gov.uk/modes/driving/congestion-charge** for more information. And if you do bring your car into London, expect to pay for parking.

NOTES

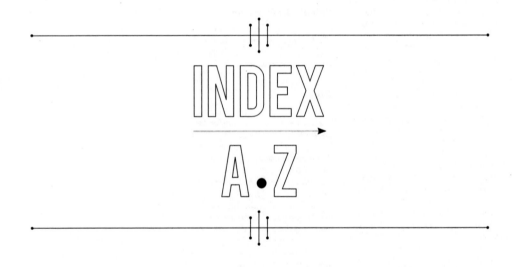

INDEX

A·Z

202 32
8 Hoxton Square 52
40 Maltby Street 69
69 Colebrooke Row 45
93 Feet East 57

A
A Child of the Jago 60
A Gold 60
A Little of What You Fancy 53
Absolute Vintage 60
Agent Provocateur 21
Agile Rabbit 69
Albam 46
Albion 53
Alexander McQueen 21
Alexander McQueen Menswear 21
Alfie's Antiques Market 21
Alibi (The) 57
Allpress Espresso 53
Ally Capellino 60
Amersham Arms (The) 71
Anchor & Hope 69
Annabel's 20
Antoni & Alison 21
Anya Hindmarch 35
Ape & Bird (The) 15
Apple Store 22
Approach (The) 52
Aquascutum 22
Artusi 69
Artwords 60
Ask for Janice 15
Attendant (The) 15

B
Babaji 15
Bad Egg 53
Bang Bang 22
Bao 15
Bar Italia 15
Bar Pepito 45
Bar Story 71
Bar Termini 20
Barbican 14
Barbour Heritage 22
Barnyard 15
Barrafina Adelaide Street 15
Barts 34
Battersea Car Boot Sale 72
Beach Blanket Babylon 34
Beagle 53
Ben Sherman 22
Ben's Canteen 69
Berber & Q 53
Bermondsey 167 72
Bermondsey Arts Club 71
Berners Tavern 15

Bernstock Speirs 32
Bethnal Green Working Men's Club 57
Beyond Retro Dalston 60
Bird of Smithfield 15
Birdhouse 69
Birthdays 57
Bistrothèque 53
Blackout II 22
Bleach 60
Blitz 60
Blixen 53
Blacklock 16
Blue Bar (The) 34
Bob Bob Ricard 16
Bodega Negra 16
Bone Daddies 16
Book Club (The) 57
Bookmarc 22
Borough Market 72
Boxpark 60
Brawn 53
Breakfast Club 53
Brick Lane Beigel Bake 53
Brick Lane Bikes 60
Brick Lane Market 60
Brilliant Corners 53
Brindisa Food Rooms 69
British Film Institute 68
British Museum 14
Brixton Cornercopia 69
Brixton Market 72
Broadway Market 60
Brompton Junction 22
Browns & Browns Focus 22
Brunswich House Café 69
Bull & Gate (The) 43
Bull & Last (The) 43
Bump Caves 71
Bunga Bunga 72
Burberry 22
Burger & Lobster Mayfair 16
Burlington Arcade 26
Busaba Eathai 16

C
Café Oto 57
Call Me Mr Lucky 71
Camberwell Arms (The) 71
Cambridge Satchel Company Mens 22
Camden Arts Centre 42
Camden Passage Antiques Market 46
Camden Town Brewery 45
Canton Arms (The) 69
Caravan Exmouth 16
Caravan King's Cross 43
Carnaby Street 26
Casa Brindisa 32
Cat & Mutton 57
Catch 57
Cây Tre 53

Cecil Sharp House 42
Céline 72
Ceviche 16
Cha Cha Moon 16
Charing Cross Road Bookshops 26
Charlotte Olympia 22
Chelsea Arts Club 34
Chelsea Physic Garden 37
Chiltern Firehouse 16
Chin Chin Labs 43
Christopher Kane 22
Churchill Arms 34
Cirque le Soir 20
City Social 16
Claire de Rouen Books 22
Claude's Kitchen 32
Climpson & Sons 53
Clove Club 54
Coach & Horses 20
Coco de Mer 22
Cocomaya 16
Columbia Road Market 60
Coma y Punto 69
Compagnie des Vins Surnaturels 20
Conran Shop 35
Cooper & Wolf 54
Copita 16
Coronet Theatre 72
Corsica Studios 72
Cos 23
Couverture & the Garbstore 35
Cow (The) 34
Cowshed 35
Craft London 69
Crate Brewery 54
Crazy Homies 34
Curzon Soho 14
Cutler & Gross 35

D
Dabbous 16
Dairy (The) 69
Dalston Roof Park 54
Dalston Superstore 57
Dandelyan 72
Darkroom 23
Daunt Books 23
David Roberts Art Foundation 42
David Zwirner 14
Daylesford Organic 35
De Beauvoir Deli 43
Delaunay (The) 17
Delfina Delettrez 23
Delhi Grill 43
Dennis Severs House 52
Dept of Coffee & Social Affairs 17
Design Museum 68
Diner (The) 54
Dinner by Heston 32
Dirty Bones 35

Dirty Burger	43
Disco	20
Dishoom Shoreditch	54
Dishoom King's Cross	43
Diverse	46
Dock Kitchen	32
Dolls House (The)	45
Dove (The)	57
Dover Street Market	22
Dream Bags Jaguar Shoes	57
Drink Shop & Do	43
Duck & Rice	17
Ducksoup	16
Duke of Cambridge	43
Dukes Brew & Que	58
Dulwich Picture Gallery	68
Dunhill	23

E

E Pellicci	54
E5 Bakehouse	60
East London Liquor Company	58
Electric Cinema	35
Electric Diner	33
Elliot's	69
Evans & Peel Detective Agency	35
Everyman Cinema	42
Experimental Cocktail Club	20

F

Fabric	20
Fabrique Bakery	60
Farm: Shop	61
Fashion & Textile Museum	68
Federation Coffee	69
Fernandez & Wells	17
Fingers Crossed Café	43
Fish & Chip Shop (The)	43
Flesh & Buns	17
Floyd's	54
Folk	22
Folklow	43
Fortnum & Mason	23
Four O Nine	70
Foyles	23
Franco Manca	70
Fred Perry	61
French House	20
Freud Museum (The)	42

G

Gagosian Gallery	42
George & Dragon (The)	58
Ginger & White	43
Globe-Trotter	23

Glory (The)	58
Goodhood Store	61
Gourmet Burger Kitchen	33
Grain Store	43
Grant Museum of Zoology	42
Gymkhana	17

H

Haché Burger Connoisseurs	44
Hackney City Farm	62
Hackney Picture House	52
Haggerston	58
Hakkasan Mayfair	17
Hampstead Heath Swimming Ponds	47
Hannah Barry Gallery	68
Happiness Forgets	58
Harrods	35
Harvey Nichols	35
Hauser & Wirth	14
Hawksmoor	54
Hawley Arms	45
Heaven	21
Herald St	52
Hereford Rd	33
Heritage Routemaster	37
Highgate Cemetery	47
High Water	58
Hix	17
Hix City	54
Hixter Bankside	70
Hoi Polloi	54
Holborn Dining Room	17
Holly Bush (The)	45
Honest Burgers	70
Honest Jon's	36
Hornet's	36
Horniman Museum & Gardens	68
Hostem	61
House of Hackney	61
Hoxley & Porter	44
Hoxton Square Bar & Kitchen	58
Hub	61
Hubbard & Bell	17
Hub Men	46
Hub Women	46
Hunter	23
Hyde Park	37

I

I Knit London	73
ICA	14
Idler Academy (The)	36
Ivy (The)	17

J

J Sheekey Oyster Bar	17
Jaeger	22
Jago	54
Jasper Morrison Shop	61
John Doe	33

K

Kate MacGarry	52
Kerb	44
Kew Gardens	73
King's Head (The)	58
Kings Place	42
Kitty Fisher's	17
Koenig Books	23
KOKO	45
Kokon To Zai	23
Kokon To Zai Notting Hill	36
Koya Bar	18
Kurobuta	17
Kyoto Garden	37

L

L'Atelier Dalston	54
L'Eau à la Bouche	54
L'Entrepôt	54
Lab G	70
Labour & Wait	61
Ladies & Gentlemen	45
Lardo	54
Lassco	73
Launceston Place	33
Lazarides	14
Lazy Oaf	23
Ledbury (The)	33
Leftovers	73
Leila's Shop	55
Les 3 Garçons	55
Lexington (The)	45
Liberty	23
Library (The)	36
Life	18
Linda Farrow Gallery	24
Lisson Gallery	42
Little Georgia	55
LN-CC	60
Loewe	24
London Eye (The)	73
London Fields	61
London Particular (The)	70
London Zoo	47
Look Mum No Hands!	18
Lounge Bohemia	58
Loungelover	58
Lucky Pig (The)	21
Lucky Seven Diner	33

Lulu Guinness	36
Luna & Curious	61
Lyle's	55

M

Macbeth (The)	58
Machine A	24
Magazine	33
Magma	24
Mahiki	20
Maison Bertaux	18
Maltby Street Market	73
Mama Lan	70
Mangal II	55
Manolo Blahnik	36
Manor (The)	70
Margaret Howell	24
Marine Ices	44
Mark's Bar	21
Marksman Public House	55
Matches	36
Maureen Paley	52
Max's Sandwich Shop	44
Mayor of Scaredy Cat Town (The)	58
Mazi	33
Merchant Archive	36
Merci Marie	55
MHL Shop	61
Miller (The)	71
Mishkin's	18
Modern Pantry (The)	18
Momo	21
Monmouth Coffee	18
Monmouth Coffee (Borough Market)	70
Monocle Café	18
Monocle Shop	23
Morito	18
Moro	18
Mouki Mou	24
Mr Fogg's	21
Mr Hare	24
Mulberry	24
Museum of London	14
Music & Goods Exchange	36

N

National Gallery	14
National Maritime Museum	68
National Portrait Gallery	14
Natural History Museum	32
Naughty Piglets	70
Neal's Yard Dairy	24
Neal's Yard Remedies	24
New Evaristo Club	21
Nicholas Kirkwood	24
Nicole Farhi	24
Nightjar	58

Nopi	18
Nordic Bakery	18
Notting Hill Arts Club	35
Number 90 Main Yard	57

O

Odette's	44
Old Blue Last (The)	58
Old Operating Theatre, Museum & Herb Garrett	68
Oldroyd	44
Old Shoreditch Station	55
Old Spitalfields Market	61
Olive Loves Alfie	46
Oliver Spencer	24
Ombra	55
Opening Ceremony	24
Original Sin	45
Oslo	59
Other Criteria	24
Other Shop	25
Ottolenghi	44
Ottolenghi (Notting Hill)	33
Oui Monsieur	44

P

Pacific Social Club	55
Palomar (The)	18
Paradise Garage	55
Paul A Young Fine Chocolates	45
Paul Smith	36
Paxton & Whitfield	24
Peg & Patriot	59
Pelicans & Parrots	61
Penhaligon's	25
Percival	25
Philip Treacy	25
Phoenix Cinema	42
Phonica Records	25
Photographers' Gallery (The)	14
Pig & Butcher	44
Pizza East	55
Pizza East Portobello	33
Plan B	72
Pollen Street Social	18
Polpetto	18
Polpo Notting Hill	33
Polpo Soho	19
Poppies Fish & Chips	55
Portland	19
Portobello Road Market	36
Portobello Star	35
Poste Mistress	25
Power Lunches Arts Café	59
Present	61
Primeur	44
Princess of Shoreditch (The)	59

Pringle of Scotland	25
Prince of Wales (The)	72
Princi	19
Proud	45
Providores & Tapa Room (The)	19

Q

Queenswood	71
Quo Vadis	19

R

Radio Days	73
Rawduck	55
Red Lion	59
Regency Café	18
Regent's Canal Walk	47
Regent's Park	47
Rellik	36
Rich Mix	52
Richmond (The)	55
Riding House Café	19
Ridley Road Market Bar	59
Rigby & Peller	25
Rio Cinema	52
Rita's Bar & Dining	56
Ritzy Cinema	68
River Café	33
Rivington Bar & Grill	56
Roast	70
Rochelle Canteen	56
Roksanda	25
Roland Mouret	25
Rooftop Café	70
Rookery (The)	70
Rosa's	34
Rosie's Deli Café	70
Roti Chai	19
Rotorino	56
Rough Trade	36
Roundhouse (The)	45
Royal Academy of Arts	14
Royal China Queensway	34
Royal Court Theatre	32
Royal Oak	59
Ruby Dock	44
Rupert Sanderson	25

S

Saatchi Gallery	32
Sadie Coles HQ	14
Sadler's Wells	42
Sake No Hana	19
Santo	34
Science Museum	32
Scootercaffe	70

Scotch of St James (The)	21	The Canton Arms (The)	69	Wormwood	34
SCP	61	Tom Dixon	36	Worship St Whistling Shop	59
Sea Cow	71	Tombo	34	Wright Brothers Oyster & Porter House	71
Sebright Arms	59	Tonkotsu East	56	Wright Brothers Spitalfields	57
Selfridges	25	Tooting Bec Lido	73		
Serpentine Gallery	32	Tooting Tram & Social	71		
Serpentine Sackler Gallery	32	Topman General Store	62	X	
Seven at Brixton	71	Topshop	26	Xoyo	60
Shacklewell Arms	59	Towpath	44		
Shakespeare's Globe	68	Tracey Neuls	26		
Shop at Bluebird (The)	36	Tramshed	56	Y	
Shoreditch Grind	56	Trangallan	44		
Shoreditch House	59	Troubadour (The)	34	Yashin Sushi	34
SHOWstudio Shop	25	Typing Room	56	Yauatcha	19
Shri Swaminarayan Mandir	42			York & Albany	45
Shrimpy's	44			You Don't Bring Me Flowers	71
Simmons	45	U		Young Vic	68
Sir John Soane's Museum	14				
Sister Ray	25	Union Street Café	71		
Sketch	19	Urban Outfitters	26	Z	
Smokehouse	44				
Smoking Goat	19			Zetter Townhouse	21
Smythson	25	V		Zucca	71
Social (The)	21				
Social Eating House	19	V&A	32		
Solange Azagury-Partridge	25	V&A Museum of Childhood	52		
Somerset House	15	Verde & Company	56		
Southbank Centre	68	Victoria Beckham	26		
South London Gallery	68	Victoria Miro	52		
Space	52	Viktor Wynd Museum of Curiosities	52		
Spring	19	Vilma Gold	52		
Spuntino	19	Vintage Showroom (The)	26		
Spurstowe Arms	59	Violet Cakes	62		
St John	20	Vogue Fabrics	59		
St John Bakery Room	71	Voodoo Ray's	56		
St John Bread & Wine	56	Vortex Jazz Club	59		
St. James's Park	26				
St Pancras Grand	44				
St. Paul's Cathedral	26	W			
Stables Market	46				
Start	61	Wah Nails Topshop	26		
Stella McCartney	26	Waiting Room (The)	46		
Stephen Friedman	15	Wallace Collection (The)	15		
Stephen Jones Millinery	26	Wellcome Collection	42		
Story Deli	56	Wenlock Arms (The)	46		
Strut	46	West Thirty Six	34		
Strut Broadway	61	What the Butler Wore	73		
Stuart Shave / Modern Art	15	White Cube Bermondsey	68		
Sunspel	62	White Cube Mason's Yard	15		
Sushi Tetsu	20	White Lyan	59		
		White Rabbit	57		
		Whitechapel Gallery	52		
T		Wild Caper	71		
		Wilkinson Gallery	52		
Tabernacle	35	Wilton Way Café	57		
Taberno Do Mercado	56	Windle & Moodie	26		
Table	71	Windsor Castle (The)	35		
Tate Modern	68	Wolf & Badger	36		
Tate Britain	32	Wolseley (The)	20		
Tatty Devine	26	Workshop	20		
Tayyabs	56	World's End	37		

NOTES

AFTERNOON TEA

Cocomaya	16
Dishoom Shoreditch	54
Fortnum & Mason	23
Four O Nine	70
Sketch	19
Wolseley (The)	20
Yauatcha	19

AMERICAN

Chiltern Firehouse	16
Diner (The)	54
Dirty Bones	35
Electric Diner	33
Hubbard & Bell	17
Lucky Seven Diner	33
Rita's Bar & Dining	56
Shrimpy's	44
Spuntino	19

ANTIQUES

Alfie's Antiques Market	21
Camden Passage Antiques Market	46
Lassco	73
Portobello Road Market	36
Viktor Wynd Museum of Curiosities	52

ART

Approach (The)	52
Barbican	14
Camden Arts Centre	42
Charing Cross Road Bookshops	26
David Roberts Art Foundation	42
David Zwirner	14
Dulwich Picture Gallery	68
Gagosian Gallery	42
Hannah Barry Gallery	68
Hauser & Wirth	14
Herald St	52
ICA	14
Kate MacGarry	52
Kings Place	42
Lazarides	14
Lisson Gallery	42
Maureen Paley	52
National Gallery	14
National Maritime Museum	68
National Portrait Gallery	14
Other Criteria	24
Photographers' Gallery (The)	14
Saatchi Gallery	32
Sadie Coles HQ	14
Serpentine Gallery	32
Serpentine Sackler Gallery	32
SHOWstudio Shop	25
Somerset House	15
South London Gallery	68
Stephen Friedman	15
Space	52
Stuart Shave / Modern Art	15
Tate Britain	32
Tate Modern	68
Victoria Miro	52
Vilma Gold	52
Wellcome Collection	42

Whitechapel Gallery	52
White Cube Bermondsey	68
White Cube Mason's Yard	15
Wilkinson Gallery	52

BAGS

Ally Capellino	60
Anya Hindmarch	35
Cambridge Satchel Company Mens	22
Charlotte Olympia	22
Dunhill	23
Globe-Trotter	23
Loewe	24
Lulu Guinness	36
Mulberry	24
Paul Smith	36
Smythson	25

BAR

40 Maltby Street	69
69 Colebrooke Row	45
Alibi (The)	57
Ape & Bird (The)	15
Ask for Janice	15
Bad Egg	53
Bar Pepito	45
Bar Story	71
Bar Termini	20
Barts	34
Beach Blanket Babylon	34
Beagle	53
Bermondsey Arts Club	71
Berners Tavern	15
Bethnal Green Working Men's Club	57
Bird of Smithfield	15
Birthdays	57
Bodega Negra	16
British Film Institute	68
Bump Caves	71
Bunga Bunga	72
Café Oto	57
Call Me Mr Lucky	71
Camden Town Brewery	45
Ceviche	16
Chelsea Arts Club	34
City Social	16
Clove Club	54
Coach & Horses	20
Compagnie des Vins Surnaturels	20
Craft London	69
Crate Brewery	54
Crazy Homies	34
Dabbous	16
Dalston Roof Park	54
Dandelyan	72
Dirty Bones	35
Dishoom King's Cross	43
Dolls House (The)	45
Dream Bags Jaguar Shoes	57
Drink, Shop & Do	43
East London Liquor Company	58
Electric Cinema	35
Evans & Peel Detective Agency	35
French House	20
Glory (The)	58

Grain Store	43
Hackney Picture House	52
Happiness Forgets	58
High Water	58
Hix City	54
Hixter Bankside	70
Hoi Polloi	54
Holborn Dining Room	17
Hoxley & Porter	44
Hoxton Square Bar & Kitchen	58
Hubbard & Bell	17
I Knit London	73
Ivy (The)	17
Ladies & Gentlemen	45
Life	18
Look Mum No Hands!	18
Lounge Bohemia	58
Loungelover	58
Lucky Pig (The)	21
Manor (The)	70
Mark's Bar	21
Mayor of Scaredy Cat Town (The)	58
Momo	21
Mr Fogg's	21
Nightjar	58
Number 90 Main Yard	57
Old Shoreditch Station	55
Ombra	55
Original Sin	45
Oslo	59
Peg & Patriot	59
Portobello Star	35
Power Lunches Arts Café	59
Proud	45
Quo Vadis	19
Rich Mix	52
Richmond (The)	55
Ridley Road Market Bar	59
Rita's Bar & Dining	56
Ritzy Cinema	68
River Café	33
Rookery (The)	70
ScooterCaffè	70
Seven at Brixton	71
Shacklewell Arms	59
Shoreditch House	59
Simmons	45
Smoking Goat	19
Social (The)	21
Social Eating House	19
St Pancras Grand	44
Tonkotsu East	56
Tooting Tram & Social	72
Trangallan	44
Troubadour (The)	34
Union Street Café	71
Viktor Wynd Museum of Curiosities	52
Vortex Jazz Club	59
West Thirty Six	34
White Lyan	59
Worship St Whistling Shop	59
Young Vic	68
Zetter Townhouse	21

BBQ
Smoking Goat 19

BEAUTY
Bleach 60
Cowshed 35
Neal's Yard Remedies 24
Penhaligon's 25

BEER
Camden Town Brewery 45
Crate Brewery 54
Duck & Rice 17
Dukes Brew & Que 58
John Doe 33
Miller (The) 72
Smokehouse 44

BIKES
Brick Lane Bikes 60
Brompton Junction 22

BOOKS
Artwords 60
Blitz 60
Bookmarc 22
British Film Institute 68
Charing Cross Road Bookshops 26
Claire de Rouen Books 22
Clove Club 54
Daunt Books 23
Foyles 23
Idler Academy (The) 36
Koenig Books 23
Library (The) 36
Magma 24
Music & Goods Exchange 36
Olive Loves Alfie 46
Other Criteria 24
Serpentine Gallery 32
Tate Modern 68
Wellcome Collection 42
White Cube Bermondsey 68

BREAD
Albion 53
E5 Bakehouse 60
Fabrique Bakery 60
L'Eau à la Bouche 54
Leila's Shop 55
Princi 19
St John Bakery Room 71
Quo Vadis 19
Wild Caper 71

BREAKFAST
202 32
8 Hoxton Square 52
Albion 53
Allpress Espresso 53
Ask for Janice 15
Attendant (The) 15
Bad Egg 53
Ben's Canteen 69
Berners Tavern 15

Bird of Smithfield 15
Birdhouse 69
Blixen 53
Book Club (The) 57
Breakfast Club 53
Caravan Exmouth 16
Caravan King's Cross 43
Climpson & Sons 53
Dalston Roof Park 54
De Beauvoir Deli 43
Diner (The) 54
Dirty Burger 43
Dishoom Shoreditch 54
Dishoom King's Cross 43
Drink, Shop & Do 43
Egg Break 32
Electric Diner 33
Elliot's 69
E Pellicci 54
Fernandez & Wells 17
Fingers Crossed 43
Floyd's 54
Ginger & White 43
Hoi Polloi 54
Holborn Dining Room 17
Hubbard & Bell 17
L'Eau à la Bouche 54
Koya Bar 18
Leila's Shop 55
London Particular (The) 70
Lucky Seven Diner 33
Lyle's 55
Merci Marie 55
Monocle Café 18
Number 90 Main Yard 57
Ottolenghi (Notting Hill) 33
Pacific Social Club 55
Princi 19
Queenswood 71
Quo Vadis 19
Rawduck 55
Regency Café 18
Rivington Bar & Grill 56
Rooftop Café 70
Roast 70
Rochelle Canteen 56
Rosie's Deli Café 70
Ruby Dock 44
Seven at Brixton 71
Shoreditch Grind 56
St John Bakery Room 71
St John Bread & Wine 56
Table 71
Towpath 44
West Thirty Six 34
Wilton Way Café 57
Wolseley (The) 20
Workshop 20
York & Albany 45

BRITISH
A Gold 60
Albion 53
A Little of What You Fancy 53
Anchor & Hope 69

Ape & Bird (The) 15
Ask for Janice 15
Barnyard 15
Beagle 53
Berners Tavern 15
Bird of Smithfield 15
Brixton Cornercopia 69
Bull & Gate (The) 43
Bull & Last (The) 43
Canton Arms (The) 69
Churchill Arms 34
City Social 16
Claude's Kitchen 32
Clove Club 54
Craft London 69
Daylesford Organic 35
Dinner by Heston 32
Dolls House (The) 45
Duke of Cambridge 43
Elliot's 69
Fish & Chip Shop (The) 43
Hereford Rd 33
Hix 17
Hix City 54
Hixter Bankside 70
Holborn Dining Room 17
John Doe 33
Kitty Fisher's 17
Launceston Place 33
London Particular (The) 70
Lyle's 55
Odette's 44
Paradise Garage 55
Pig & Butcher 44
Poppies Fish & Chips 55
Quo Vadis 19
Regency Café 18
Riding House Café 19
Rivington Bar & Grill 56
Roast 70
Rochelle Canteen 56
Rooftop Café 70
Rosie's Deli Café 70
St John 20
St John Bread & Wine 56
St Pancras Grand 44
Typing Room 56
White Rabbit 57
Wilton Way Café 57
York & Albany 45

BRUNCH
202 32
Attendant (The) 15
Babaji 15
Bad Egg 53
Ben's Canteen 69
Bistrothèque 53
Bob Bob Ricard 16
Breakfast Club 53
Brunswich House Café 69
Bunga Bunga 72
Caravan Exmouth 16
Caravan King's Cross 43
Chick 'n Sours 53

Chiltern Firehouse	16
Claude's Kitchen	32
Dalston Superstore	57
Duck & Rice	17
Dukes Brew & Que	58
Egg Break	32
Electric Diner	33
Fingers Crossed	43
Fernandez & Wells	17
Foxlow	43
Ginger & White	43
Hawksmoor	54
Hubbard & Bell	17
Koya Bar	18
London Particular (The)	70
Max's Sandwich Shop	44
Modern Pantry (The)	18
Number 90 Main Yard	57
Ottolenghi	44
Providores & Tapa Room (The)	19
Rita's Bar & Dining	56
Rivington Bar & Grill	56
Roast	70
Rooftop Café	70
Rosie's Deli Café	70
Seven at Brixton	71
St Pancras Grand	44
Table	71
White Rabbit	57
Wilton Way Café	57
Workshop	20
Wright Brothers Oyster & Porter House	71

BUDGET

93 Feet East	57
Agile Rabbit	69
Allpress Espresso	53
Amersham Arms (The)	71
Bar Italia	15
Bar Story	71
Breakfast Club	53
Brick Lane Beigel Bake	53
Busaba Eathai	16
Café Oto	57
Cha Cha Moon	16
Charing Cross Road Bookshops	26
Climpson & Sons	53
Diner (The)	54
Delhi Grill	43
E Pellicci	54
Fernandez & Wells	17
French House	20
Gourmet Burger Kitchen	33
Haché Burger Connoisseurs	44
Kerb	44
Look Mum No Hands!	18
Mama Lan	70
Mangal II	55
Marine Ices	44
Music & Goods Exchange	36
Nordic Bakery	18
Regency Café	18
Table	71
Towpath	44
Wilton Way Café	57

BURGERS

Bob Bob Ricard	16
Burger & Lobster Mayfair	16
Diner (The)	54
Dirty Burger	43
Dukes Brew & Que	58
Gourmet Burger Kitchen	33
Electric Diner	33
Haché Burger Connoisseurs	44
Honest Burgers	70
Hoxton Square Bar & Kitchen	58
Lucky Seven Diner	33

BYO

BYOC	20
Merci Marie	55
Tayyabs	56

CABARET

Bistrothèque	53

CAKES

A Gold	60
Albion	53
Allpress Espresso	53
Caravan Exmouth	16
Cocomaya	16
E5 Bakehouse	60
Fabrique Bakery	60
Fernandez & Wells	17
Fortnum & Mason	23
L'Eau à la Bouche	54
Leila's Shop	55
Look Mum No Hands!	18
Maison Bertaux	18
Monocle Café	18
Nordic Bakery	18
Ottolenghi	44
Ottolenghi (Notting Hill)	33
Paul A Young Fine Chocolates	46
St John Bakery Room	71
Violet Cakes	62
Yauatcha	19

CDS

Rough Trade	36
Sister Ray	25

CEMETERY

Highgate Cemetery	47

CHEESE

Neal's Yard Dairy	24
Paxton & Whitfield	25

CHINESE

Cha Cha Moon	16
Duck & Rice	17
Hakkasan Mayfair	17
Mama Lan	70
Royal China Queensway	34

CHIPS

Dove (The)	57
E Pellicci	54

CHOCOLATE (continued header)

Gourmet Burger Kitchen	33
Haché Burger Connoisseurs	44
Royal Oak	59
Sebright Arms	59
Windsor Castle (The)	35

CHOCOLATE

A Gold	60
Cocomaya	16
Paul A Young Fine Chocolates	46
Verde & Company	56

CHOPS

Blacklock	16

CLUB

93 Feet East	57
Alibi (The)	57
Bethnal Green Working Men's Club	57
Birthdays	57
Cirque le Soir	20
Catch	57
Coronet Theatre	72
Corsica Studios	72
Dalston Superstore	57
Disco	20
Fabric	20
Heaven	21
KOKO	45
Mahiki	21
New Evaristo Club	21
Notting Hill Arts Club	35
Plan B	72
Power Lunches Arts Café	59
Proud	45
Scotch of St James (The)	21
Social (The)	21
Vogue Fabrics	59
Xoyo	60

COCKTAILS

69 Colebrooke Row	45
Ask for Janice	15
Barnyard	15
Bar Termini	20
Barts	34
Beach Blanket Babylon	34
Beagle	53
Berber & Q	53
Bird of Smithfield	15
Bistrothèque	53
Blixen	53
Blue Bar (The)	34
Book Club (The)	57
Breakfast Club	53
Brunswich House Café	69
Bull & Gate (The)	43
Bump Caves	71
Call Me Mr Lucky	71
Cha Cha Moon	16
Chick 'n Sours	53
City Social	16
Compagnie des Vins Surnaturels	20
Craft London	69
Crazy Homies	34

Dandelyan 72
Dirty Bones 35
Dishoom Shoreditch 54
Dishoom King's Cross 43
Dolls House (The) 45
Dream Bags Jaguar Shoes 57
East London Liquor Company 58
Evans & Peel Detective Agency 35
Experimental Cocktail Club 20
Floyd's 54
Foxlow 43
French House 20
Grain Store 43
Hakkasan Mayfair 17
Happiness Forgets 58
Hawksmoor 54
High Water 58
Hix 17
Hix City 54
Hixter Bankside 70
Hoi Polloi 54
Hoxley & Porter 44
Hubbard & Bell 17
Kitty Fisher's 17
Ladies & Gentlemen 45
Lounge Bohemia 58
Loungelover 58
Lucky Pig (The) 21
Mahiki 21
Mark's Bar 21
Mayor of Scaredy Cat Town (The) 58
Momo 21
Mr Fogg's 21
Nightjar 58
Original Sin 45
Oui Monsieur 44
Peg & Patriot 59
Portobello Star 35
Rita's Bar & Dining 56
Rosa's 34
Royal Oak 59
Seven at Brixton 71
Shoreditch Grind 56
Shrimpy's 44
Simmons 45
Tonkotsu East 56
West Thirty Six 34
White Lyan 59
Worship St Whistling Shop 59
York & Albany 45
Zetter Townhouse 21

COFFEE

Allpress Espresso 53
Antoni & Alison 21
Attendant (The) 15
Bar Italia 15
Bar Termini 20
Beagle 53
Beyond Retro Dalston 60
Birdhouse 69
Caravan King's Cross 43
Chin Chin Labs 43
Climpson & Sons 53
Cooper & Wolf 54

Dalston Roof Park 54
Dept of Coffee & Social Affairs 17
Drink, Shop & Do 43
E5 Bakehouse 60
Elliot's 69
E Pellicci 54
Fabrique Bakery 60
Federation Coffee 69
Fernandez & Wells 17
Fingers Crossed 43
Ginger & White 43
Hubbard & Bell 17
Idler Academy (The) 36
L'Atelier Dalston 54
L'Eau à la Bouche 54
Leila's Shop 55
Look Mum No Hands! 18
Merci Marie 55
Monmouth Coffee 18
Monmouth Coffee (Borough Market) 70
Monocle Café 18
Nordic Bakery 18
Old Shoreditch Station 55
Pacific Social Club 55
Present 61
Rosie's Deli Café 70
Ruby Dock 44
Scootercaffè 70
Shoreditch Grind 56
Towpath 44
Troubadour (The) 34
Verde & Company 56
Wild Caper 71
Wilton Way Café 57
Workshop 20
You Don't Bring Me Flowers 71

COLOMBIAN

Coma y Punto 69

COMEDY

Prince of Wales (The) 72
Roundhouse (The) 45
Tabernacle 35

CONCEPT STORE

Darkroom 23
Dover Street Market 23
Mouki Mou 24
Other Shop 25
Shop at Bluebird (The) 36
Wolf & Badger 36

DANCE

Barbican 14
Sadler's Wells 42
Southbank Centre 68

DELI

A Gold 60
Brindisa Food Rooms 69
Dairy (The) 69
De Beauvoir Deli 43
Fortnum & Mason 23
Harvey Nichols 35

L'Eau à la Bouche 54
Leila's Shop 55
Mishkin's 18
Ottolenghi 44
Pizza East Portobello 33
Rosie's Deli Café 70
Tombo 34
Verde & Company 56
Wild Caper 71

DEPARTMENT STORE

Harrods 35
Harvey Nichols 35
Liberty 23
Selfridges 25

DESIGN

Alfie's Antiques Market 21
Charing Cross Road Bookshops 26
Conran Shop 35
Design Museum 68
House of Hackney 61
Jasper Morrison Shop 61
Labour & Wait 61
Luna & Curious 61
Monocle Shop 24
SCP 61
Tom Dixon 36

DIM SUM

Duck & Rice 17
Hakkasan Mayfair 17
Royal China Queensway 34
Yauatcha 19

DON'T MISS

69 Colebrooke Row 45
A Child of the Jago 60
Alexander McQueen Menswear 21
Alibi (The) 57
A Little of What You Fancy 53
Ally Capellino 60
Approach (The) 52
Artusi 69
Babaji 15
Bao 15
Barrafina Adelaide Street 15
Bar Termini 20
Beagle 53
Berners Tavern 15
Bethnal Green Working Men's Club 57
Beyond Retro Dalston 60
Bistrothèque 53
Blitz 60
Brixton Cornercopia 69
Borough Market 72
Brunswich House Café 69
Café Oto 57
Camden Arts Centre 42
Caravan King's Cross 43
Céline 72
Chiltern Firehouse 16
Christopher Kane 22
Clove Club 54
Coma y Punto 69

Compagnie des Vins Surnaturels	20	
Craft London	70	
Curzon Soho	14	
Dabbous	16	
Dandelyan	72	
David Zwirner	14	
Dover Street Market	23	
Electric Cinema	35	
Elliot's	69	
Experimental Cocktail Club	20	
Fabric	20	
Federation Coffee	69	
Franco Manca	70	
Gymkhana	17	
Hannah Barry Gallery	68	
Happiness Forgets	58	
Hix	17	
Hoi Polloi	54	
House of Hackney	61	
Hoxley & Porter	44	
Hub Women	46	
King's Head (The)	58	
Kokon To Zai	23	
Labour & Wait	61	
Ladies & Gentlemen	45	
Leila's Shop	55	
Lisson Gallery	42	
London Particular (The)	70	
Lounge Bohemia	58	
Lyle's	55	
Maison Bertaux	18	
Maltby Street Market	73	
Manor (The)	70	
Mark's Bar	21	
Marksman Public House	55	
Max's Sandwich Shop	44	
Monmouth Coffee	18	
Mr Hare	24	
Natural History Museum	32	
New Evaristo Club	21	
Old Spitalfields Market	61	
Oliver Spencer	24	
Opening Ceremony	24	
Original Sin	45	
Other Shop	25	
Ottolenghi	44	
Ottolenghi (Notting Hill)	33	
Palomar (The)	18	
Paradise Garage	55	
Paul Smith	36	
Paxton & Whitfield	25	
Photographers' Gallery (The)	14	
Portland	19	
Portobello Road Market	36	
Primeur	44	
Riding House Café	19	
Ritzy Cinema	68	
River Café	33	
Rookery (The)	70	
Royal China Queensway	34	
Sadie Coles HQ	14	
Serpentine Gallery	32	
Shacklewell Arms	59	
Sir John Soane's Museum	14	
Sketch	19	
Smokehouse	44	
Somerset House	15	
South London Gallery	68	
St John	20	
St John Bakery Room	71	
St John Bread & Wine	56	
Strut Broadway	61	
Sushi Tetsu	20	
Tate Modern	68	
Tatty Devine	26	
Tayyabs	56	
Tooting Tram & Social	72	
V&A	32	
V&A Museum of Childhood	52	
Violet Cakes	62	
Vintage Showroom (The)	26	
White Cube Bermondsey	68	
White Cube Mason's Yard	15	
World's End	37	
Yashin Sushi	34	
Zetter Townhouse	21	

EXCHANGE

Bang Bang	22
Music & Goods Exchange	36

EYEWEAR

Cutler & Gross	35
Linda Farrow Gallery	24

FASHION

A Child of the Jago	60
Alexander McQueen	21
Ally Capelino	60
Antoni & Alison	21
Aquascutum	22
Barbour Heritage	22
Bermondsey 167	72
Blackout II	22
Browns & Browns Focus	22
Burberry	22
Burlington Arcade	26
Céline	72
Christopher Kane	22
Coco de Mer	22
Cos	23
Darkroom	46
Diverse	23
Dover Street Market	23
Fashion & Textile Museum	68
Folk	23
Fred Perry	61
Goodhood Store	61
Hub	61
Hub Women	46
Hunter	23
Jaeger	22
Kokon To Zai	23
Kokon To Zai Notting Hill	36
Lazy Oaf	23
Liberty	23
LN-CC	60
Loewe	24
Machine A	24
Margaret Howell	24
Matches	36
Merchant Archive	36
MHL Shop	61
Monocle Shop	24
Mouki Mou	24
Mulberry	24
Nicole Farhi	24
Olive Loves Alfie	46
Opening Ceremony	24
Other Shop	25
Paul Smith	36
Pelicans & Parrots	61
Pringle of Scotland	25
Roksanda	25
Roland Mouret	25
Sunspel	62
Start	61
Stella McCartney	26
Stephen Jones Millinery	26
Strut	46
Topshop	26
Urban Outfitters	26
Victoria Beckham	26
World's End	37

FILM

Barbican	14
British Film Institute	68
Curzon Soho	14
Electric Cinema	35
Everyman Cinema	42
Hackney Picture House	52
ICA	14
Phoenix Cinema	42
Rio Cinema	52
Ritzy Cinema	68

FISH & CHIPS

Fish & Chip Shop (The)	43
Poppies Fish & Chips	55
Sea Cow	71

FLOWERS

Columbia Road Market	60
House of Hackney	61
You Don't Bring Me Flowers	71

FREE ENTRY

Hackney City Farm	62
Horniman Museum & Gardens	68
Natural History Museum	32
Saatchi Gallery	32
Science Museum	32
Serpentine Gallery	32
Serpentine Sackler Gallery	32
Tate Britain	32
V&A	32
V&A Museum of Childhood	52
Whitechapel Gallery	52

FRENCH

Bistrothèque	53
Brawn	53
L'Eau à la Bouche	54
Les 3 Garçons	55

Merci Marie 55
Oui Monsieur 44

FUSION
Chick 'n Sours 53
Magazine 33

GREEK
Mazi 33

GROCERY
Brixton Cornercopia 69

GRUNGY
93 Feet East 57
Alibi (The) 57
Corsica Studios 72
Fabric 20
George & Dragon (The) 58
Haggerston 58
New Evaristo Club 21
Notting Hill Arts Club 35
Power Lunches Arts Café 59
Shacklewell Arms 59
Spuntino 19

HAIR
Bleach 60
Windle & Moodie 26

HATS
Bernstock Speirs 60
Philip Treacy 25
Stephen Jones Millinery 26

ICE CREAM
Chin Chin Labs 43
Lab G 70
Marine Ices 44

INDIAN
Delhi Grill 43
Dishoom Shoreditch 54
Dishoom King's Cross 43
Gymkhana 17
Roti Chai 19
Tayyabs 56

INTERIORS
Alfie's Antiques Market 21
Bermondsey 167 72
Blitz 60
Conran Shop 35
Darkroom 23
Goodhood Store 61
House of Hackney 61
Jasper Morrison Shop 61
Labour & Wait 61
L'Atelier Dalston 54
Luna & Curious 61
Merchant Archive 36
Monocle Shop 24
Paul Smith 36
Pelicans & Parrots 61
Radio Days 73

SCP 61
Stables Market 46
Tom Dixon 36
Urban Outfitters 26

ISRAELI
Palomar (The) 18

ITALIAN
Artusi 69
Bar Italia 15
Bunga Bunga 72
E Pellicci 54
Lardo 54
Ombra 55
Pizza East 55
Pizza East Portobello 33
Polpetto 18
Polpo Notting Hill 33
Polpo Soho 19
Princi 19
River Café 33
Rotorino 56
Scootercaffe 70
Story Deli 56
Union Street Café 71
Zucca 71

JAPANESE
Bone Daddies 16
Brilliant Corners 53
Café Oto 57
Flesh & Buns 17
Koya Bar 18
Kurobuta 17
Life 18
Sake No Hana 19
Sushi Tetsu 20
Tombo 34
Tonkotsu East 56
Yashin Sushi 34

JAZZ
Haggerston 58
Southbank Centre 68
Vortex Jazz Club 59
Waiting Room (The) 46
Wenlock Arms (The) 46

JEWELLERY
Camden Passage Antiques Market 46
Darkroom 23
Delfina Delettrez 23
Other Criteria 24
Solange Azagury-Partridge 25
Tatty Devine 26

KIDS
Ginger & White 43
Hackney City Farm 62
Horniman Museum & Gardens 68
Lucky Seven Diner 33
Marine Ices 44
Natural History Museum 32
Olive Loves Alfie 46

Regent's Park 47
Rio Cinema 52
Science Museum 32
Stella McCartney 26
Tooting Bec Lido 73

KNICK KNACKS
Labour & Wait 61
Luna & Curious 61
Other Criteria 24
SHOWstudio Shop 25

KNITTING
I Knit London 73

LATE
Bar Italia 15
Barbican 14
Breakfast Club 53
Brick Lane Beigel Bake 53
Haggerston 58
ICA 14
Mangal II 55
Pizza East 55
Shacklewell Arms 59
St Pancras Grand 44
Voodoo Ray's 56

LATES
British Museum 14
Camden Arts Centre 42
South London Gallery 68
Tate Modern 68
V&A 32

LINGERIE
Agent Provocateur 21
Coco de Mer 22
Rigby & Peller 25
Stella McCartney 26
Sunspel 62

LITERARY EVENTS
Book Club (The) 57
Chelsea Arts Club 34
Idler Academy (The) 36
Shoreditch House 59
Tabernacle 35

LIVE MUSIC
93 Feet East 57
Agile Rabbit 69
Amersham Arms (The) 71
Barbican 14
Birthdays 57
Book Club (The) 57
Bull & Gate (The) 43
Bunga Bunga 72
Brilliant Corners 53
Café Oto 57
Catch 57
Cecil Sharp House 42
Coronet Theatre 72
Corsica Studios 72
Dolls House (The) 45

Glory (The)	58	Nopi	18	Topman General Store	62
Haggerston	58	Wormwood	34	Urban Outfitters	26
Heaven	21			Vintage Showroom (The)	26
Hoxton Square Bar & Kitchen	58	**MEMBERS CLUB**		What the Butler Wore	73
ICA	14	Annabel's	20	World's End	37
Kings Place	42	Chelsea Arts Club	34		
KOKO	45	Dolls House (The)	45	**MEXICAN**	
Lexington (The)	45	King's Head (The)	58	Bodega Negra	16
Life	18	Shoreditch House	59	Crazy Homies	34
Macbeth (The)	58			Santo	34
Miller (The)	72	**MENS**			
Nightjar	58	A Child of the Jago	60	**MODERN EURO**	
Old Blue Last (The)	58	Albam	46	40 Maltby Street	69
Oslo	59	Alexander McQueen	21	8 Hoxton Square	52
Power Lunches Arts Café	59	Alexander McQueen Menswear	21	Berners Tavern	15
Prince of Wales (The)	72	Ally Capellino	22	Blixen	53
Proud	45	Aquascutum	22	Camberwell Arms (The)	71
Rich Mix	52	Barbour Heritage	22	Cow (The)	34
Ritzy Cinema	68	Ben Sherman	22	Dabbous	16
Roundhouse (The)	45	Bermondsey 167	72	Delaunay (The)	17
Sebright Arms	59	Blackout II	22	Dairy (The)	69
Shacklewell Arms	59	Browns & Browns Focus	22	Dock Kitchen	32
Southbank Centre	68	Burberry	22	Ducksoup	16
Smoking Goat	19	Cambridge Satchel Company Mens	22	Egg Break	32
Tabernacle	35	Christopher Kane	22	Floyd's	54
Tooting Tram & Social	72	Cos	23	Four O Nine	70
Troubadour (The)	34	Darkroom	23	Hoi Polloi	54
Vortex Jazz Club	59	Diverse	46	Ivy (The)	17
Waiting Room (The)	46	Dover Street Market	23	Ledbury (The)	33
Wenlock Arms (The)	46	Dunhill	23	Manor (The)	70
Xoyo	60	Folk	23	Marksman Public House	55
		Fred Perry	61	Naughty Piglets	70
MALL		Globe-Trotter	23	Oldroyd	44
Boxpark	60	Goodhood Store	61	Portland	19
		Hornet's	36	Primeur	44
MARKET		Hostem	61	Queenswood	71
Agile Rabbit	69	Hub	61	Richmond (The)	55
Battersea Car Boot Sale	72	Hub Men	46	Social Eating House	19
Borough Market	60	Hunter	23	Sketch	19
Brick Lane Market	60	Jaeger	22	Smokehouse	44
Brindisa Food Rooms	69	Kokon To Zai	23	Spring	19
Brixton Cornercopia	69	Kokon To Zai Notting Hill	36	West Thirty Six	34
Brixton Market	72	Lazy Oaf	23		
Broadway Market	60	Library (The)	36	**MONUMENT**	
Camden Passage Antiques Market	46	LN-CC	60	London Eye (The)	73
Columbia Road Market	60	Loewe	24	St. Paul's Cathedral	26
Coma y Punto	69	Machine A	24		
Federation Coffee	69	Margaret Howell	24	**MOROCCAN**	
Franco Manca	70	MHL Shop	61	Momo	21
Honest Burgers	70	Monocle Shop	24		
Kerb	44	Mouki Mou	24	**MULTIBRAND**	
Lab G	70	Mr Hare	24	Browns & Browns Focus	22
Leftovers	73	Music & Goods Exchange	36	Diverse	46
Maltby Street Market	73	Oliver Spencer	24	Goodhood Store	61
Mama Lan	70	Opening Ceremony	24	Hostem	61
Monmouth Coffee (Borough Market)	70	Other Shop	25	Hub	61
Old Spitalfields Market	61	Paul Smith	36	Hub Men	46
Portobello Road Market	36	Pelicans & Parrots	61	Hub Women	46
Seven at Brixton	71	Percival	25	Kokon To Zai	23
St John Bakery Room	71	Present	61	Kokon To Zai Notting Hill	36
Stables Market	46	Pringle of Scotland	25	LN-CC	60
		Radio Days	73	Machine A	24
MEDITERRANEAN		Sunspel	62	Matches	36
Berber & Q	53	Start	61	Other Shop	25
Jago	54	Strut	46	Present	61

Start	61	Bao	15	Wild Caper	71
Urban Outfitters	26	Bar Termini	20		
		Berber & Q	53	**OYSTERS**	
MUSEUM		Blacklock	16	J Sheekey Oyster Bar	17
British Museum	14	Blixen	53	Richmond (The)	55
Design Museum	68	Bull & Gate (The)	43	St Pancras Grand	44
Fashion & Textile Museum	68	Cambridge Satchel Company Mens	22	Wright Brothers Oyster & Porter House	71
Freud Museum (The)	42	Chick 'n Sours	53	Wright Brothers Spitalfields	57
Grant Museum of Zoology	42	Chiltern Firehouse	16		
Horniman Museum & Gardens	68	Christopher Kane	22	**PACIFIC RIM**	
Museum of London	14	City Social	16	Caravan Exmouth	16
National Gallery	14	Craft London	69	Modern Pantry (The)	18
Natural History Museum	32	Dandelyan	72	Providores & Tapa Room (The)	19
National Maritime Museum	68	Delfina Delettrez	23		
National Portrait Gallery	14	Dishoom King's Cross	43	**PARKS & GARDENS**	
Old Operating Theatre, Museum		Dolls House (The)	45	Chelsea Physic Garden	37
& Herb Garrett	68	Duck & Rice	17	Hampstead Heath Swimming Ponds	47
Royal Academy of Arts	14	Egg Break	32	Horniman Museum & Gardens	68
Science Museum	32	Glory (The)	58	Hyde Park	37
Shakespeare's Globe	68	High Water	58	Kew Gardens	73
Sir John Soane's Museum	14	Hubbard & Bell	17	Kyoto Garden	37
Tate Britain	32	Ivy (The)	17	London Fields	62
V&A	32	Jago	54	Regent's Park	47
V&A Museum of Childhood	52	John Doe	33	St. James's Park	26
Viktor Wynd Museum of Curiosities	52	Kitty Fisher's	17		
Wallace Collection (The)	15	Ladies & Gentlemen	45	**PERFUME**	
Wellcome Collection	42	Oui Monsieur	44	Penhaligon's	25
		Manor (The)	70		
MYTHIC		Marksman Public House	55	**PERUVIAN**	
Annabel's	19	Max's Sandwich Shop	44	Ceviche	16
Bar Italia	15	Naughty Piglets	70		
Ben Sherman	22	Oldroyd	44	**PHOTO**	
Brick Lane Beigel Bake	53	Original Sin	45	Claire de Rouen Books	22
British Film Institute	68	Oslo	59	National Portrait Gallery	14
Browns & Browns Focus	22	Paradise Garage	55	Photographers' Gallery (The)	14
Burlington Arcade	26	Peg + Patriot	59	Proud	45
Carnaby Street	26	Portland	19		
Chelsea Arts Club	34	Primeur	44	**PIZZA**	
Coach & Horses	20	Queenswood	71	Agile Rabbit	69
E Pellicci	54	Richmond (The)	55	Bunga Bunga	72
Fabric	20	Rosa's	34	Crate Brewery	54
French House	20	Rotorino	56	Dream Bags Jaguar Shoes	57
George & Dragon (The)	58	Smoking Goat	19	Floyd's	54
Globe-Trotter	23	Spring	19	Franco Manca	70
Heritage Routemaster	37	Taberno Do Mercado	56	Lardo	54
Highgate Cemetery	47	Tonkotsu East	56	Marine Ices	44
Honest Jon's	36	Typing Room	56	Pizza East	55
Hornet's	36	Victoria Beckham	26	Pizza East Portobello	33
Liberty	23	Viktor Wynd Museum of Curiosities	52	Prince of Wales (The)	72
Maison Bertaux	18	West Thirty Six	34	Princi	19
Paxton & Whitfield	25			Story Deli	56
Regency Café	18	**ORGANIC**		Voodoo Ray's	56
Rough Trade	36	Chick 'n Sours	53	York & Albany	45
Saatchi Gallery	32	Claude's Kitchen	32		
Sadler's Wells	42	Daylesford Organic	35	**POP-UP**	
Shakespeare's Globe	68	Duke of Cambridge	43	Boxpark	60
St John	20	Farm: Shop	61		
World's End	37	Launceston Place	33	**PORTUGUESE**	
		Leila's Shop	55	Taberno Do Mercado	56
NAILS		London Particular (The)	70		
Wah Nails Topshop	26	Merci Marie	55	**PUB**	
		Neal's Yard Remedies	24	Amersham Arms (The)	71
NEW		Story Deli	56	Anchor & Hope	69
Babaji	15	Table	71	Ape & Bird (The)	15
Bad Egg	53	Violet Cakes	62	Bull & Gate (The)	43

Bull & Last (The) 43
Camberwell Arms (The) 71
Canton Arms (The) 69
Cat & Mutton 57
Churchill Arms 34
Cow (The) 34
Dove (The) 57
Duck & Rice 17
Duke of Cambridge 43
George & Dragon (The) 58
Haggerston 58
Hawley Arms 45
Holly Bush (The) 45
Lexington (The) 45
Macbeth (The) 58
Marksman Public House 55
Miller (The) 72
Old Blue Last (The) 58
Pig & Butcher 44
Prince of Wales (The) 72
Princess of Shoreditch (The) 59
Red Lion 59
Royal Oak 59
Sebright Arms 59
Smokehouse 44
Spurstowe Arms 59
Waiting Room (The) 46
Wenlock Arms (The) 46
Windsor Castle (The) 35

QUIZ NIGHTS
Lexington (The) 45
Waiting Room (The) 46
Wenlock Arms (The) 46

RUSSIAN
Little Georgia 55

SCANDINAVIAN
Cooper & Wolf 54
Nordic Bakery 18
Oslo 59

SEAFOOD
Wright Brothers Spitalfields 57

SHERRY
Bar Pepito 45
Morito 18

SHOES
Burlington Arcade 26
Charlotte Olympia 22
Folk 23
Hunter 23
Manolo Blahnik 36
Mr Hare 24
Music & Goods Exchange 36
Nicholas Kirkwood 24
Olive Loves Alfie 46
Paul Smith 36
Poste Mistress 25
Rupert Sanderson 25
Stella McCartney 26
Tracey Neuls 26

SMALL PLATES
8 Hoxton Square 52
Bao 15
Caravan King's Cross 43
Egg Break 32
Jago 54
Oui Monsieur 44
Polpo Notting Hill 33
Polpo Soho 19
Primeur 44
Rotorino 56
Taberno Do Mercado 56
Wormwood 34

SPA
Cowshed 35

SPANISH
Barrafina Adelaide Street 15
Brindisa Food Rooms 69
Casa Brindisa 32
Copita 16
Morito 18
Moro 18
Seven at Brixton 71
Trangallan 44

SSHHH
69 Colebrooke Row 45
Barts 34
Call Me Mr Lucky 71
Ducksoup 16
Evans & Peel Detective Agency 35
Experimental Cocktail Club 20
King's Head (The) 58
Lounge Bohemia 58
Mayor of Scaredy Cat Town (The) 58
Merci Marie 55
New Evaristo Club 21
Rochelle Canteen 56
Worship St Whistling Shop 59

STATIONERY
Smythson 25

STEAK
Foxlow 43
Hawksmoor 54
Hixter Bankside 70
Tramshed 56

SUNDAY ROAST
Amersham Arms (The) 71
Anchor & Hope 69
Churchill Arms 34
Dolls House (The) 45
Dove (The) 57
Foxlow 43
Hawley Arms 45
Holly Bush (The) 45
Hubbard & Bell 17
Marksman Public House 55
Number 90 Main Yard 57
Pig & Butcher 44
Roast 70

Royal Oak 59
Windsor Castle (The) 35
York & Albany 45

SUSHI
Sake No Hana 19
Sushi Tetsu 20
Yashin Sushi 34

SWIMMING
Hampstead Heath Swimming Ponds 47
Tooting Bec Lido 73

TAIWANESE
Bao 15

TAKE AWAY
Agile Rabbit 69
A Gold 60
Bad Egg 53
Brick Lane Beigel Bake 53
Brindisa Food Rooms 69
Brixton Cornercopia 69
Caravan King's Cross 43
Casa Brindisa 32
Cha Cha Moon 16
Climpson & Sons 53
Cocomaya 16
Dairy (The) 69
Daylesford Organic 35
De Beauvoir Deli 43
Delhi Grill 43
Dept of Coffee & Social Affairs 17
Dirty Burger 43
Drink, Shop & Do 43
Federation Coffee 69
Fernandez & Wells 17
Fingers Crossed 43
Fish & Chip Shop (The) 43
Fortnum & Mason 23
Ginger & White 43
J Sheekey Oyster Bar 17
Kerb 44
Lab G 70
L'Eau à la Bouche 54
Max's Sandwich Shop 44
Merci Marie 55
Monmouth Coffee 18
Monmouth Coffee (Borough Market) 70
Modern Pantry (The) 18
Ottolenghi (Notting Hill) 33
Poppies Fish & Chips 55
Rita's Bar & Dining 56
Rosa's 34
Roti Chai 19
Ruby Dock 44
Sea Cow 71
St John Bakery Room 71
St Pancras Grand 44
Stables Market 46
Story Deli 56
Table 71
Tramshed 56
Wild Caper 71
York & Albany 45

TAPAS
Bar Pepito 45
Barrafina Adelaide Street 15
Casa Brindisa 32
Copita 16
Morito 18
Ombra 55
Pollen Street Social 18
Seven at Brixton 71
Trangallan 44

TEQUILA
Crazy Homies 34
Dukes Brew & Que 58

TERRACE
202 32
8 Hoxton Square 52
Albion 53
Bar Italia 15
Barts 34
Beach Blanket Babylon 34
Beagle 53
Bird of Smithfield 15
Blixen 53
British Film Institute 68
Corsica Studios 72
Crate Brewery 54
Dalston Roof Park 54
Duke of Cambridge 43
Electric Diner 33
Four O Nine 70
Ginger & White 43
Grain Store 43
Hawley Arms 45
Hoxton Square Bar & Kitchen 58
L'Eau à la Bouche 54
Leila's Shop 55
Little Georgia 55
Macbeth (The) 58
Mazi 33
Miller (The) 72
Quo Vadis 19
Red Lion 59
River Café 33
Rochelle Canteen 56
Rookery (The) 70
Shrimpy's 44
Southbank Centre 68
Towpath 44
Troubadour (The) 34
West Thirty Six 34
Wright Brothers Spitalfields 57
Young Vic 68

THAI
Busaba Eathai 16
Churchill Arms 34
Smoking Goat 19
Rosa's 34

THEATRE
Roundhouse (The) 45
Royal Court Theatre 32
Shakespeare's Globe 68
Young Vic 68

TURKISH
Babaji 15
Mangal II 55

VEGETARIAN
Grain Store 43
Merci Marie 55
Nopi 18
Ottolenghi 44
Ottolenghi (Notting Hill) 33
Pollen Street Social 18
Queenswood 71
Rivington Bar & Grill 56
Workshop 20

VIETNAMESE
Cây Tre 53

VIEW
City Social 16
Dandelyan 72
Dalston Roof Park 54
Kew Gardens 73
London Eye (The) 73
River Café 33
Rooftop Café 70
Rookery (The) 70
St. Paul's Cathedral 26
Towpath 44

VINTAGE
Absolute Vintage 60
A Child of the Jago 60
Alfie's Antiques Market 21
Bang Bang 22
Battersea Car Boot Sale 72
Beyond Retro Dalston 60
Blackout II 22
Blitz 60
Brick Lane Market 60
Camden Passage Antiques Market 46
Cutler & Gross 35
Hornet's 36
Lassco 73
L'Atelier Dalston 54
Leftovers 73
Merchant Archive 36
Music & Goods Exchange 36
Pelicans & Parrots 61
Por tobello Road Market 36
Radio Days 73
Rellik 36
Stables Market 46
Strut 46
Strut Broadway 61

Vintage Showroom (The) 26
What the Butler Wore 73

VINYL
Honest Jon's 36
Music & Goods Exchange 36
Phonica Records 25
Rough Trade 36
Sister Ray 25

WHISKY
Tonkotsu East 56

WINE BAR
Brawn 53
Brilliant Corners 53
L'Entrepôt 54
Naughty Piglets 70
Providores & Tapa Room (The) 19

WOW
Barbican 14
Blue Bar (The) 34
Bob Bob Ricard 16
Burlington Arcade 26
Dinner by Heston 32
Kyoto Garden 37
Les 3 Garçons 55
Lucky Pig (The) 21
Magazine 33
Nicholas Kirkwood 24
Roundhouse (The) 45
Serpentine Gallery 32
Serpentine Sackler Gallery 32
SHOWstudio Shop 25
Shri Swaminarayan Mandir 42
Sketch 19
St Pancras Grand 44
St. Paul's Cathedral 26
Tate Modern 68
Tooting Bec Lido 73
Wolf & Badger 36
Wolseley (The) 20

ZOO
London Zoo 47
Regent's Park 47

**GOGOPARIS
& GOGOLONDON
ALSO AVAILABLE
ON THE APPSTORE**

NOTES

Galerie 1900-2000 • *Paris*
303 Gallery • *New York*
Miguel Abreu • *New York*
A Gentil Carioca • *Rio de Janeiro*
Air de Paris • *Paris*
Applicat-Prazan • *Paris*
Raquel Arnaud • *São Paulo*
Art : Concept • *Paris*
Alfonso Artiaco • *Napoli*
Balice Hertling • *Paris*
Catherine Bastide • *Brussels*
Baudach • *Berlin*
Hervé Bize • *Nancy*
Tanya Bonakdar • *New York*
Bortolami • *New York*
Isabella Bortolozzi • *Berlin*
Luciana Brito • *São Paulo*
Broadway 1602 • *New York*
Gavin Brown's enterprise • *New York*
Galerie Buchholz • *Berlin, Köln*
Campoli Presti • *London, Paris*
Capitain Petzel • *Berlin*
carlier | gebauer • *Berlin*
Casas Riegner • *Bogotá*
Cherry and Martin • *Los Angeles*
Mehdi Chouakri • *Berlin*
C L E A R I N G • *New York, Brussels*
Sadie Coles HQ • *London*
Continua • *San Gimignano, Beijing,
Boissy-le-Châtel, La Habana*
Paula Cooper • *New York*
Pilar Corrias • *London*
Cortex Athletico • *Bordeaux, Paris*
Chantal Crousel • *Paris*
Ellen de Bruijne Projects • *Amsterdam*
Massimo De Carlo • *Milano, London*
Dependance • *Brussels*
Dvir Gallery • *Tel Aviv*
Eigen+Art • *Berlin, Leipzig*
Frank Elbaz • *Paris*
Essex Street • *New York*

Konrad Fischer • *Düsseldorf, Berlin*
Peter Freeman, Inc. • *Paris, New York*
House of Gaga • *México D.F.*
Gagosian Gallery • *Paris,
New York, London, Beverly Hills,
Hong Kong*
Gaudel de Stampa • *Paris*
gb agency • *Paris*
GDM • *Paris*
François Ghebaly • *Los Angeles*
Gladstone Gallery • *New York,
Brussels*
Elvira González • *Madrid*
Marian Goodman • *Paris, New York,
London*
Bärbel Grässlin • *Frankfurt*
Greene Naftali • *New York*
Karsten Greve • *Paris, Köln,
St. Moritz*
Hauser & Wirth • *Zürich, London,
New York*
Max Hetzler • *Berlin, Paris*
Xavier Hufkens • *Brussels*
In Situ - Fabienne Leclerc • *Paris*
Jablonka • *Köln*
Jeanne Bucher Jaeger • *Paris*
Jousse Entreprise • *Paris*
Annely Juda Fine Art • *London*
Karma International • *Zürich*
kaufmann repetto • *Milano, New York*
Anton Kern • *New York*
Kraupa-Tuskany Zeidler • *Berlin*
Andrew Kreps • *New York*
Krinzinger • *Wien*
Kukje Gallery/Tina Kim Gallery • *Seoul,
New York*
kurimanzutto • *México D.F.*
Labor • *México D.F.*
Landau Fine Art • *Montreal*
Simon Lee • *London, Hong Kong*
Lehmann Maupin • *New York,*

Hong Kong
Lelong • *Paris, New York*
Lisson • *London, New York, Milano*
Loevenbruck • *Paris*
Florence Loewy • *Paris*
Long March Space • *Beijing*
Luhring Augustine • *New York*
Mai 36 Galerie • *Zürich*
Marcelle Alix • *Paris*
Giò Marconi • *Milano*
Matthew Marks • *New York,
Los Angeles*
Gabrielle Maubrie • *Paris*
Fergus McCaffrey • *New York*
Mendes Wood DM • *São Paulo*
kamel mennour • *Paris*
Metro Pictures • *New York*
Meyer Riegger • *Berlin, Karlsruhe*
mfc-michèledidier • *Brussels, Paris*
Massimo Minini • *Brescia*
Victoria Miro • *London*
Mitchell-Innes & Nash • *New York*
The Modern Institute • *Glasgow*
Monitor • *Roma, New York*
mor.charpentier • *Paris*
Jan Mot • *Brussels, México D.F.*
Nächst St. Stephan
Rosemarie Schwarzwälder • *Wien*
Nagel Draxler • *Berlin, Köln*
Nahmad Contemporary • *New York*
Nature Morte • *New Dehli*
Neu • *Berlin*
Neue Alte Brücke • *Frankfurt*
neugerriemschneider • *Berlin*
New Galerie • *Paris*
Franco Noero • *Torino*
Nathalie Obadia • *Paris, Brussels*
Office Baroque • *Brussels*
Guillermo de Osma • *Madrid*
Overduin & Co. • *Los Angeles*
Pace • *New York, London, Beijing*
Parra & Romero • *Madrid, Ibiza*
Françoise Paviot • *Paris*
Peres Projects • *Berlin*
Galerie Perrotin • *Paris, New York,
Hong Kong*
Francesca Pia • *Zürich*
Plan B • *Cluj, Berlin*
Gregor Podnar • *Berlin*
Eva Presenhuber • *Zürich*
ProjecteSD • *Barcelona*
Proyectos Monclova • *México D.F.*
RaebervonStenglin • *Zürich*
Almine Rech • *Paris, Brussels*
Reena Spaulings Fine Art • *New York*
Regen Projects • *Los Angeles*
Michel Rein • *Paris, Brussels*
Rodeo • *Istanbul, London*
Thaddaeus Ropac • *Paris, Salzburg*
Andrea Rosen • *New York*

Sophie Scheidecker • *Paris*
Esther Schipper • *Berlin*
Micky Schubert • *Berlin*
Gabriele Senn • *Wien*
Natalie Seroussi • *Paris*
Sfeir-Semler • *Beirut, Hamburg*
ShanghART • *Shanghai, Beijing,
Singapore*
Jessica Silverman • *San Francisco*
Skarstedt • *New York, London*
Pietro Sparta • *Chagny*
Sprüth Magers • *Berlin, London*
Luisa Strina • *São Paulo*
Micheline Szwajcer • *Brussels*
Daniel Templon • *Paris, Brussels*
The Third Line • *Dubai*
Tornabuoni Arte • *Paris, Firenze,
Milano*
UBU Gallery • *New York*
Valentin • *Paris*
Georges-Philippe & Nathalie Vallois • *Paris*
Van de Weghe • *New York*
Vedovi • *Brussels*
Vilma Gold • *London*
Vitamin Creative Space • *Guangzhou,
Beijing*
Waddington Custot • *London*
Nicolai Wallner • *Copenhagen*
Michael Werner • *New York, London*
White Cube • *London, Hong Kong,
São Paulo*
Jocelyn Wolff • *Paris*
Xippas • *Paris, Genève,
Montevideo, Punta del Este*
Thomas Zander • *Köln*
Zeno X • *Antwerp*
ZERO… • *Milano*
Galerie Zlotowski • *Paris*
David Zwirner • *New York, London*

AVEC LE SOUTIEN DU
GROUPE GALERIES LAFAYETTE

Allen • *Paris*
Arcade • *London*
Arratia Beer • *Berlin*
Callicoon Fine Arts • *New York*
Chert • *Berlin*
Lars Friedrich • *Berlin*
Hollybush Gardens • *London*
Josh Lilley • *London*
Jérôme Poggi • *Paris*
Real Fine Arts • *New York*

*Index 06/07/2015
Information — info@fiac.com
www.fiac.com*

22-25 OCTOBRE 2015

fiac…

GRAND PALAIS ET HORS LES MURS, PARIS

fiac.com

Organisé par

Reed Expositions

Partenaire officiel

———•———

GOGO CITY GUIDES
www.gogocityguides.com

PARIS
6 rue Thorel, 75002 Paris, France
info@gogocityguides.com

———•———

UK
Pinnacle House, 1st Floor,
31 Cross Lances Road, Hounslow, TW3 2AD.
london@gogocityguides.com

Gogo City Guides is a digitally driven publishing company editing
new-generation guides, in print and for iPhone, to London and Paris.

Founding Editor
Kate van den Boogert, kate@gogocityguides.com

Editorial Assistant
Chloe Gu, editorial@gogocityguides.com

London Editor
Caroline Kinneberg, london@gogocityguides.com

Editor at Large
Clodagh Kinsella, clodagh@gogocityguides.com

Photographer at Large
Anna Watts, anna@gogocityguides.com

Branding & Communications
sydney@gogocityguides.com

Designed & Typeset by
Alice Gazio & Doris Hémar, hello@alicegazio.com

Thanks to
Natasha Davis, Tatsuo Hino, Heidi Knudsen, Charlotte Olympia Dellal.

Find our complete list of stockists here:
www.gogocityguides.com/stockists

Lightning Source UK Ltd.
Milton Keynes UK
UKOW03f0626060915

258124UK00001B/1/P